Final Cut Express Solutions

Final Cut® Express Solutions™

Jason Cranford Teague

David Teague

San Francisco • London

Associate Publisher: Dan Brodnitz
Acquisitions Editor: Mariann Barsolo
Developmental Editor: Pete Gaughan
Production Editor: Dennis Fitzgerald
Technical Editor: Dorne Pentes
Copyeditor: Sharon Wilkey
Compositor: Franz Baumhackl
DVD Coordinator: Dan Mummert
DVD Technician: Kevin Ly
Proofreaders: Emily Hsuan, Eric Lach, Nancy Riddiough
Indexer: Lynnzee Elze
Cover Designer and Photographer: John Nedwidek, Emdesign

Copyright © 2003 SYBEX Inc., 1151 Marina Village Parkway, Alameda, CA 94501. World rights reserved. No part of this publication may be stored in a retrieval system, transmitted, or reproduced in any way, including but not limited to photocopy, photograph, magnetic, or other record, without the prior agreement and written permission of the publisher.

Library of Congress Card Number: 2003106710

ISBN: 0-7821-4248-6

SYBEX and the SYBEX logo are either registered trademarks or trademarks of SYBEX Inc. in the United States and/or other countries.

The DVD interface was created using Macromedia Director, COPYRIGHT 1994, 1997-1999 Macromedia Inc. For more information on Macromedia and Macromedia Director, visit http://www.macromedia.com.

TRADEMARKS: SYBEX has attempted throughout this book to distinguish proprietary trademarks from descriptive terms by following the capitalization style used by the manufacturer.

The author and publisher have made their best efforts to prepare this book, and the content is based upon final release software whenever possible. Portions of the manuscript may be based upon pre-release versions supplied by software manufacturer(s). The author and the publisher make no representation or warranties of any kind with regard to the completeness or accuracy of the contents herein and accept no liability of any kind including but not limited to performance, merchantability, fitness for any particular purpose, or any losses or damages of any kind caused or alleged to be caused directly or indirectly from this book.

Manufactured in the United States of America

10 9 8 7 6 5 4 3 2 1

Software License Agreement: Terms and Conditions

The media and/or any online materials accompanying this book that are available now or in the future contain programs and/or text files (the "Software") to be used in connection with the book. SYBEX hereby grants to you a license to use the Software, subject to the terms that follow. Your purchase, acceptance, or use of the Software will constitute your acceptance of such terms.

The Software compilation is the property of SYBEX unless otherwise indicated and is protected by copyright to SYBEX or other copyright owner(s) as indicated in the media files (the "Owner(s)"). You are hereby granted a single-user license to use the Software for your personal, noncommercial use only. You may not reproduce, sell, distribute, publish, circulate, or commercially exploit the Software, or any portion thereof, without the written consent of SYBEX and the specific copyright owner(s) of any component software included on this media.

In the event that the Software or components include specific license requirements or end-user agreements, statements of condition, disclaimers, limitations or warranties ("End-User License"), those End-User Licenses supersede the terms and conditions herein as to that particular Software component. Your purchase, acceptance, or use of the Software will constitute your acceptance of such End-User Licenses.

By purchase, use or acceptance of the Software you further agree to comply with all export laws and regulations of the United States as such laws and regulations may exist from time to time.

Software Support

Components of the supplemental Software and any offers associated with them may be supported by the specific Owner(s) of that material, but they are not supported by SYBEX. Information regarding any available support may be obtained from the Owner(s) using the information provided in the appropriate read.me files or listed elsewhere on the media.

Should the manufacturer(s) or other Owner(s) cease to offer support or decline to honor any offer, SYBEX bears no responsibility. This notice concerning support for the Software is provided for your information only. SYBEX is not the agent or principal of the Owner(s), and SYBEX is in no way responsible for providing any support for the Software, nor is it liable or responsible for any support provided, or not provided, by the Owner(s).

Warranty

SYBEX warrants the enclosed media to be free of physical defects for a period of ninety (90) days after purchase. The Software is not available from SYBEX in any other form or media than that enclosed herein or posted to www.sybex.com. If you discover a defect in the media during this warranty period, you may obtain a replacement of identical format at no charge by sending the defective media, postage prepaid, with proof of purchase to:

SYBEX Inc.
Product Support Department
1151 Marina Village Parkway
Alameda, CA 94501
Web: http://www.sybex.com

After the 90-day period, you can obtain replacement media of identical format by sending us the defective disk, proof of purchase, and a check or money order for $10, payable to SYBEX.

Disclaimer

SYBEX makes no warranty or representation, either expressed or implied, with respect to the Software or its contents, quality, performance, merchantability, or fitness for a particular purpose. In no event will SYBEX, its distributors, or dealers be liable to you or any other party for direct, indirect, special, incidental, consequential, or other damages arising out of the use of or inability to use the Software or its contents even if advised of the possibility of such damage. In the event that the Software includes an online update feature, SYBEX further disclaims any obligation to provide this feature for any specific duration other than the initial posting.

The exclusion of implied warranties is not permitted by some states. Therefore, the above exclusion may not apply to you. This warranty provides you with specific legal rights; there may be other rights that you may have that vary from state to state. The pricing of the book with the Software by SYBEX reflects the allocation of risk and limitations on liability contained in this agreement of Terms and Conditions.

Shareware Distribution

This Software may contain various programs that are distributed as shareware. Copyright laws apply to both shareware and ordinary commercial software, and the copyright Owner(s) retains all rights. If you try a shareware program and continue using it, you are expected to register it. Individual programs differ on details of trial periods, registration, and payment. Please observe the requirements stated in appropriate files.

Copy Protection

The Software in whole or in part may or may not be copy-protected or encrypted. However, in all cases, reselling or redistributing these files without authorization is expressly forbidden except as specifically provided for by the Owner(s) therein.

For Pat and Ken, my biggest fans
—*Jason Cranford Teague*

For Stan Brakhage
—*David Teague*

 ## Acknowledgments

Thanks to our Parents without whom we would never have met.

Thanks to Neil Salkind, Jessica Richards, and the team at Studio B.

Great thanks to Dan Brodnitz, Mariann Barsolo, Pete Gaughan, Dennis Fitzgerald, Sharon Wilkey, Franz Baumhackl, all our proofreaders, and the rest of the staff at Sybex. Thanks to Dorne Pentes for his insightful feedback while providing technical commentary.

Thanks to Allison Garber and Kyle McCabe for their help in the production of the DVD tutorial video. Thanks to the Prospect Park Zoo in Brooklyn, New York, for providing the location for the tutorial video. And thanks to Sean Travers for composing the music for that video. Thanks to Joseph Linaschke at Apple Computer.

From David

Thanks of course to my brother, Jason, for another hard-working collaboration that leaves us closer. Thanks to Allison for opening my eyes to what's around me and for her love and support through all those nights of writing. Thanks to Kyle, who was simultaneously writing his own book and whose late-night phone calls of solidarity were invaluable. And thanks to my family for their support and constant love.

Thanks also to the amazing movie theatres of New York City that continually provide me inspiration with their programming: Film Forum, Anthology Film Archives, BAM, and the rest.

And very importantly to all my close friends who put up with me during the writing of this book and whose support, creativity, and collaboration I wouldn't be able to live and work without—thanks to all of you, especially Nat, Cathryn, Justin, Caitlin, Linden, St. John, Jean, and Sean.

From Jason

Thanks to David for his hard work on this and for always agreeing with me; my family and friends for their support; my wife, Tara, for her patience and love; and my kids, Jocelyn and Dashiel, for making me laugh when everything looks bleak. Thanks to Thomas for talking to me about something other than video editing.

Also, thanks to those who inspire me: Trent Reznor, Matt Johnson, Monty Python, Gustav Klimt, John William Waterhouse, Pablo Picasso, Dave McKean, Frank Miller, Neil Gaiman, Carl Sagan, Philip K. Dick, William Gibson, ZBS Studios (for *Ruby*), National Public Radio, and, of course, Douglas Adams.

Contents

Introduction xi

Chapter 1 **The Hardware Setup** 1

Finding the Right Mac 2

Using Powerful Hard Disks 5

Choosing a DVD Burner. 6

Using Multiple Monitors and Speakers 8
Adding a Second Monitor   8
Using a Reference Monitor   9
Adding Speakers   10

Choosing Your Camera. 11
Which DV Format Should I Use?   11

Hooking Up a DV Deck 12

The Supporting Cast:
Other Useful Equipment You Might Need on a Shoot. 13

Chapter 2 **The Software** 15

Getting Started 16
Starting the Program for the first time   16
Options, Options Everywhere: Using Contextual Menus   19

Working in the Browser 20
The Project Tab   20
The Effects Tab   22

Working in the Viewer 23

Working in the Timeline 25

Working in the Canvas 27

Working with the Tool Palette and Audio Meters. 28

The Supporting Cast: Other Useful Software You Might Need 30

Chapter 3 **Gathering Your Media** 33

Starting a New Project 34

Capturing Video 35
Setting Preferences for Capture   36
Preparing to Capture   38
Setting Markers   43
Capturing Video Clips   44

	Importing Clips	51
	Using Import to Get Media Files	51
	Dragging and Dropping Media Files	53
	Organizing Your Project	54
	Creating a New Bin	54
	Organizing with Bins	55
	Setting Properties of a Clip or Sequence	56
Chapter 4	**Editing Basics**	**59**
	Navigating the Timeline	60
	Changing Your View	60
	Setting In and Out Points in the Timeline	61
	Working with Markers	63
	Using Sequences	66
	Creating a New Sequence	66
	Naming and Opening a Sequence	67
	Getting Started with Clips	68
	Setting In and Out Points in the Viewer	68
	Bringing Clips into the Timeline	71
	Moving Clips in the Timeline	77
	Copying and Pasting Footage with the Clipboard	78
	Creating Sub-Clips	79
	Editing with Multiple Tracks	82
	Adding Tracks	83
	Setting Target Tracks	85
	Deleting Tracks	86
Chapter 5	**Cutting Your Video**	**89**
	Snapping and Linking Clips	90
	Snapping Tracks into Position	90
	Linking Audio and Video Tracks	91
	Deleting Clips and Gaps	94
	Cutting Clips with the Razor Blade	96
	Getting a Closer Look: The Zoom Tools	97
	Making Quick Trims	98
	Trimming with the Mouse	98
	Extending an Edit	100
	Trimming Clips: Roll, Ripple, Slip, and Slide	101
	Understanding the Trim Edit Window	103
	Using Roll Edits to Trim	106
	Using Ripple Edits to Trim	108
	Using Slip Edits to Trim	110
	Using Slide Edits to Trim	111
Chapter 6	**Adding Transitions**	**115**
	Adding a Transition	116
	Editing a Transition	119
	Changing the Transition's Duration in the Timeline	119

	Changing the Transition's Duration Numerically	120
	Changing a Transition's Alignment	121
	Rendering Effects	**122**
	Editing with the Transition Edit Window	124
	Trimming in the Transition Edit Window	125
	Creating a Quick Fade to Black	**126**
	Using Other Transitional Effects	**127**
Chapter 7	**Adding Video Effects**	**133**
	Adding Effects with Filters	**134**
	Adding a Filter: Desaturate	134
	Adding Multiple Filters	138
	Managing Filter Effects	139
	Adding Special Effects	**140**
	Inverting Your Images	141
	Distorting the Image	143
	Blurring the Image	144
	Changing the Perspective	146
	Adding a Border	147
	Stylizing Your Footage	149
	Working with Color Correction	**150**
	Brightening or Darkening the Image	150
	Fixing Poor White Balance	153
	Manipulating the Image with Motion Controls	**156**
	Changing Size, Position, and Orientation	156
	Cropping the Image	160
	Distorting the Image	161
	Changing the Opacity	163
	Adding a Drop Shadow	165
	Working with Composite Modes	**167**
Chapter 8	**Adding Audio**	**175**
	Combining and Splitting Stereo Pairs	**176**
	Adjusting Audio Levels and Spread	**178**
	Using Keyframes to Adjust Audio Levels over Time	181
	Adding Keyframes in the Timeline	183
	Editing Video and Audio Independently: Split Edits	**184**
	Editing Split Edits in the Viewer	186
	Adding Audio Transitions	**187**
	Adding a Pause	**189**
	Importing Audio	**189**
	Adding Imported Audio	190
	Adding Filters to Audio	**191**
	Sweetening the Audio with Audio Filters	191
	Using Special-Effects Audio Filters	193

Chapter 9	**Adding Titles and Finishing Up**	197
	Changing a Clip's Speed	198
	Playing a Clip in Slow Motion, Fast Motion, or Reverse	198
	Creating a Freeze-Frame	199
	Adding a Voice-Over	201
	Using Keyframes to Animate a Clip	203
	Creating a Motion Path	204
	Editing the Motion Path	207
	Adding Titles	209
	Creating Basic Titles	210
	Using Advanced Title Techniques	217
	Setting Item Properties	223
	Setting Project Properties and Item Comments	223
	Changing Sequence Settings	224
	Setting Item (Clip and Sequence) Properties	226
	Reconnecting Media	227
Chapter 10	**Outputting Your Project**	231
	Preparing Your Project for Output: Putting It All Together	232
	The Juxtaposition of Shots	233
	Laying Down the Edits	234
	Adding Transitions	236
	Adding Filters and Other Effects	238
	Adding Titles and the Soundtrack	239
	Nesting Sequences	242
	Exporting a Sequence	243
	Exporting as a Final Cut Movie	243
	Exporting as a QuickTime (or Other Format) Movie	245
	Exporting Still Images	247
	Printing to Video	251
	Using the Print To Video Command	251
	Recording Directly from the Timeline	253
	Burning to DVD	254
	Saving Your Project for DVD	254
	Creating a DVD Data Disc	257
	Exporting to the Web (or Other Multimedia)	257
	Saving Your Project for the Web	258
	Placing Your Video in a Web Page	261
Glossary of Terms		265
	Index	*272*

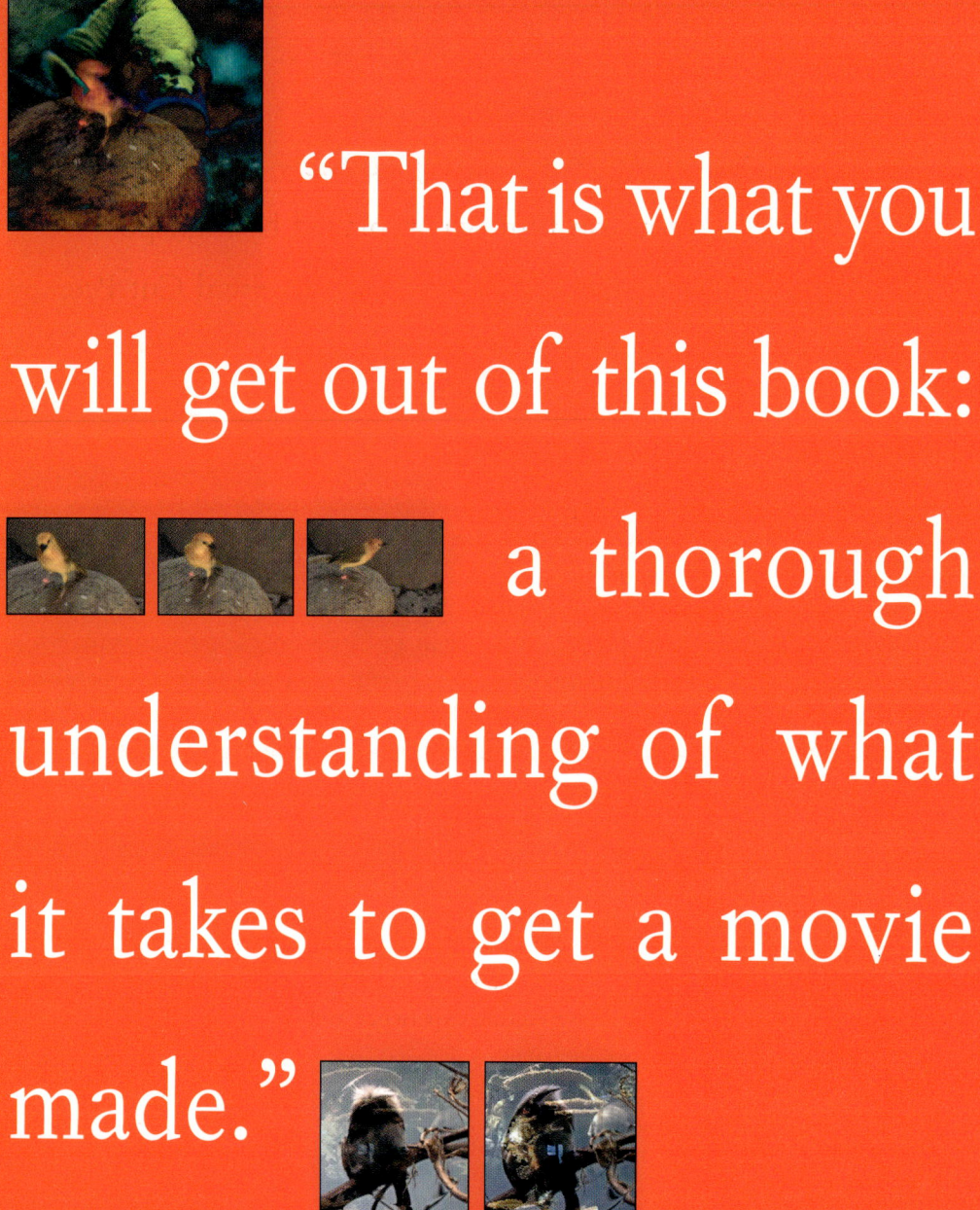

"That is what you will get out of this book: a thorough understanding of what it takes to get a movie made."

Introduction

Editing movies digitally with a computer has revolutionized the industry of filmmaking. In just a few years, the age-old practice of editing on film was replaced by high-powered computers with editing software such as Final Cut Pro, Avid, and Premiere. However, despite the digital revolution, setting up a digital editing suite took more than know-how; it took a major investment. At first, a professional, broadcast-quality edit system required tens of thousands of dollars to build.

With Apple Computer's introduction of Final Cut Pro, the price tag dropped to a thousand dollars for the program plus the cost of a G3 or G4 Mac computer, which brought professional digital editing to a much wider audience. However, there were still many individuals and small businesses who wanted to cut videos—ranging from short narrative films to industrials to vacation videos—but found Final Cut Pro too expensive and too loaded with unneeded functions. Their only option was Apple's iMovie or other rudimentary editing software that was just too simplistic.

Why Final Cut Express?

Enter Final Cut Express. Responding to the need for consumer and prosumer editing software at an affordable price, Apple refashioned their powerful Final Cut interface for use by people who did not have editing experience and who did not need a lot of the bells and whistles of the Pro version.

Beyond providing a suite of tools for nonprofessionals who want to give their home movies good-looking production values, Final Cut Express also opens the door to small businesses to create their own videos. Projects that once called for expensive outsourcing could now be handled on the premises with a digital video camera and Final Cut Express's easy-to-use yet high-grade tools.

> ### What Is Nonlinear Editing?
>
> You will often hear Final Cut Express described as a digital nonlinear editing system. What does this mean? *Digital* obviously pertains to the digital format of the video (using 1s and 0s instead of a chemical or magnetic recording process). But *nonlinear* is a less obvious term.
>
> To understand it, look at an earlier form of editing, called *linear* editing, that was common with video tape-to-tape cutting. When editing tape to tape, you would lay out your first clip, then follow it with a second clip, then follow it with a third clip, and so on until you had a finished piece. If you wanted to make a change, you couldn't without scrapping everything afterward because you were locked into the linear nature of the video tape. You couldn't insert or switch shots.
>
> *Nonlinear* editing does not have these limitations. It enables you to remove a shot and close the gap left by that shot immediately. It lets you switch shots and insert new shots in the middle of your edit. It lets you think of editing in a nonlinear way, so you are not locked into a series of stacked shots that cannot be moved around.

Even though Final Cut Express is touted as a "mid-level" editing software, it is still an incredibly high-powered tool that makes programs such as iMovie look like kid's stuff. When Apple simplified the interface of Final Cut Pro, they left most of the interface intact, cutting only some of the more advanced functions. The biggest change is that Express is geared solely for editing digital video (DV), whereas FCP allows for cutting other formats such as analog and film. For DV users, this is good news, because Express cuts out a lot of unnecessary choices and windows that can be confusing. The setup has also been streamlined and is much easier for a beginner to use.

So why Final Cut Express? When Apple conceived of the software, they designed the program for users who needed a program more advanced than iMovie yet not as complex as Final Cut Pro. They also wanted to provide an editing program with a price tag that was more affordable to home users, who were reluctant to spend the money for Final Cut Pro knowing they wouldn't be using a lot of Pro's advanced functions.

Final Cut Express offers a strong interface for basic cutting and then some. In fact, when the program was released, we were both surprised by how much Apple had left in—making Final Cut Express a simpler but still very sophisticated piece of software.

What Is This Book About?

Final Cut Express places the tools of editing at your disposal in a single package that will run on a Mac, all for a fraction of the cost traditionally associated with video editing. Because many Final Cut Express users will be editing movies for the first time, *Final Cut Express Solutions* has taken extra care to highlight editing basics—both technical and theoretical. Whether you are cutting together a video of your beach trip or making a promotional video for your business, this book will not only guide you through the use of Final Cut Express, but also help you understand the skills needed to create compelling and tightly edited movies.

While preparing to write this book, we recognized that using Final Cut Express follows the 80/20 rule. That is, you will use about 20 percent of its features 80 percent of the time and the other 80 percent of the features no more than 20 percent of the time. Even though Apple has trimmed down the interface and cut many functions of the original Final Cut, the Express version retains a hefty number of the tools, effects, and generators of the professional version. This book focuses on getting you immediately up and running with editing, and in later chapters we look at some of the more advanced skills. When you get right down to it, video editing should be a matter of instinct and craft, and it should not require constant referral to a manual.

The goal of this guide is to get your feet wet in video editing by using step-by-step instructions and hundreds of color illustrations to show you what you should be seeing while you are working. We want to show you the features you'll use every day that should, eventually, become second nature. It is crucial when learning a new system—especially one with as many options as Final Cut Express—that you become well grounded in the basics first and then build on those skills as a foundation. That is what you will get out of this book: a thorough understanding of what it takes to get a movie made with Final Cut Express.

Beyond that, this book is designed to help you explore and discover Final Cut Express and learn how to make it work best for you. No two editors will work the same, and no editor works the same on every project. Final Cut Express is powerful because of its versatility and user-friendly style. We have included information to help you understand how to get the most out of the program without becoming overwhelmed by all of the possibilities.

Who Is This Book For?

Final Cut Express is a flexible program that can be used by many kinds of people. The three main types of people who use Final Cut Express are home users, students, and small-business users. A home user might be someone who wants to create a wedding video that looks nice and slick—with titles and effects—without spending thousands of dollars for a professional edit job. Or they might be an amateur moviemaker who wants to shoot their own short film but doesn't need the higher-level tools of a professional editing facility.

Final Cut Express is also a great way for film students to cut their teeth on editing skills. Because the transition from Express to Final Cut Pro is especially smooth, learning on Express can help a film student to focus on the basic mechanics of editing without being confused by extra tools and functions, before moving on to the Pro version.

Small-business users will also find Final Cut Express a great investment. Commercials, tutorials, and promotional videos can all be edited on Final Cut Express and can take full advantage of the software's professional-looking graphics capabilities and effects.

How Is This Book Organized?

Final Cut Express Solutions covers everything you need to know to make effective use of Final Cut Express. Although we have included a DVD with footage and exercises for you to practice with, this book is designed to help you edit your own movie. To help organize the information, we have split the book into 10 chapters that will take you through step-by-step examples. Unlike many manuals, this is not just a reference book. Each chapter builds on previous lessons and takes you through the editor's job, from setup to the output of the final project, by using clips and sequence examples from the DVD. Here's a run-down of the chapters and what we cover in each:

Chapter 1 introduces you to setting up your Mac and Final Cut Express for optimum efficiency, and offers some tips on accessories to enhance your editing process.

Chapter 2 takes a close look at the interface, introducing you to the different windows and tools you'll be using to edit.

Chapter 3 takes you through capturing your footage, which is the process of bringing your digital video into the computer. You'll also look at how to import clips from other programs.

Chapter 4 covers the basics of editing, from reviewing your clips to making simple edits.

Chapter 5 takes the editing one step further, looking at editing techniques such as ripple, roll, slip, and slide.

Chapter 6 adds transitions to the mix—the ability to have one shot transition to the next with a dissolve, wipe, or many other built-in effects.

Chapter 7 looks at video effects and how to add them to your footage. This can be done to fix problem footage or to stylize your video to give it a certain look

Chapter 8 examines audio concepts, for example, changing sound levels and using audio filters to manipulate your sound.

Chapter 9 brings titles, graphics, and advanced motion effects to your repertoire.

Chapter 10 concludes with methods of outputting your video—back to tape or for the Web, and gives some tips on making movies for DVDs.

Each chapter in this book covers a specific topic important to video editors. We have avoided making this book simply a laundry list of features (you can get that from the manual) and have instead concentrated on the real-world everyday tasks that editors face, showing you how to use Final Cut Express to full advantage for those tasks. Each chapter begins with an overview introduction to help explain some of the reasoning and theory that the specific tasks in each section of the chapter cover. Nearly every step in these instructions also includes an illustration that shows what you should be seeing on the screen during the step.

Each chapter concludes with a special sidebar called "Movie Night." These sidebars recommend various movies from cinema history that are noteworthy for their editing and usually have some attribute that relates to the topics of that chapter. The best education any editor can get is to watch a lot of movies—all kinds of movies—from the dawn of filmmaking to the latest feature playing at the theatre.

What Tools Do You Need for This Book?

Obviously, for a book about Final Cut Express, you are going to need a copy of Final Cut Express—as of this writing, there is only one version of the program available—and a Macintosh computer capable of running Final Cut Express and QuickTime Pro. The exact Mac system you use can vary widely, although video editing is what the faster G4 Macs were designed to handle (we discuss this in more detail in Chapter 1). You can also use a PowerBook, which is handy if you are editing on the road.

You will also need some way to generate your own footage. You might be getting this from someone else or you might have your own digital video camera. The exact source of the footage that you will eventually edit is not important in the scope of this book; you'll learn how to capture from digital video.

Other than that, we recommend some equipment in Chapter 1, but there's nothing that you *must* have to start using Final Cut Express. We also recommend that you have an image-editing program (such as Adobe Photoshop) to help create graphic files that you will use with Final Cut Express. Again, this is not required to use Express but it can significantly increase the production values of your movie.

What Came Before Final Cut Express?

Editing is an art form that stretches back to the end of the nineteenth century with the invention of motion picture technology. The first forms of editing were all on film, with strips of film physically cut and spliced (either with glue or tape) to make up a finished piece. This method is still in use and was the dominant form of editing until video technology became widely accessible and affordable in the late 1960s. With video, editing was a tape-to-tape editing process. You would take a source tape, choose a clip from it that you wanted to use, and then copy it to another tape. The downside of video-to-video editing was that every time you made an edit, the quality of the video would degrade because you were making a copy from another tape.

With the advent of fast computers, editing moved into the digital realm, and software such as Premiere, Avid, and Final Cut Pro emerged as leading industry standards for digital editing. Now, with the release of Final Cut Express, much of the same power is available at a cost well within the reach of any budding video editor.

Contacting the Authors

In addition to providing the DVD, we have set up a website to provide additional materials for the book, where you can download updates, read frequently asked questions, and view the video created in Chapter 10. You can find the site at http://www.webbedenvironments.com/fce.

If you want to reach us with questions about the book, Final Cut Express, or digital video editing in general, feel free to write us at fce@webbedenvironments.com.

You can also find additional information about this book, provide feedback, or read updates at www.sybex.com.

About the Authors

Jason Cranford Teague has written and contributed to several best-selling computer design books including *DHTML and CSS for the World Wide Web*, *Final Cut Pro 3 and the Art of Filmmaking*, and *Photoshop 7 at Your Fingertips*. He has been a multimedia designer for more than 10 years—starting in print and migrating to the virtual world—working for clients including Coca-Cola, Virgin, CNN, Kodak, and WebMD. In addition, he has written for the Apple Developers Center, Adobe, Macworld, and C|Net and has appeared on TechTV's *The Screen Savers*. Jason is currently the creative director for Bright Eye Media (www.brighteyemedia.com) and teaches design classes online and in the classroom.

David Teague works as a writer, filmmaker, film curator, and teacher. His film work includes documentaries, features, shorts, and music films. David teaches video making, editing, and media literacy to adults and teenagers, and is the coauthor of the best-selling book *Final Cut Pro 3 and the Art of Filmmaking*. Working as a cinematographer and editor, he has shot and edited documentaries for PBS's *Live from Lincoln Center* and music videos for artists such as David Bowie, Laurie Anderson, and the Kronos Quartet. He also runs a bimonthly film show at New York's Knitting Factory called *Flicker*, which features new Super-8 and 16mm work (www.flickernyc.com). David lives in Brooklyn, and when he is not working you can usually find him riding the Cyclone out at Coney Island.

Dear Reader,

Thank you for choosing *Final Cut Express Solutions*. This book is part of a new wave of Sybex digital video books, all written by outstanding authors—artists and professional teachers who really know their stuff, and have a clear vision of the audience they're writing for.

At Sybex, we're committed to producing a full line of quality books on a variety of digital imaging and video topics. With each title, we're working hard to set a new standard for the industry. From the paper we print on, to the visual examples our authors provide, our goal is to bring you the best books available.

I hope you see all that reflected in these pages. I'd be very interested in hearing your feedback on how we're doing. To let us know what you think about this, or any other Sybex book, please visit us at www.sybex.com. Once there, go to the product page, click on Submit a Review, and fill out the questionnaire. Your input is greatly appreciated.

Best regards,

Dan Brodnitz
DAN BRODNITZ
Associate Publisher
Sybex Inc.

The Hardware Setup

It used to be the case that an editing suite contained a giant flatbed film editor, shelves crammed with film reels, and cavernous trim bins bulging over with loose strips of film. This was the original nonlinear editing system. Over the past decade, as digital editing has become more available and affordable, the editing room has changed. Now instead of film reels and splicers, the editing suite is filled with computers, monitors, video decks, maybe an extra hard disk and, of course, Final Cut Express. In this chapter, we discuss the best way to set up an editing suite for digital video editing in Final Cut Express, and the various peripheral elements you can add depending on your needs and budget.

Chapter Contents
Finding the right Mac
Knowing what peripherals you
  need and how to pick them
Choosing your camera
Hooking up a DV deck
Other tools of the trade

Finding the Right Mac

Your computer is your tool. It is the device you will be using to create—to sculpt—your video. More than likely, you did not purchase this book unless you already own a computer, so we are not going to waste time telling you what to buy. However, you might not be sure whether your computer can handle Final Cut Express. Not all computers sporting the Mac logo will be able to run Final Cut Express, so you'll need to make sure that your Macintosh has the following:

G3 or G4 processor (300MHz or faster) You will need a G4 processor to use real-time effects. Obviously, the faster your processor, the faster you will be able to work. However, don't be afraid to use older machines if that's what you have to edit with. What counts are your skills.

OS X Jaguar (v.10.2) or higher This is the standard Mac OS shipping with all new machines. If you are using OS 9 or older versions of OS X (10.0–10.1), you will need to upgrade.

256MB of RAM This is the bare minimum you need for OS X and Final Cut Express, but you will need at least 384 megabytes (MB) if you want G4 real-time effects to work correctly. It is especially true with digital filmmaking that the more memory you have, the faster you can edit. In addition, more memory will help prevent the problem of dropped frames. Memory is relatively cheap these days, so stock up.

40MB free hard-disk space This is the bare minimum needed to install Final Cut Express, but you will obviously need more space while working to house the large media files.

One or more FireWire ports These ports are used to capture and export video. (Although useful for downloading digital photographs, USB (Universal Serial Bus) is too slow for video.)

QuickTime 6.1 or higher installed You will need to install or upgrade to QuickTime Pro, but the software is included with Final Cut Express.

Apple Computer offers several Mac models that either come out-of-the-box ready for video editing or can be tricked out to at least the bare minimum. Generally speaking, all new Macs will be able to handle Final Cut Express to varying degrees of proficiency. However, older models might or might not be able to handle the program:

iMac Although thought of as a consumer-level machine, iMacs (see Figure 1.1), even the older multicolored ones, are often used as basic video editing stations. Also keep in mind that the newer flat-panel iMacs are at least as fast as the fastest Macs of just a few years ago. The major drawbacks of the iMac for video editing are lack of expandability, slower speed, and small screen size on older iMacs.

Note: The cable television channel Oxygen uses multiple iMacs running Final Cut Pro to enable producers and editors to quickly create rough-cuts of their programs.

Figure 1.1
The Apple iMac

eMac   Primarily intended for the education audience (which is where it gets that cute little *e* from), the eMac (see Figure 1.2) has the basics needed for Final Cut Express, although you might need to add more RAM. The major drawbacks of the eMac for video editing are lack of speed and expandability.

Figure 1.2
The Apple eMac

iBook   Older (clamshell) iMacs are not recommended because of their lack of speed, smaller hard drives and lack of FireWire support. However, newer iBooks (see Figure 1.3) have the bare minimum credentials for video editing. The major drawbacks of the iBook for video editing are small screen size (on smaller iBooks), lack of speed, and lack of expandability.

Figure 1.3
The Apple iBook

PowerBook If you need to edit on the road, the PowerBook is your best bet. It provides most of the power of the desktop Power Mac and incredible portability. Final Cut Express will work on later model "Bronze" PowerBooks (black casing) or with any of the newer "Titanium" PowerBooks (see Figure 1.4). The major drawback for video editing with PowerBooks is lack of expandability.

Figure 1.4
The Apple (Titanium) PowerBook with a whopping 17-inch monitor

 Note: Most of the video created for this book was edited on Titanium PowerBooks.

Power Mac The powerhouse for video editing is the desktop Power Mac (see Figure 1.5). Newer models include dual processors, which will speed any editing job. In addition, Power Macs are far more expandable than any other Mac model, enabling you to add or change graphic cards, use internal disks, or add other third-party expansion cards such as an analog-to-digital capture card. The major drawback of the Power Mac for video editing is lack of portability.

Figure 1.5
The desktop-bound Apple Power Mac

Using Powerful Hard Disks

Digital video consumes massive amounts of disk space. Just 15 minutes of uncompressed video footage can eat 3 gigabytes (GB) of disk space. You will also need extra hard-disk space to store your raw media as you capture it from your digital video tapes. Although computers are coming with increasingly large hard disks, we strongly recommend that you use an external or separate internal hard disk to devote exclusively to media storage. This is because capturing media to your primary internal hard disk (the one that came with the machine) can cause problems such as program crashes and corrupted video files if that disk is also being used to run programs (including Final Cut Express).

You have two basic choices for adding extra hard disks:

Internal disk (Power Macs only.) This type of disk is installed in any empty media bay. The advantage is that internal disks take up less space than external disks and do not require an extra power socket. Internal disks tend to be cheaper, but you lose out on the portability factor of the external. Although it might seem daunting to pry open your precious computer to install a new internal hard disk, it is actually remarkably easy. Desktop Macs are designed to be easily opened, and additions can be simply snapped into place.

External FireWire disk (Requires FireWire.) This disk is installed by plugging into any open FireWire port. The advantage of external disks is that they are hot-swappable, which means you can plug in and unplug the disks while the computer is running and you can link multiple disks together to create a chain of disks, cameras, or other devices all accessible at the same time.

FireWire disks are relatively cheap. You can now buy disks with storage in the range of 120GB for only a few hundred dollars. When you are deciding how much space you need, remember that 1GB can hold roughly 5 minutes of captured video.

Because digital video relies on timing, you need to consider several features about any hard disk you are using. These are listed in Table 1.1.

Table 1.1 Recommended Hard-Disk Features

Feature	Value
Rotational speed	5,400rpm minimum but 7,200rpm or higher recommended. Hard-disk speed is measured in rpm (rounds per minute), just like a vinyl record. FireWire video runs at 4,200 rpm, so you'll want to make sure the disk you buy is faster than that.
Buffer	2MB minimum, but 6MB or higher recommended
Access time	8.9 milliseconds (ms)
Data transfer rate	50MB

Note: Although designed as a highly portable MP3 player, Apple's iPod includes a FireWire hookup that enables you to transfer any file type (even video), enabling it to double as a pocket-size hard disk. The iPod can store up to 20GB, which is plenty of space for a short film, even uncompressed.

Older Technology: SCSI Hard Disks

Another, costlier option is to use SCSI disks, which can have a faster and more reliable connection than FireWire. SCSI disks are also much more expensive by several hundred dollars and require a SCSI PCI card on your computer. For the most efficient editing, you can get SCSI disks that spin as fast as 10,000rpm.

Like FireWire disks, SCSI disks can be linked in a chain, but are not hot-swappable (this means you have to reboot your computer to plug in the disk). SCSI disks also require special software to daisy-chain them together if you want to link more than one disk to the computer at the same time. SCSI disks have the advantage of being more reliable than FireWire. FireWire disks will more likely "drop frames" when capturing media. This means that not all of the frames from the source tape are making it onto the computer, which is obviously a big problem you will want to avoid!

Choosing a DVD Burner

In addition to your hard disks, you will also need a DVD-RW (read and write)—often referred to as a DVD burner—if you plan on putting your films on DVD. Many Macs come with the SuperDrive, which allows for CD and DVD burning. However, if you have purchased a Mac without a DVD burner, then you will need to purchase an external disk or, if you have a desktop machine with an open bay (a slot for media disks), you can purchase an internal disk. External DVD disks will hook up to your machine through a FireWire connection, but will have a separate power supply requiring its own plug in your electrical outlet, not to mention space on your desktop. Internal DVD disks, on the other hand, are mounted within a Power Mac desktop machine in any of the available media bays, thus not taking any additional desk space or requiring a power plug.

> **Note:** For more information on DVD burning, ↪ Chapter 10, "Outputting Your Video."

If you are purchasing a DVD burner, look for the following features:

Is compatible with Macs Not all DVD players on the market can run with the Macs.

Can use 4.7GB DVD-R discs This is the standard DVD disc format that you will find in most stores.

Reads DVDs at 8x or greater This is how fast the DVD drive can play DVDs back. Slower speeds will skip more often.

Writes DVDs at 4x This is how fast the DVD drive can burn information to the disc.

Has a 4MB buffer or greater Although 2MB will do, for serious video encoding it might slow you down.

You will also want to make sure that your DVD burner supports DVD-Video and DVD-ROM, as well as DVD-R formats.

In addition to the DVD features, most DVD burners also double as CD burners. When evaluating your DVD burner, don't forget to check the CD features and make sure they are up to standard. Make sure that it supports the common CD formats: CD-ROM, CD-Audio, CD-R, CD-RW, CDI, CD Bridge, CD Extended, CD Mixed Mode, and Photo CD media.

What Is FireWire?

FireWire is the trademarked name Apple Computer uses to refer to the input/output (I/O) industry standard known as IEEE 1394. Apple originally developed this standard to allow high-speed connections between peripherals (such as hard disks and DV cameras) and computers. Data transfer rates reached up to 400 megabits per second (Mbps), with some newer devices allowing transfer rates up to 800Mbps. This speed is FireWire's most important advantage for video applications.

In addition, FireWire allows hot-swapping. That is, you can plug and unplug peripherals without having to turn your computer off, and the device will be immediately available to your computer with no further effort on your part.

By using FireWire, you can connect as many as 63 independent devices to a single computer. Each device hooks into the previous device, and these devices can be seen by any other computer on your network. So, you can hook a hard disk to one computer and use it over an office Ethernet with no difficulty.

Continues

> **What Is FireWire?** *(Continued)*
>
> Sony also uses the IEEE 1394 standard in most of its DV cameras; however, they call their product i.LINK instead of FireWire. Don't worry, though; whether you see FireWire, i.LINK, or IEEE 1394, these names all refer to the same thing and will use similar (if not always identical) cables and plugs to enable various peripherals to talk to one another.

Using Multiple Monitors and Speakers

You need only one monitor to work with Final Cut Express. However, having only one computer monitor is much like having only one eye: it limits your vision and can slow you down. You have two distinct options (which are not mutually exclusive) for adding monitors to your editing suite: you can add a second computer monitor, effectively creating a larger workspace, and/or add a reference monitor to watch the signal coming from your DV deck.

Adding a Second Monitor

Although you can get by with a single computer monitor, your life (and editing capabilities) will be much improved with a second computer monitor. This simply gives you more desktop space, which can be invaluable when editing larger projects. When you are editing with Final Cut Express, you will be able to watch the progress of your cuts on one computer screen. This is certainly enough to edit competently, but the image is small and cramped. A second computer monitor will enable you to spread out your work area, especially useful for the timeline, and enables you to display the video screen at larger sizes. In fact, you can simply place your tools in one screen and your video window in the other.

Most desktop models have a port for a second monitor so that you need simply plug it in, and OS X makes it insanely easy to control two monitors. To set up a second monitor, plug the monitor into your computer, open the Display control panel (see Figure 1.6), and click the Detect Displays button. All monitors currently connected to the machine will appear.

Note: Mirroring displays enables you to have both monitors show the same image, which is useful when teaching. However, you will generally want to make sure that mirroring is off when working in Final Cut Express.

In the Display control panel, you can also click the Show Displays In Menu Bar option to select it (see Figure 1.7). A new icon will appear in your menu bar, in the top-right corner of the screen, and will display extra monitors if they are connected to your computer. This menu provides quick access to the Detect Displays option and enables you to set the monitor resolutions independently or use mirroring to have both monitors show the same signal.

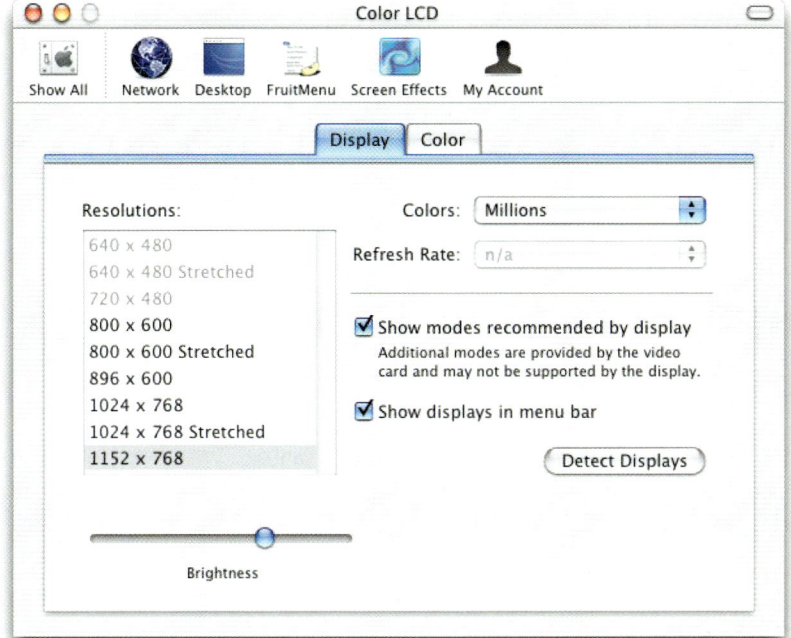

Figure 1.6
The Display control panel

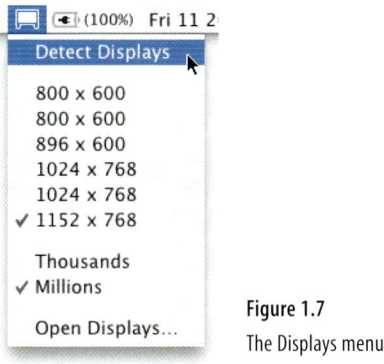

Figure 1.7
The Displays menu

Using a Reference Monitor

In addition to recommending a second computer monitor, we highly recommend getting a reference monitor. Although the computer monitor can display your video, if your work will eventually be viewed on a TV screen, you need something that will show the video as it will look for a broadcast audience. But this is not just any TV. Reference monitors have been calibrated to display the image at the correct color and contrast levels. You can buy reference monitors at different screen sizes and portability, and can also use the monitor when shooting to get a better view of your shots outside the camera viewfinder.

> **Video Standards: NTSC and PAL**
>
> In the United States, the standard is for you to use an NTSC reference monitor. NTSC stands for National Television Standards Committee and is the recognized standard for North America and parts of Asia. The NTSC standard is a composite video signal that runs at 60 interlaced half-frames per second. There are 525 lines in each frame.
>
> The other major standard is PAL, which is the dominant European system. PAL stands for Phase Alternating Line and runs at 50 half-frames per second. PAL has 625 lines in each frame, which gives it a higher resolution than the NTSC standard. You'll find that a lot of American productions shooting on DV will shoot PAL because of this higher resolution, especially if the project is going to be blown up to film.

After you have your external reference monitor, you'll want to connect it to your DV deck or camera. Most DV decks and cameras have a composite (standard VCR plug) and an S-Video output. You should use S-Video if you have it, because the signal is vastly superior to composite. You can connect your deck/camera with an S-Video cable to the external monitor. Some more professional decks will have a component output, which sends a higher-quality signal than S-Video.

With your reference monitor hooked up to your DV deck, and your DV deck in kind hooked up to your computer via FireWire, you'll now be able to view your edits on the external reference monitor in real time as you cut with Final Cut Express. But be warned, there might be a slight delay between the image on the reference monitor and the image on the computer screen. This is normal, and due to the lag time of sending the signal over so many cables.

Adding Speakers

It's a real luxury to have external speakers to edit with. Let's face it, the computer's built-in speakers sound tinny, and if you're cutting anything to music or are doing any kind of audio cleanup work, it can be difficult to make informed audio edits with built-in speakers are. Buying external speakers or a good set of head phones can really change the impact of your piece, so you can make informed decisions about sound design as you cut.

We recommend the Monsoon speakers set (www.monsoonpower.com/index_mmedia.htm), which comes in a left and right package with a subwoofer box. If you are editing with a reference monitor, you'll need to plug the mini-plug from the speaker system directly into your deck or camera (the same place where you would plug in headphones), and your audio will now be played over a nice set of speakers with a real range and depth of bass instead of the tinny computer speakers. If you are not using a reference monitor, then after you've captured, you'll want to plug your speakers' plug directly into the computer's mini-plug input.

Choosing Your Camera

Unless you are simply going to be editing footage shot by someone else, you are also going to need a digital video camera (DV camera). DV cameras can range from cheap home use models that are very small and portable with built-in microphones, to professional cameras that take in microphone inputs, sport excellent lenses, and offer a host of in-camera effects. When looking for a Mini-DV camera, determine what kind of features you need (see the following section on DV formats) and how much you're willing to pay. Digital video cameras can be divided into three broad categories based on cost and quality:

Consumer   Primarily intended for home and nonprofessional uses, these cameras will cost less than cameras in the other two categories but have lower resolutions and thus produce lower-quality images.

Prosumer   Although a step up in quality (and price), these cameras are directed at amateur filmmakers who are shooting more than home movies. Sony's TRV line of cameras are comparatively inexpensive ($800–$1,500), but still good-quality cameras producing great results in the right hands.

Professional   Although not quite film, professional DV cameras can get pretty close. The cameras are expensive (several thousand dollars at least) but worth it if you are a full-time filmmaker. The Canon XLS cameras and Sony's PD cameras are great for broadcast-quality shooting.

Which DV Format Should I Use?

Another important consideration is the format that the camera records in. There are three main formats:

Digital 8   This is an older format that is a holdover from Hi8. Digital 8 (D8) was created so that digital video cameras could also use the more traditional Hi8 tapes. Although still used in many consumer and a few prosumer cameras, this format is being phased out in favor of Mini-DV.

Mini-DV   The most common digital video cameras support the Mini-DV format. Mini-DV records the digital signal on tape. Tapes can come in a variety of lengths, but the most common tapes run 60 minutes at SP (standard play) speed.

DVCAM   This is a platform that records on the same kind of tape as Mini-DV, with one difference. Unlike Mini-DV, the DVCAM tape has an intrinsic link between the audio and video. This allows for crystal sync while capturing long clips of video, whereas Mini-DV can drift sync as the sound and video run side by side with the same timecode, but are not locked together. Sony's PD-150 supports both Mini-DV and DVCAM. DVCAM tapes use more tape stock to record the same amount of footage than Mini-DV tapes. For example, a tape that runs 60 minutes recording Mini-DV will run only 40 minutes recording DVCAM.

Although Final Cut Express will work with any of these formats, we recommend purchasing a camera with the Mini-DV format, unless you still need to work with older Hi8 tapes. We shot video for this book by using the Canon XLS (Mini-DV) and the Sony DCR-TRV320 (D8).

Hooking Up a DV Deck

Although you can use your camera as the playback device while capturing your video, this can dramatically add to the wear and tear of your camera, substantially shortening its useful lifetime as a recording device. So, what you need is a device devoted to playing back the video. What you need is a DV deck (see Figure 1.8). A DV deck enables you to play and record DV tapes, and comes with a four-pin FireWire connection that will connect directly into your computer. The advantage of DV decks is that they can communicate directly with Final Cut Express and be controlled from within the program.

 Note: In reality, you might not be able to afford a separate deck; a camera works fine, especially when you are on a budget or on the road!

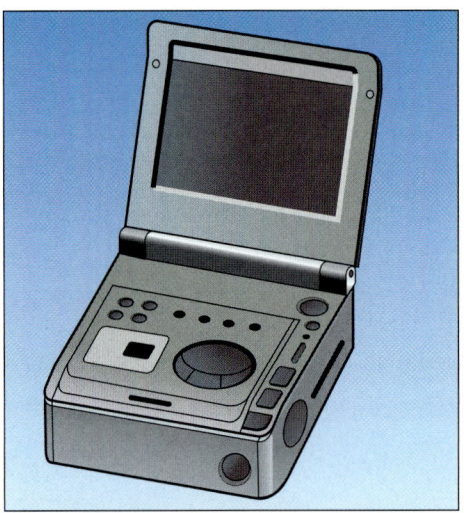

Figure 1.8 We recommend the Sony DV clams, which provides quality Mini-DV and DVCAM playback and recording and can come with an LCD display.

Figure 1.9 FireWire cables with the 6-pin connection that goes to your computer (left) and the 4-pin connection for your deck (right).

Whether you use a DV deck or a camera as a deck, you will need to connect it to your computer with a FireWire cable. FireWire plugs come in two sizes: four-pin and six-pin. The plug on your computer is the larger six-pin connection, and the connection on your deck or camera is the smaller four-pin (see Figure 1.9). This means you'll need to make sure that the cable you get has a four-pin plug on one end and a six-pin on the other.

To connect your deck or camera to your computer, simply plug the four-pin end of your FireWire cable into the deck/camera, and plug the six-pin end of the cable into your computer. Your computer will immediately recognize the connection, and when you start Final Cut Express, it will acknowledge the connection to the deck/camera. If it can't find the deck, it will tell you and prompt you to hook one up.

After you've successfully connected your camera/deck to your computer, you're ready to bring in media from your digital video tapes and edit them with Final Cut Express!

The Supporting Cast:
Other Useful Equipment You Might Need on a Shoot

Although all you need to create video is a camera, a good computer, and the right editing software, you might need other equipment to create high-quality work:

Lights If you are shooting, for example, an interview for a documentary or a scene for a short narrative film, you might want to bring in special lighting. Often the available light (the term for the daylight, lamps, and so forth, that already provide illumination in a location) might not be bright enough or in the right places for your shoot. Digital video is more sensitive than film to light, and so you can get by with minimal lighting and still get a good exposure by opening the aperture. Typically, lighting a single subject works in a three-point lighting system: a brighter key light and a softer fill light in front of the subject on either side, and one light behind and off to the side to bring relief between the subject and the background. Good quality DV lights that are portable and affordable are the Omni lights, which can be bought individually or in kits.

Microphones The internal microphones of most DV cameras aren't bad, but if you need to use a boom (a pole with a microphone on the end that can pick up sound from a specific spot) or want to use a lavalier (a special tiny microphone that hooks onto a person's collar—the standard sit-down interview microphone), you'll have to buy an external microphone. If your DV camera has a special XLR input (like the Sony PD-150 cameras), then you can plug any standard professional microphone directly into your camera. If your camera, like most commercial cameras, doesn't have the XLR input, then you'll need to buy a Beechtek box. This little black box fastens to the bottom of your camera and converts XLR to mini—the small plug that is the audio input plug on most commercial cameras.

Movie Night!

Breathless (À Bout de Souffle), 1960

Director: Jean-Luc Godard

Starring: Jean-Paul Belmondo, Jean Seberg

The movies were never the same after Godard's first feature film. Ushering in the French New Wave along with other filmmakers such as Agnes Varda and Francois Truffaut, Godard made a lyric homage to American gangster movies that took the conventions of a Hollywood crime thriller and turned them inside out. The editing of *Breathless* is perhaps its biggest legacy, as Godard's use of jarring jump cuts and rapid montage opened the door to a looser and more playful kind of moviemaking. When it was released, the film's unorthodox structure and irreverent style caused quite a stir and almost overnight changed the way a movie could be made. Everything from Arthur Penn's *Bonnie and Clyde* to today's omnipresent jittery MTV cutting style owe something to *Breathless*. But half a century of imitations haven't dulled its impact.

When you watch the film, notice how Godard shortens scenes by snipping out middle sections and how this affects the rhythm and tone of the scenes. The editing style not only gives an immediate, documentary feel but also emphasizes the mechanics of movie-making.

The Software

Final Cut Express has an interface based around a series of windows that work together to help you edit your digital video. There are four main windows: the Browser, the Viewer, the Timeline, and the Canvas. To make your cut, you'll be using all four windows at different times. This chapter gives you an overview of each window and of all their individual buttons and functions.

Chapter Contents
Getting started
Working in the Browser
Working in the Timeline
Working in the Viewer
Working in the Canvas
Working with the Tool palette
   and Audio Monitor
Using additional software

Getting Started

Every project that you create with Final Cut Express starts the same way: you have to open the program and start editing your film in a new project file. This section teaches you how to start Final Cut Express and then takes you on a quick tour of the interface. The rest of the chapter explores the interface in more depth.

Starting the Program for the first time

Unless you are very patient person indeed, you have probably already started Final Cut Express at least once, possibly several times, before buying this book. Generally speaking, Final Cut Express is started much like any other program. However, the first time you run it, there are a few special considerations for how your system is set up. If you have already run the Final Cut Express for the first time, then you can skip down to step 3 after starting the program.

Note: If you want that first-time feeling when starting Final Cut Express for this exercise, delete the Final Cut Express preferences file: User Account > Library > Preferences > Final Cut Express User Data > Final Cut Express 1.0 Prefs. This will reset Final Cut Express back to factory fresh conditions (you will not need to reenter your serial number).

1. To start Final Cut Express, double-click the program's icon. Alternatively, you can double-click any Final Cut Express project file icon.
2. If this is the first time you have run Final Cut Express, you see the dialog box shown in Figure 2.1. Final Cut Express has default setup configurations to get you editing quickly, enabling you to choose from a list of preset video setups (↪ "Understanding the Setup" for more details). In addition, you need to choose the hard disk where all your media—the footage you bring in from your digital video tapes—will be housed. The hard disk allocated for your media files is known as a *scratch disk*. If you have a second hard disk (that is, not the hard disk with Final Cut Express on it), you will generally want to choose this one for your scratch disk.

Note: You can change the Setup For setting at any time while running Final Cut Express by choosing Final Cut Express > Easy Set Up… and then choosing a different setting from the drop-down list. You can change the settings for setup or your scratch disk after you've started Final Cut Express by using Final Cut Express > Preferences.

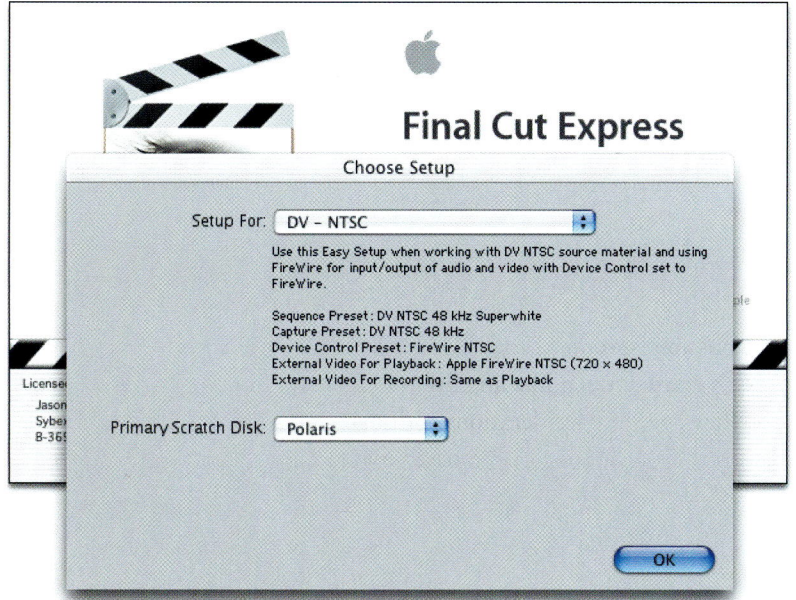

Figure 2.1 Choose from a list of preset options for your video setup (Setup For) and choose the hard disk where you want your media files saved.

Understanding the Setup

The first time you start Final Cut Express and any time you use the Easy Setup command, you will be able to choose from a list of preset video setups. The basic setup for editing in the United States is DV – NTSC. You can also choose setups for PAL video and anamorphic footage.

Underneath the pull-down menu is a list of what that preset contains. You'll notice that the common DV – NTSC option sets up Final Cut Express to capture and create sequences that use DV (digital video)—NTSC (North American standard video)—at 48kHz (standard audio sampling rate for digital video) and that you will be controlling your device (the camera or deck) through FireWire technology. The External Video For Playback item tells the computer that you will be watching your video from the computer on a deck, camera, or reference monitor and to send out that video signal from the computer through FireWire (this is the FireWire cable that is plugged into your camera or deck).

3. Every time you start Final Cut Express, the program first checks to see whether you have a digital video deck or digital video camera connected to the computer. If a device is properly connected, the Final Cut Express interface will appear and you can proceed to step 4.

If no device is found, you see the dialog box shown in Figure 2.2. If you do not have a device connected, click Continue to proceed starting up Final Cut Express. If this dialog box appears and you have a camera or deck hooked up, make sure the device is turned on and that the FireWire cable is properly plugged in. Then click the Check Again button.

Figure 2.2
If you do not have a camera or deck hooked up, click Continue.

4. If this is the first time you have run Final Cut Express, your screen looks something like Figure 2.3, with a new untitled project loaded in the Browser. The actual appearance of your window might not look exactly like Figure 2.3, depending on your monitor size. You can quickly change the layout of windows by choosing Window > Arrange and then choosing from the list of preset window configurations. If you have run Final Cut Express before, then you see all of the projects in the Browser that you had open the last time you quit the program. You are now ready to begin editing.

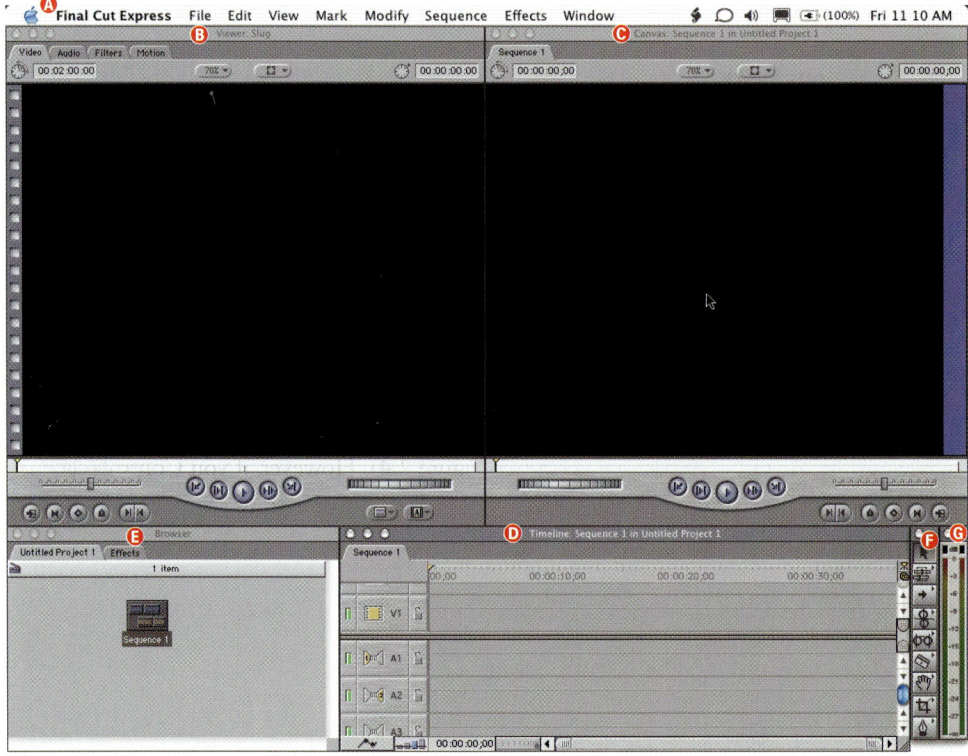

Figure 2.3 The Final Cut Express interface
Ⓐ Menu bar   Ⓑ Viewer   Ⓒ Canvas   Ⓓ Timeline   Ⓔ Browser   Ⓕ Tools   Ⓖ Audio Monitor

As you can see in Figure 2.3, the Final Cut Express interface is divided into regions that serve different functions or contain various tools:

Menu bar   The Mac interface's standard menu bar gives you access to most of Final Cut Express's tools and functions.

Viewer   (Shortcut: ⌘+1) This is like a mini-VCR that lets you preview individual clips before or after they are edited into a sequence. The Viewer also lets you trim your clip by setting In and Out points and lets you add effects.

Canvas   (Shortcut: ⌘+2) This simply acts as a monitor for the Timeline, enabling you to view what is going on in your film.

Timeline   (Shortcut: ⌘+3) This is where all the action takes place. This is where you view your sequences, where the cutting takes place, and where your clips are placed together to create your video.

Browser   (Shortcut: ⌘+4) This is where all of your clips and editing elements are organized. Video files, sound files, sequences, still images, and so forth are all housed in the Browser and can be organized in folders called *bins*.

Tools   This smaller window enables you to access Final Cut Express's tools for editing.

Audio Monitor   (Shortcut: Option+4) This provides a quick visual reference for the audio levels in the left and right channels while you are viewing a clip either in the Viewer or the Canvas.

Options, Options Everywhere: Using Contextual Menus

Even seasoned computer veterans might be slightly intimidated by the Final Cut Express interface. There is a lot going on and a lot of options. However, one often overlooked but extremely powerful feature of this application is the availability of contextual menus. These are little pop-up menus that appear when you hold down the Control key while clicking on an area with your mouse (referred to as Control+clicking, or right-clicking if you have a two-button mouse).

Many windows and icons within the interface have contextual menus that enable you to quickly access the possible options for that object. For example, if you Control+click in an empty area of the Browser, you will be able to change the view for the window from a list to icons of various sizes, or vice versa (see Figure 2.4). However, if you Control+click on a video clip within that same window, you will see options for actions that you can perform on the clip, such as cutting, copying, or viewing it in the Viewer (see Figure 2.5).

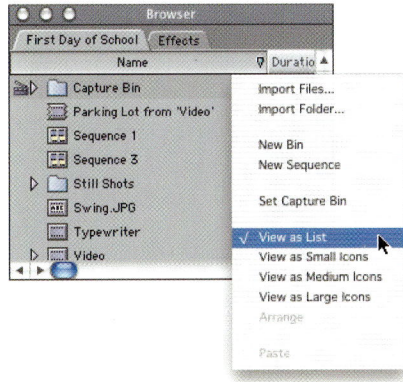

Figure 2.4
The contextual menu for the Browser window

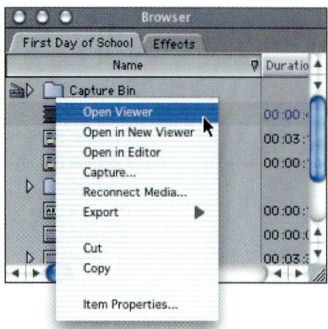

Figure 2.5
The contextual menu for a film clip

Although available in almost all applications, contextual menus are especially effective for Final Cut Express. They can not only speed your workflow, but might even remind you of options you have that are otherwise buried deep within the menu bar. Throughout this book, we highlight contextual menus with helpful shortcuts in them.

Working in the Browser

The simplest way to imagine your Browser is as a big digital filing cabinet. After you start up Final Cut Express, the Browser should already be open. If it's not, choose Window > Browser or press ⌘+4 to open it.

In a project tab, each of the items—the video clips, sequences, audio files, still images, and so forth that you will use in your cutting—is listed with pertinent information about them stored to the right of their names. In addition, the Browser contains the Effects tab, which holds all of the special effects and filters available to you while editing.

The Project Tab

When you first open Final Cut Express, you'll need to create a new project. A *project* is a file saved to your hard disk that stores all of your editing elements and decisions. No actual media files are stored in a project file, it simply records references to them, so this file is relatively small. The media files (audio, video, still images) are housed elsewhere, and the project file knows where to find them.

All of the media available for a project are in this window and represented as clip icons (see Figure 2.6). Multiple projects can be opened in Final Cut Express at the same time; each project is represented by a tab in the Browser.

 Note: Although initially presented as medium sized icons, you can ctrl+click in any blank area of the Browser and choose to view the contents as a list or to set the size of the icons (small, medium, or large).

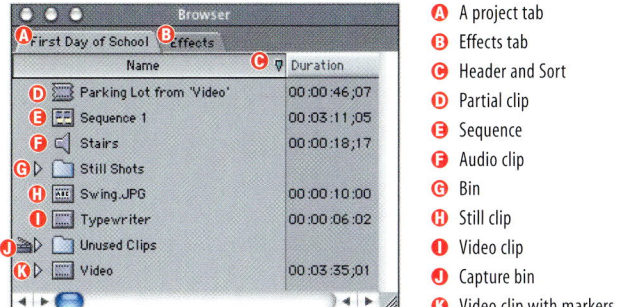

Figure 2.6 The Browser is where you store the video, still, and audio clips you will be using, in individual project tabs.

Project tabs   Each open project is represented by a tab with the project's name. You can switch back and forth between projects by clicking on these tabs. Control+click a project tab to close the project.

Effects tab   This contains bins of effects and filters that you can use with a project.

Header and Sort content   Click any of the column heads to sort the clips by that criteria. Click again to reverse the order. You can scroll horizontally to view many different columns.

Sub-clip   This is part of another clip already in the project which has been cropped based on markers in the originating clip. This acts like a clip.

Sequence   This is a collection of edited media clips, effects, and filters. Double-clicking displays the sequence in the Timeline.

Audio clip   This represents an audio-only media file, such as a voice-over file or a track imported from a CD. Double-clicking displays the audio waveform in the Viewer.

Bin   This is a folder used to store media clips.

Still clip   This represents a still image media file (no motion). Double-clicking displays the image in the Viewer.

Video clip   This represents a video media file (which can also include audio). Double-clicking displays the video in the Viewer.

Capture bin   Indicated by the clapboard, this is where all captured clips are placed.

Video clip with markers   This indicates a video clip that has markers set. Click the triangle to view the markers, which can be treated as partial clips.

You can customize how your clips will appear in the Browser. Pick between viewing them as a list or as small, medium, or large icons by choosing View > Browser Items and selecting the icon size (see Figure 2.7).

> **Note:** The icon for a media file (video, audio, or still) in your Browser does not represent the actual file on your hard disk. If you delete the icon from your Browser, you are *not* deleting it from your hard disk.

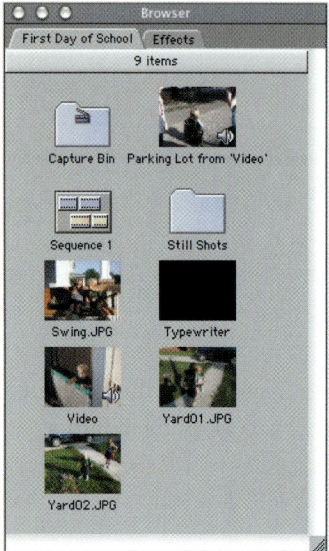

Figure 2.7
This project tab shows the clips as medium-sized icons.

Notice that you can scroll not only vertically in the window to see more clips, but also horizontally to see additional information about your clips. Here you can quickly check on your clip's duration, its source reel (the digital video tape it came from), and any notes about the clip.

The Effects Tab

The Browser also houses the Effects tab (see Figure 2.8), a window of all of Final Cut Express's built-in effects. These effects are separated into bins allocating different sorts of effect types. You can also access effects from the Effects menu on the menu bar.

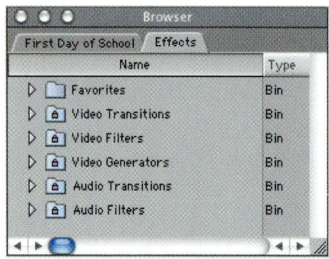

Figure 2.8
The Effects tab

The Favorites bin works like a bookmark list, where you can place effects that you use regularly. The effects will preserve whatever settings they have when dragged into the bin. The other folders contain various categories of tools:

Video Transitions   This is where you'll find effects such as the common cross-dissolve and a host of wipes and irises.

Video Filters   This folder contains a host of Photoshop-style filters such as Gaussian Blur and Desaturate.

Video Generators   Here you'll find computer-made clips such as Bars and Tone, Slugs, and Titles.

Audio Transitions   This holds cross-fades for audio clips.

Audio Filters This folder has some rudimentary graphic equalizing, hum removing, and echo effects, among others.

> **Note:** If you do not like having the effects and projects in the same window, click any of the tabs and drag it out of the Browser. The tab (Effects or a Project) will then appear in its own window. To reattach the detached tab to the Browser window, simply click and drag the tab back into the Browser window.

Working in the Viewer

A lot of important decision-making is made in the Viewer (see Figure 2.9); this is where you can preview and make changes to your clips before and after editing them into a sequence. You can open clips into the Viewer from the Browser or from the Timeline by double-clicking them. In the Viewer, you'll decide how to trim your clip and make adjustments to various attributes such as audio levels and motion, as well as customize effects on individual clips. Remember that you can have only one clip open at a time in the Viewer, and so the changes you make in the Viewer are affecting only one clip.

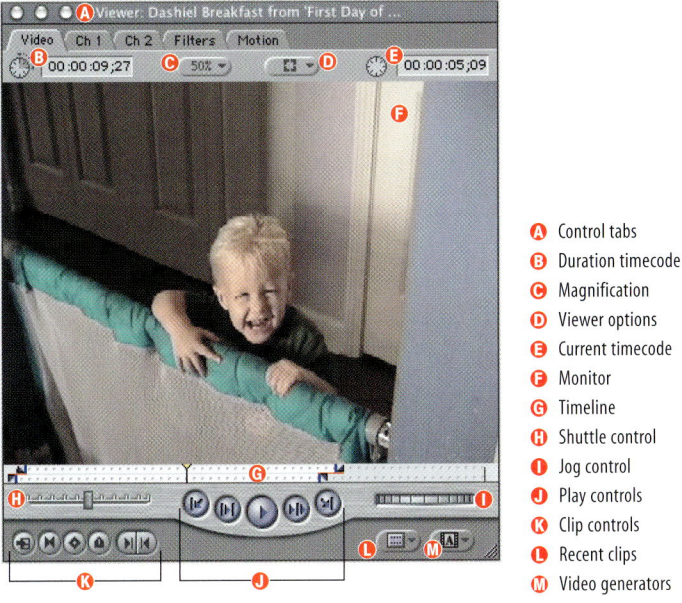

- **A** Control tabs
- **B** Duration timecode
- **C** Magnification
- **D** Viewer options
- **E** Current timecode
- **F** Monitor
- **G** Timeline
- **H** Shuttle control
- **I** Jog control
- **J** Play controls
- **K** Clip controls
- **L** Recent clips
- **M** Video generators

Figure 2.9 The Final Cut Express Viewer is where you preview clips before placing them into a sequence.

As shown in Figure 2.9, the viewer is made up of the following parts:

Control tabs These are tabs to access controls for the Video (shown in Figure 2.9), (either Audio *or* Ch 1 and Ch 2 depending on whether the audio tracks are stereo-pairs or mono), Filters, and Motion windows. Text clips have a special tab called Controls. Each tab has different controls.

Duration timecode This indicates the duration of the clip from a set In point to a set Out point. If no In and Out points are set, the duration listed is for the full clip.

Magnification   This indicates the percentage magnification at which you view the video. As a default, you should stick with Fit To Window. Magnification does not affect the size of the final output.

Viewer options   Choose to have a Wireframe overlay or a Title Safe guide.

Current timecode   This displays the timecode where your playhead is resting. The timecode relates to the timecode from your source material.

Monitor   This is the main area where you view the footage in motion or as an individual frame.

Timeline   This thin white strip underneath the monitor is a representation of the entire clip. You can scrub along it to view your clip by dragging the playhead.

Shuttle control   When you click and drag to the left (backward) or right (forward), this control allows you to move through the clip at a variable rate. The farther you move in a direction, the faster the clip is played.

Jog control   By clicking and dragging this control to the left or right, you move through the footage one frame at a time, forward or backward.

Play controls   Click these to move the playhead around or start playing from particular points in the clip. These buttons are described in Table 2.1 (listed from left to right) with shortcut keys if the Viewer is the frontmost window.

▶ **Table 2.1** Play Controls

Control	Shortcut Key	Action
Previous Edit		Moves the playhead to the preceding edit or In/Out point on the clip
Play In To Out	Shift+\	Plays only the part of the clip designated by In and Out points to preview your trimmed clip
Play	spacebar	Plays and pauses your clip at normal speed
Play Around Current	\	Plays a few seconds before and after the current location of your playhead
Next Edit		Moves the playhead to the next edit or In/Out point in the clip

Clip controls   Click these to move the playhead around or start playing from particular points in the clip. These buttons are described in Table 2.2 (listed from left to right) with shortcut keys if the Viewer is the frontmost window.

▶ **Table 2.2** Clip Controls

Control	Shortcut Key	Action
Match Frame	F	Synchs the Timeline's playhead with the Viewer's playhead for the current clip shown. This button is not available if the clip has been opened directly from the browser.
Mark Clip	X	Sets the In point and an Out points at the beginning and end of the clip, respectively
Add Keyframe	Control+K	Sets a keyframe at the current frame of the clip
Add Marker	M	Places a marker at the current frame of the clip open in the Viewer
Mark In	I	Sets an In point at the current frame of the clip
Mark Out	O	Sets an Out point at the current frame of the clip

Recent clips   Choose from a list of recently viewed clips to quickly load them into the Viewer.

Video generators   Choose from lists of common video-generated clips (such as Bar and Tone) to quickly load them into the Viewer.

> ### Controlling Video from Your Keyboard
>
> Final Cut Express wisely offers some easy keyboard shortcuts to shuttle through and preview your footage. These shortcuts are universal throughout Final Cut Express, meaning they work while logging clips, in the Timeline, in the Canvas, and in the Viewer:
>
> **Spacebar** plays or pauses your video.
>
> **Shift+spacebar** plays your video backward.
>
> **J** rewinds your video. Double- or triple-tap the key for faster rewinding while viewing the footage.
>
> **K** pauses your video. By holding the K key down in conjunction with the J or L key, your video moves forward or backward one frame at a time.
>
> **L** fast-forwards your video. Double- or triple-tap the key for faster fast-forwarding while viewing the footage.
>
> **Left arrow key** moves back one frame.
>
> **Right arrow key** moves forward one frame.
>
> **M** sets an In point at the playhead location.
>
> **O** sets an Out point at the playhead location.

Working in the Timeline

The Timeline is where the magic happens (see Figure 2.10). In this window, you will be bringing your separate clips together to create the montage. Video clips, sound clips, still images, graphics—all of these elements are combined in the Timeline to make the cut of your movie. The Timeline is set up like a highway, with tracks for video and audio laid out like lanes on a road. As you bring in clips, you'll be laying them out on these tracks and putting them side by side to make an edit between one clip to the next. If you do not see the Timeline, you can open it by choosing Window > Timeline or by pressing ⌘+3

Figure 2.10   The Timeline is where you add different clips (video, stills, and audio) to create your video.

The Timeline is where you will be editing individual sequences in a Project. Each sequence has its own series of audio and video tracks. With Final Cut Express, you can have up to 99 video and audio tracks in one sequence. As you cut, you're able to mix audio on multiple tracks and lay video on multiple tracks for organizational purposes, and to create composite or transition effects.

Sequence tabs Each sequence open in the Timeline has its own tab. By clicking the tab, you make that sequence active and ready for cutting.

Video tracks These tracks are used to add video into your movie. Click the green rectangle to hide a video track from playback. Click the film clip icon to make that the designated video track (the selected film strip icon is yellow) so that new video is automatically added to that track. Click the lock icon to prevent the track from being edited.

Audio tracks These are used to add audio into your movie. Click the green rectangle to disable audio in that track. Click the left or right speaker icon to designate the stereo channel for that track (the selected channel icon is yellow). Click the lock icon to prevent the track from being edited.

Playhead This indicates which frames are currently playing in your sequence, or if you are paused, and shows which frame you are currently viewing. The timecode at the bottom of the Timeline shows where the playhead is resting.

Clip This is a representation of a clip (audio, video, graphic) that can be trimmed and moved to change your cut.

Snapping toggle This enables you to "snap" your playhead or a clip to an edit point, marker, or In or Out point.

Linking toggle This toggle turns the linking of all clips on or off.

Clip overlay This turns on or off an overlay that shows a clip's opacity and audio levels.

Track height This adjusts the visible height of the tracks and the clips on the tracks, to change the size of the clip thumbnail.

Clip width This enables you to zoom in or out of your sequence by changing the relative width of clips.

The horizontal scroll bar at the bottom of the Timeline enables you to scroll forward or backward along your sequence. Clicking and dragging the tabs at either end of the scroll bar enables you to adjust the clip width rather than scroll.

Note: Whenever you open a sequence from the Browser by double-clicking it, that sequence is automatically loaded into the Timeline.

The horizontal scroll bar at the bottom of the Timeline enables you to scroll forward or backward along your sequence. Clicking and dragging the tabs at either end of the scroll bar enables you to adjust the clip width rather than scroll.

Working in the Canvas

The Canvas window is really just an extension of the Timeline (see Figure 2.11). Acting as a monitor for the Timeline, the Canvas plays the clips as edited in the Timeline's active sequence. Without the Canvas, you wouldn't be able to see what your movie looks like with all the cuts you've made.

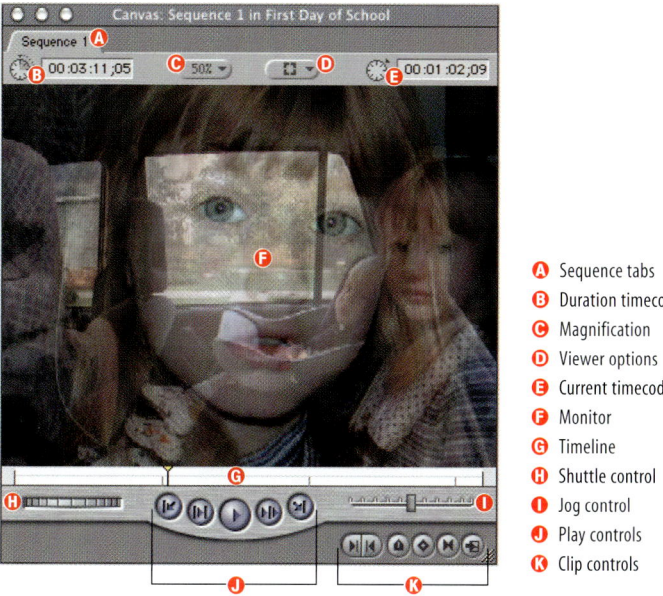

- **A** Sequence tabs
- **B** Duration timecode
- **C** Magnification
- **D** Viewer options
- **E** Current timecode
- **F** Monitor
- **G** Timeline
- **H** Shuttle control
- **I** Jog control
- **J** Play controls
- **K** Clip controls

Figure 2.11 The Canvas is where you view the results of the Timeline.

Click the sequence tabs at the top of the Canvas (Sequence 1, for example) to move among different sequences open in the Timeline. Beyond that, the controls for the Canvas are virtually identical to those shown in Figure 2.9 in the Viewer (although mirrored), and the same keyboard shortcuts are used when the Canvas is the active window.

Quick Edit Overview

We've covered the four windows you will be working with (the Browser, the Viewer, the Timeline, and the Canvas) separately so you can see what they are really made of. But when you are editing, you'll be using all of these windows together to make your movie.

Although you'll use all four in any number of combinations, the basic progress of a clip through the interface goes like this:

1. A clip is captured from a digital video tape and brought into the Browser.
2. The clip is opened in the Viewer so it can be reviewed and trimmed.
3. After the clip is ready, it is brought into the Timeline so it can be edited in with other clips.
4. The clips edited in the Timeline are watched in the Canvas monitor.
5. Voila—the clip has made its journey into your final edited movie.

Working with the Tool Palette and Audio Meters

The Audio Meters (see Figure 2.12) displays the current audio levels in the left and right channels for the clip playing in the Viewer or Canvas. Keep an eye on this while editing to ensure that your audio does not become distorted. If you do not see the Audio Meters, choose Window > Audio Meters (or press Option+4).

Figure 2.12
The Audio Meters is used to check the audio levels while a clip is playing.

If you've used Photoshop or Illustrator before, then Final Cut Express's Tool palette (see Figure 2.13) will look familiar. It's a collection of specific tools that enable you to change the icon of your cursor to perform different kinds of tasks. It will help you make faster decisions while cutting and enable you to navigate within the Final Cut Express multiple window environment.

Although you'll be looking in more depth at some of these functions in later chapters (⌘ Chapter 5, "Cutting Your Video"), Table 2.3 provides a quick reference for the Tool palette's many features.

Figure 2.13
The basic Tool palette

▶ **Table 2.3** Features of the Tool Palette

Icon	Tool	Keyboard Shortcut	Description
	Selection	A	Selects any clip, tab, or window that the cursor clicks
	Edit Selection	G	Selects an edit instead of a clip and opens the Trim Edit window to change the selected edit
	Group Selection	GG	Selects multiple clips at the same time
	Range Selection	GGG	Selects a part of a clip
	Select Track Forward	T	Selects all clips on a single video track to the right of the cursor
	Select Track Backward	TT	Selects all clips on a single video track to the left of the cursor
	Select Track	TTT	Selects all clips on a single track
	Select All Tracks Forward		Selects all clips on all tracks to the right of the cursor
	Select All Tracks Backward		Selects all clips on all tracks to the left of the cursor
	Ripple Edit	RR	Performs a ripple edit
	Roll Edit	R	Performs a roll edit
	Slip Item	S	Performs a slip edit
	Slide Item	SS	Performs a slide edit
	Razor Blade	B	Makes a cut in a clip, turning it into two individual clips
	Razor Blade All	BB	Makes a cut in all clips at a particular point in the Timeline
	Zoom In	Z	Magnifies the Timeline scale for precision editing
	Zoom Out	ZZ	Reduces the Timeline to view more of the sequence
	Hand	H	Navigates over a magnified image in the monitor of the Canvas or Viewer
	Scrub Video	HH	Scrubs back and forth through the footage of a clip in the Browser when it is in large icon mode
	Crop	C	Manually crops a video image
	Distort	D	Manually distorts a video image
	Pen	P	Adds a keyframe
	Pen Delete	PP	Deletes a keyframe
	Pen Smooth	PPP	Smooths a keyframe

For more information on the Ripple Edit, Roll Edit, Slip Item, and Slide Item tools, ↻ Chapter 5. For more on the Pen tools, see Chapter 7, "Adding Video Effects."

> **Organizing Your Windows**
>
> Dealing with all of the windows and palettes in the Final Cut Express interface can be an organizational nightmare. Of course, you can always place your tools in a second monitor (if you have one). One recommended strategy with a second monitor is to use the split mode and keep your Browser in the second monitor so that you have a large space to view your many clips and bins. In your first monitor, have your Timeline take up the bottom half, and split the top half between the Canvas and the Viewer, with the Viewer on the left and the Canvas on the right. This is especially useful if one monitor is smaller than the other, for instance if you are using a PowerBook. Of course, you can set up the layout however you want, and you might want to try some different styles before settling on the one that is most comfortable.
>
> However, if you don't have the luxury of a second monitor, Final Cut Express comes with several preset window arrangements that can help you optimize your work environment. Access these by choosing Window > Arrange. You can choose recommended setups based on whether you are doing more capturing, color correcting, or editing. You can then take these presets and tailor them to your own needs.

The Supporting Cast: Other Useful Software You Might Need

Although everything you need for video editing is included with Final Cut Express, it can't do everything. Here are some of the programs you might want to have in your arsenal:

Apple iPhoto This photo management program comes standard on all newer Macs running OS X. Although not integrated into Final Cut Express, you can drag pictures from one program to the other. We talk more about using iPhoto for still images in Chapter 5.

Apple QuickTime With this standard video program for Macs, you can view a Final Cut Express movie or export a QuickTime file. We look more at QuickTime Pro in Chapter 10, "Outputting Your Video."

Apple iDVD This free DVD creation package includes an interface as simple to use as iPhoto but made for creating DVD interfaces to show your videos. We discuss this program in greater detail in Chapter 10.

Apple DVD Studio Pro If you need more than buttons on screens for your DVD interface, you need DVD Studio Pro. This program can be used to create professional-quality DVDs with high-quality audio and video and sophisticated navigation, without having to learn complex programming commands. We look more at DVD Studio Pro in Chapter 10.

Adobe Photoshop or Photoshop Elements The standard for image editing software, Photoshop and Photoshop Elements are regularly used to create titles for films. We discuss these in greater detail in Chapter 9, "Adding Titles."

Adobe After Effects A powerful motion graphics program that enables you to create very sophisticated animated effects. You can use After Effects to make animated titles, moving colorful backgrounds, logos, and so on. Final Cut Express can import After Effects sequences.

Adobe Illustrator As with Photoshop, you can use Illustrator to create still graphics and titles that are far more intricate and sophisticated than you can in Final Cut Express's graphics or title tools. Final Cut Express can import image files from Illustrator as clips.

Film Gimp Film Gimp is used specifically to retouch digital video sequences and can be used in conjunction with Final Cut Express to perform tasks such as removing book mikes or other announces. Sony has used it on many major motion pictures, including *Harry Potter* and *Stuart Little*. Even better, the program is free!

Boris filters Final Cut Express comes with several filters and effects from Boris. However, there are many more in the Boris Continuum Complete and Boris Red packages, which include vector animation, 3-D compositing, several incredible filters, and other special effects. For example, if you need a flaming hand, it's easy with Boris. We talk more about Boris in Chapter 7.

Movie Night!

The Thin Blue Line

Director: Errol Morris

In today's world, the documentary film is more and more often associated with a talking head and illustrated with stock photography and footage, a style popularized by Ken Burns in films such as *The Civil War* and *Jazz*. However, the documentary form has a very rich history and has often been on the forefront of movie-making techniques such as editing.

In his documentary *The Thin Blue Line*, Errol Morris takes a look at a murder trial in Texas and comes up with a movie that is nonfiction but often feels like a Hollywood crime film. Through judicious editing, Morris mixes studio-lit interviews with the accused murderer, the police, the lawyers, and other characters with stylized reenactments that have actors play out different versions of what happened the night of the murder. With his mannered and often eccentric style, Morris edits his documentary to bring out the quirks of the characters, letting his interview subjects speak for long periods of time. Morris not only made a thrilling documentary that mixes film styles, he also made such a good case for the accused man's innocence that, prompted by the film, the case was appealed and the guilty verdict was overturned.

Gathering Your Media

Capturing is the first step an editor takes when working on a project. It will provide you the materials—the pieces—that you will fit together later as you edit a final movie. Capturing isn't just about the technical process of transferring video from tape to hard disk; in addition, there are a lot of creative and organizational decisions to be made that will help you to create a better finished product.

Chapter Contents
Starting a new project
Adding markers
Capturing video clips
Importing media files
Organizing your project media

Starting a New Project

A "Project" is a file that you save on your hard drive where references to all of your clips are stored as well as individual sequences that you are working on. When you first open Final Cut Express, a blank project is shown in the Browser window (with a blank sequence) that you can begin to add clips to. However, if you need to create a new project file, follow these steps:

1. Choose File > New Project (⌘+E). A new project appears as a tab in the Browser window. By default, the new project is called Untitled Project with a number. The project automatically includes a blank sequence called Sequence 1 (see Figure 3.1). For the exercises in chapters 4 through 10 of this book, you will be using the project called "Land, Sea, & Air" which is on the DVD. For this exercise, just practice creating a new project of your own.

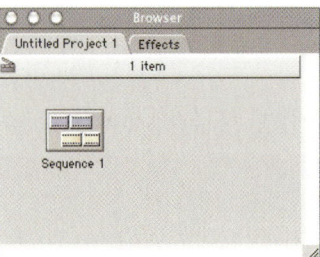

Figure 3.1
A new project in the Browser

 Note: Remember that you can Control+click in any empty area of the Browser window to choose whether to view files in a list or as icons.

2. Choose File > Save Project As and name your file (see Figure 3.2). This can be any standard filename you want. Now choose where you want to save your project file. The name of the project is now shown in the Browser tab.

You are now ready to start editing your movie. However, your project has no media files to be edited. You need to either capture video footage from DV tape or import media from a hard disk.

 Note: When saving a project, it's a good idea not to save it on the external or internal separate disks where your media is kept. This way, if your media disk drive becomes corrupt (or gets dropped or eaten by your dog), you will still have the project file with all of the editing decisions saved. You would then have to go back to your source tapes to bring in the footage again, but you won't have to recut, because the project file retains that information.

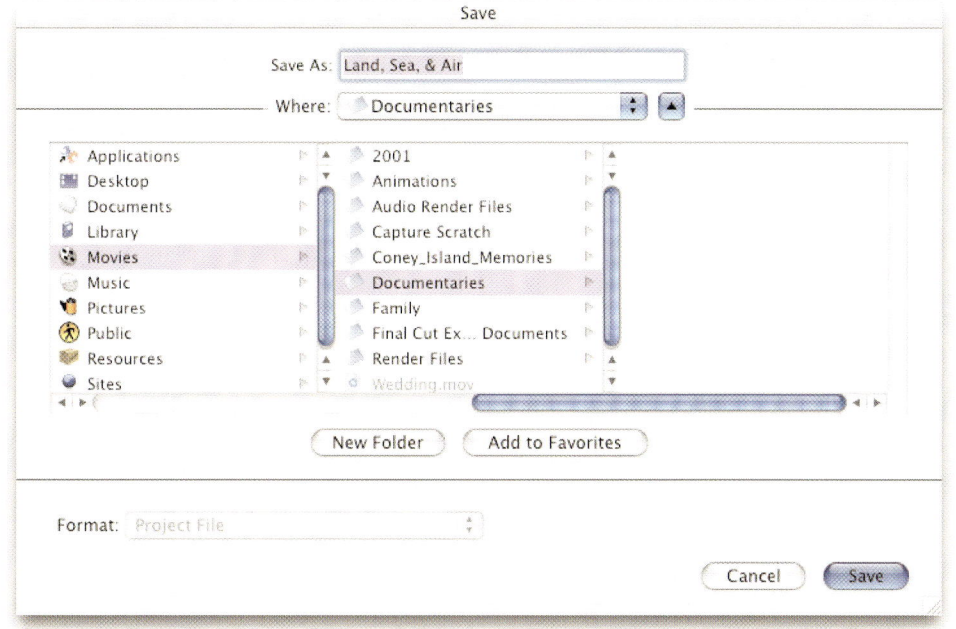

Figure 3.2 Save your projects in a logical location such as the Movies folder on your main hard disk.

Capturing Video

Before you can start to edit your movie, you need to bring the video footage from your digital videotape into the computer. This process is called *capturing*, as it takes the video image and sound from the tape and creates a new computer file on your hard disk. A *clip* is an individual media file that lives on your hard disk and that can be manipulated and edited with Final Cut Express. Each time you bring in footage from videotape into the computer, you create a *video clip*, which includes moving images and can also include audio. In the clip icon shown here, notice the little speaker icon indicating that this clip includes audio tracks.

Before you start bringing your footage into the computer, there are a few things you will want to double-check and set. By setting certain preferences, you can make sure you don't lose any stray frames of video due to memory problems. You will also need to tell Final Cut Express where to store the media after it is captured.

Setting Preferences for Capture

The Preferences window in Final Cut Express contains two categories of preferences that are important for capturing your footage: General preferences, and Scratch Disk preferences. Before capturing, it's a good idea to check whether they are set the way you want them. To set preferences for capturing, choose Final Cut Express > Preferences (Option+Q).

In the General tab (see Figure 3.3), you will find several options.

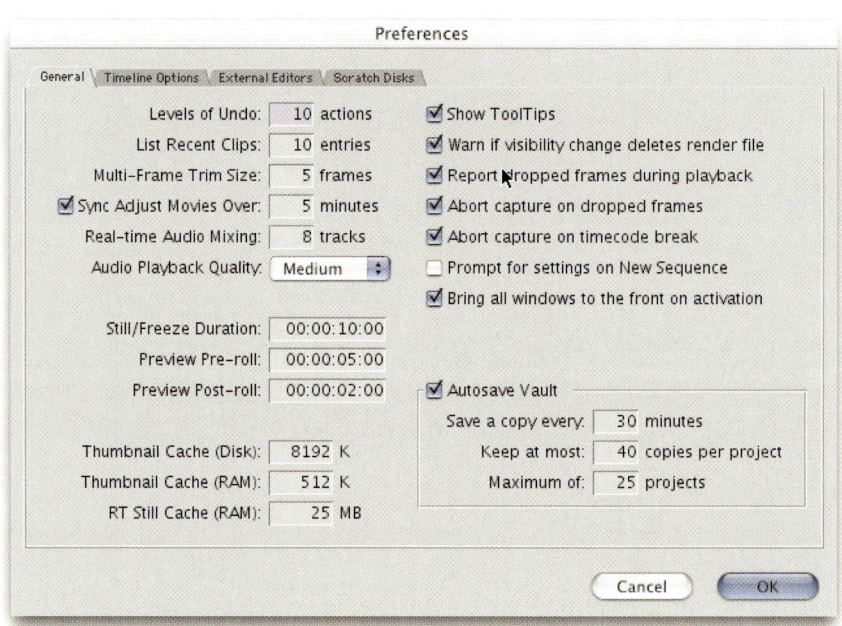

Figure 3.3 The General Preferences

We recommend that you select these check boxes in particular:

Sync Adjust Movie Over X Minutes   When video and audio are captured from a Mini-DV tape, the signals are sent together, but not connected (that is, there is no intrinsic link). Therefore, a drift in sync can occur over time. It's recommended to always keep this option selected unless you are capturing from DVCAM, which has an intrinsic lock between audio and video. The minutes setting should reflect the length of the clips that you are bringing in.

Abort Capture On Dropped Frames   This option causes Final Cut Express to monitor your input, looking for frames in the video that get lost, and to stop capturing altogether when a frame is missing (&⌒ the upcoming "What Is a *Dropped Frame* and How Can I Pick It Up?" sidebar).

Abort Capture On Timecode Break   Select this check box if you want the capturing process to stop if there is a non sequitur in the timecode. This means that the timecode on the tape breaks, which can happen when someone stops a tape while shooting and fast-forwards into the tape a bit before shooting more.

Next, click the Scratch Disks tab of the Preferences window (see Figure 3.4). At the top of the window, review your scratch disk—the disk your media will be captured to—to make sure it is set correctly (☞ Chapter 2, "The Software," for detailed instructions on setting your scratch disk). At the bottom of the window, select the Limit Capture Now To *X* Minutes check box; this sets a maximum amount of time for the Capture Now option. You should set this in accordance with the amount of memory you have—the more memory, the more footage you can capture at once without problems.

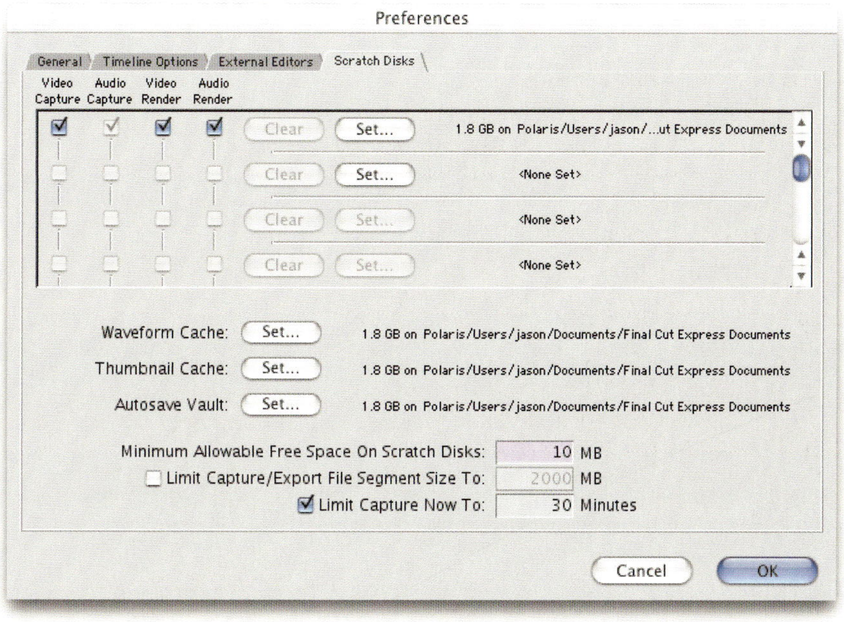

Figure 3.4 The Scratch Disk Preferences

What Is a *Dropped Frame* and How Can I Pick It Up?

A *dropped frame* is a frame from your source DV tape that didn't make it through the FireWire connection to your computer and is therefore going to be missing from your media clip. This is a big problem because it can cause your media to look jerky or like it is skipping. Typically, frames get dropped if the computer doesn't have enough memory or if you are running other applications.

Generally, if frames are dropping during capture, you will want to stop capturing and start over. If the problem persists, try saving your project, rebooting the computer, restarting Final Cut Express, and then try capturing again. If you still cannot shake dropped frames, the problem might be your external disk (not all FireWire disks are made to Apple's specifications) so you should check with the manufacturer.

Preparing to Capture

The Capture window is a special window, separate from the main Final Cut Express interface, that lets you review footage on your source DV tapes and then capture sections of the tape to create video clips on your hard disk. The Capture window (see Figure 3.5) looks remarkably like the Viewer and the Canvas and has many of the same controls (&⌢ Chapter 2 for detailed descriptions of these). In this section, you'll look under the hood of the Capture window to see how it works before jumping into using it in the following sections.

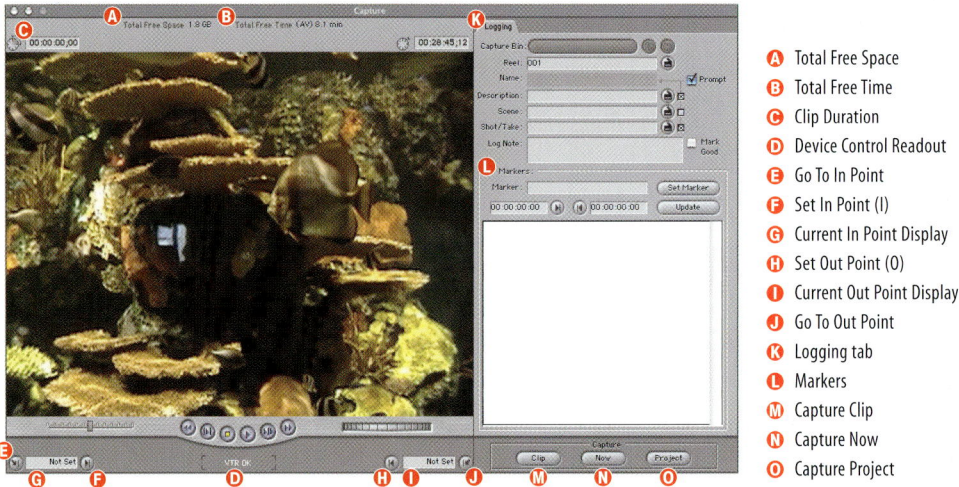

Figure 3.5 The Capture window is where your computer collects video clips.

The Capture window is made up of the following controls and readouts as shown in Figure 3.5:

Total Free Space   This shows the amount of space left on the hard disk that you have designated as your scratch disk. If you have very little space, you'll need to change your scratch disk (&⌢ Chapter 2).

Total Free Time   This indicates the amount of high-resolution video (in minutes and seconds) that can be captured to the scratch disk before it becomes full.

Clip Duration   When you set In and Out points to designate a clip, this readout shows you how long that clip runs.

Device Control Readout   This readout tells you if you have a connection to a deck (readout will say VTR OK) or if Final Cut Express cannot detect a connection to a deck (readout will say No Communication).

Go To In Point   Clicking this button shuttles the digital video tape to the timecode of the current In point.

Set In Point (I)   Clicking this button sets an In point to designate the beginning of a clip to capture.

Current In Point Display   This readout shows the timecode of the current In point. You can also type in an In point timecode value.

Set Out Point (O)   Clicking this button sets an Out point to designate the end of a clip to capture.

Current Out Point Display   This readout shows the timecode of the current Out point. You can also type in an Out point timecode value.

Go To Out Point   Clicking this button shuttles the digital videotape to the timecode of the current Out point.

Logging tab   This tab contains the set of controls to log a clip, the process by which you name and set information for individual clips.

Markers   This adds markers to highlight certain parts of the clip (🔗 the "Setting Markers" section later in this chapter).

Capture Clip   Clicking this button captures a clip after In and Out points have been set.

Capture Now   Clicking this button captures whatever is currently playing from the deck or camera.

Capture Project   Clicking this button captures everything within the open project. This is handy when you've erased your media files, but still have the project and want to bring all the media for that project back into the computer.

To begin your capture, first make sure that the project you want to capture clips into is selected in the Browser window, check that your DV deck or camera is properly connected to your computer, and make sure that you've inserted the correct videotape into your deck or camera. If you are using a camcorder, set it to VCR or VTR mode (see Figure 3.6).

Figure 3.6 The camera switch is set to VTR mode.

Now you're ready to follow these steps:

1. Choose File > Capture (⌘+8) to open the Capture window..
2. Review the tape to find the clips you want to capture. Final Cut Express gives you multiple ways to do this. Because of FireWire technology and its integration with digital video, you can control the deck or camera from Final Cut Express's interface. To review your tape, you can do any of the following:
   - Use the VCR-style controls at the bottom of the monitor to play, fast-forward, and rewind through the tape.

- Use the J, K, L, and spacebar keys to move through the footage. Remember: J rewinds, K stops, L fast-forwards, and the spacebar plays and pauses.
- Use the Shuttle and Jog controls on either side of the monitor.
- Use the controls on the deck and camera itself, although this is probably the most cumbersome method.

Changing the Timecode View

The Capture, Viewer, and Canvas windows all include readouts showing timecodes for different purposes (Clip Duration, Current Timecode, and In and Out points). You can set how the timecode for each of these is displayed by Control+clicking the timecode box and selecting one of these options from the contextual menu:

View As Non-Drop Frame Shows timecode in the non-drop frame style. Although common wisdom is that video runs at 30 frames per second, it actually runs at 29.97 frames per second. (They really made this easy, didn't they?) Non-drop frame is a type of timecode that has not been adjusted for this fractional frame speed and runs at 30fps. Non-drop frame is denoted by colon increment dividers.

View As Drop Frame Shows timecode in the drop frame style. This timecode method adjusts for the 29.97fps rate by leaving out occasional frames to keep the rate accurate. Drop frame timecode leaves out the 1 and 0 frame on the first second of every minute, except for minutes that can be divided by 10. Drop frame timecode is denoted by a semicolon as the minute and frame increment divider.

View As Frame Lists timecode only in frames. Instead of dividing the timecode with minutes and seconds, the readout simply shows you the number of frames that have passed.

3. To create a new capture bin (the bin that newly captured clips are placed into) or to set an existing bin to be the capture, you do one of the following:
   - In the Capture window, click Up One Level to change the capture bin to the bin around it. If the current bin is not inside another bin, then the Browser itself is used as the capture bin.
   - In the Capture window, click the Create New Bin buttons to add a new bin to the Browser that will be used as the capture bin.
   - In the Browser, control+click an existing bin that you want to become the capture bin ("Organizing with Bins" later in this chapter) or Control+click in a blank area within the Browser and select Set Capture Bin. If clicking in a blank area, the top level of the Browser window is where new clips are placed.

   For this exercise, create a new bin called **Unused Clips** and set this to be the capture bin. All of the newly captured clips will go into this bin. Then, as you use them in your film, you can move them from this bin to other bins.

4. Enter the Reel name by clicking in the field next to the label Reel and typing a new name. The Reel name is the name or code number for the original source DV tape that you pull the clip from. The Default name is 001. If you are editing from footage shot by someone else for a big project, they might give you a tape that is already coded (for example, TAPE CC001), so you would follow this code. For this exercise, we are using the Reel name Aquarium Tape 1 (see Figure 3.7).

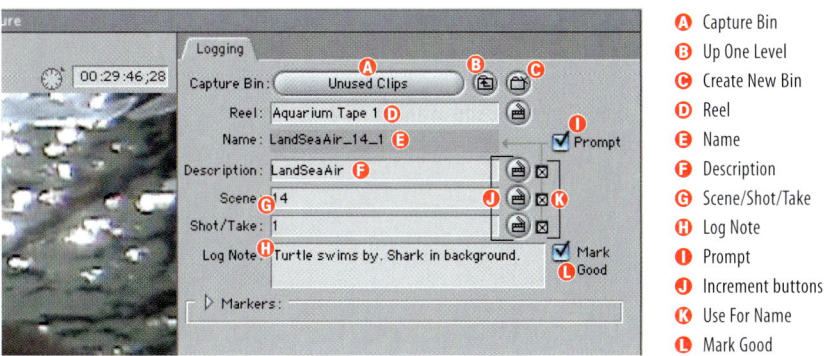

Figure 3.7 The Logging tab in action

The Logging tab has the following controls:

Capture Bin This shows you the project and bin you will capture your clip into.

Up One Level Click this to set the capture bin one level above the current level.

Create New Bin Click this to create a new bin inside the current logging bin and sets it as the capture bin.

Reel Enter the name or code for the digital video source tape you are capturing from.

Name Enter the name you want to use for the clip being captured.

Description You can enter an optional description of a clip for more detailed cataloging.

Scene and Shot/Take Enter information here if you are organizing shots by a camera log of scenes and takes.

Log Note This option provides an optional note for any concerns, thoughts, or flags for that clip.

Prompt If this check box is selected, you will be prompted when logging or capturing to enter a name for the clip. If you already entered a name in the Name field, that will be used as the default.

Increment buttons Click to incrementally increase the numbers or letters used in the Description, Scene, and/or Shot/Take fields.

Use For Name Check to use the Description, Scene, and/or Shot/Take will to create the name automatically.

Mark Good Check this box to indicate that you liked this clip for whatever reason.

5. Type a name for the clip. There are several ways to describe a particular clip: Name, Description, Scene, and/or Shot/Take. Try to come up with something succinct but descriptive. It's best with larger projects to come up with a coding system.

Note: You'll probably want to organize your clips alphabetically or numerically, sorting by the first characters of the name you assign.

To save time typing, you can have Final Cut Express construct the name for you automatically by using the Description, Scene, and Shot/Take information you type (separated by an underscore). To do this, select the check box next to each. In this example, we are logging the first take of scene 14 in a film called *Land, Sea, & Air*, so we set the name as LandSeaAir_14_1.

6. In the Log Note, you can add additional text, such as whether the clip is cut short or runs the full length, if the lighting was bad, if anything went wrong, if the take is very good, and so forth.

After setting up the clip in the Logging tab, you are ready to either add markers or to start capturing.

FAQ on Capturing

Here are some frequently asked questions about setting up to capture video:

What is the capture bin for?   When a clip is captured and brought into Final Cut Express, it is housed in the Browser. You can have multiple projects open at the same time, and you can have many bins (folders that organize clips) within the same project. To help you keep a project organized, Final Cut Express allows you to designate a capture bin. This is the target bin, where all the clips you capture will automatically be housed. The current capture bin is listed at the top of the Logging tab in the Capture window and is indicated by a clapboard icon in the Browser.

Why can't I see the video controls in the Capture window?   If your DV deck or camera is not properly hooked up and you try to open the Capture window, you will first see an alert letting you know that the device was not found. Click OK. Then you will see the Capture Hardware dialog box. Check your connections and click Check Again. If you click Continue instead and proceed without a device properly attached, you will still see the Capture window, but will not have any video controls and will see only test bars in the monitor area.

Why is setting the Reel name important?   If you lose your media file or if you need to delete it for some reason, you'll want to have a reference to the tape that a clip comes from so you can recapture the media. If you don't have the right reel number listed, you won't know what tape to use!

Why are the folders called *bins*?   Although they look and act like folders, Final Cut Express calls its organizational units *bins* in reference to the actual large bins used in film editing. When cutting film, the trims of film that would later be spliced together to make the movie are hung from hooks over big bins that fill with masses of curled film. So even though Final Cut Express doesn't use large cardboard boxes lined with garbage bags to hold its clips, the term has stuck.

Setting Markers

In addition to setting the other logging information, you can also set markers for a clip. Markers are helpful tools to make frame-specific marks and notes. This function in the Capture window lets you mark parts within the clip to identify specific moments. For example, you might want to mark when someone steps in front of the camera and ruins the sound, or when the shot goes out of focus, or when a cloud passes overhead and changes the lighting. You can, of course, add markers later when the footage is captured, but it is often helpful while logging to go ahead and mark the clips.

Another great advantage of marking clips is that each marker can be treated as a clip when editing your film. This enables you to drag and drop the part of the clip delineated by the marker to use it in your video without having to trim it first in the Viewer.

To set markers, follow these steps:

1. Have your footage set at the frame you want to designate as the In point for your marker. Open the Markers area by clicking the arrow to the left of the Markers title (see Figure 3.8).

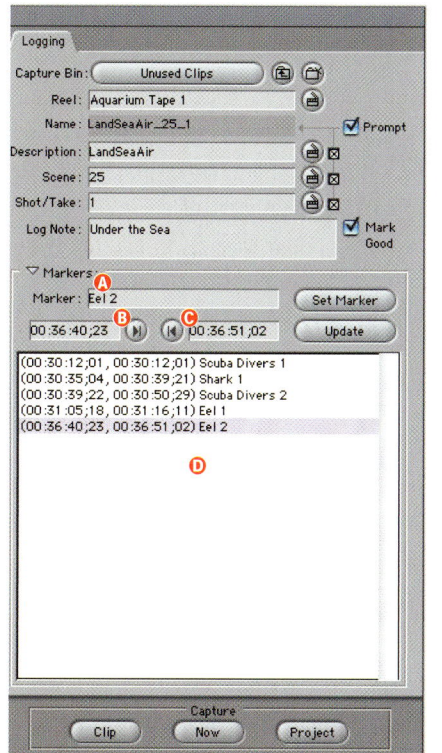

Figure 3.8

Markers set for a clip

Ⓐ Marker name
Ⓑ Set Mark In button
Ⓒ Set Mark Out button
Ⓓ Marker list

2. Click the Mark In button. This sets the opening point for the marker to the current location in the clip.

3. Fast-forward through the footage, to where you want the marked section to end, and click the Set Marker Out button button. You can now type the name that you want to identify this marker in the Marker text box. This name should indicate what you are marking, for example, Eel 2.

4. Click the Set Marker button. Your marker is added to the clip by using the set In and Out points and will appear as a list in the window below the marker controls.

Repeat steps 1–4 for as many markers as desired. After you finish setting your markers, you are ready to begin capturing your clips.

Note: If you want to make changes to a marker in your list, click the marker, make the changes by typing in the new information, and click the Update button.

Capturing Video Clips

With all your settings in place, the deck or camera hooked up to your computer, the DV tape in the deck, and the Capture window open, it's time to start capturing your footage. When you do so, Final Cut Express gives you a couple of options. Remember that when you capture, you are not taking in the whole tape as one long piece (although technically you can if you want to). You're choosing select parts of the tape and giving them individual names. These new selects are called clips. Let's look at the different methods for capturing clips.

Note: Clips should always be at least 10 seconds long. Shorter clips might have a problem capturing.

Deciding Where Captured Files Go

When installing Final Cut Express, a new folder called Final Cut Express Documents is created on your hard disk in the Documents folder. This is the default location for captured files, located in this folder are several other folders including one called Capture Scratch. Every project opened in Final Cut Express will have its own folder created within the Capture Scratch folder, and that is where you will find your raw clip files (see Figure 3.9).

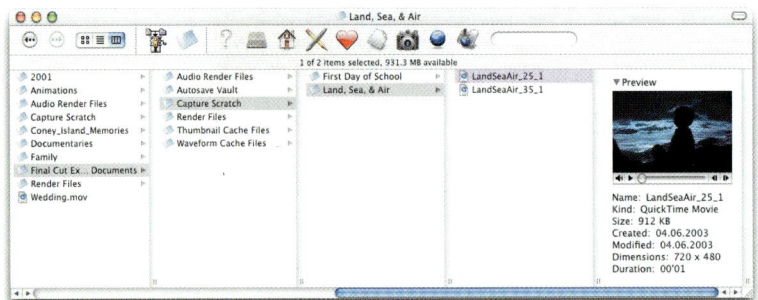

Figure 3.9
Clips are located in the Capture Scratch Folder

To change the location of the Final Cut Express Documents folder, open the Scratch Disks tab in the Preferences window (Option+Q), click the Set button, navigate to the folder on your hard disk where you want the auxiliary files saved (we prefer the Movies folder), and click Choose.

Using Capture Now

The simplest and quickest way to capture footage is to use the Now button. Capture Now is a function that immediately starts capturing whatever footage is currently playing on your deck or camera (and therefore whatever is currently showing in the Capture window's monitor).

> **Note:** The Capture Now method is good for bringing in footage on the fly, or bringing in long clips when you don't need to be exactly accurate in which section of the tape you are taking in.

To capture footage by using Capture Now, follow these steps:

1. Use the Capture window video controls to scan through the tape to the beginning of the clip that you want to capture.
2. Set a marker at this point (↩ "Setting Markers" earlier). Then rewind the tape to about 15 to 20 seconds before the first frame you want to start with.
3. Start the footage playing by clicking the Play button (spacebar).
4. Click the Now button in the Capture area to begin capturing the footage from the tape. This will obviously capture several seconds before your intended starting point, but this gives you what is called *pre-roll* footage to allow smoother edits. A large window appears, showing the footage as it is being captured (see Figure 3.10). The resolution of the image shown as it is being captured is always much lower than the resolution of the final clip.

Figure 3.10 The clip is being captured. Press Escape to stop capturing.

5. Press Escape when you want to stop capturing footage. You might want to wait a few seconds after the end of the footage that you are capturing to give the clip a *post-roll*. A new video clip appears in your bin, containing the video footage you just captured.

Note: You can rename the clip by clicking its icon in the Browser, waiting a fraction of a second, and clicking again (do *not* double-click). You can then type the new name for the clip.

Repeat steps 1–5 for as many clips as desired.

Using Capture Clip

If you need a more precise way of choosing a clip to take from your source tape, you should use the Capture Clip method, which enables you to set exact In and Out points for a clip by using the timecode on the source tape. This way, you can pick exactly—to the frame—what section of a tape you want to bring in as a clip.

This method is helpful when you are taking in lots of short clips, or when you are editing a narrative movie and are pulling specific scenes and takes from a series of shots.

To use the Capture Clip method, follow these steps:

1. Preview your tape and find the footage that you want to be the beginning of your clip.
2. Set the tape on the exact frame that you want to designate as the first frame of your clip and click the Set In Point button (I). A timecode value now appears in the Current In Point window. Now you need to set the last frame of your clip (see Figure 3.11).

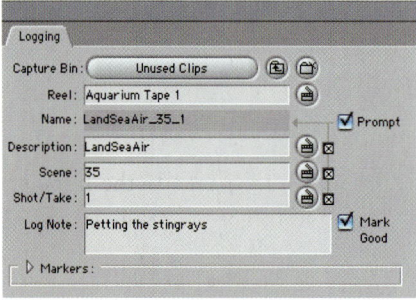

Figure 3.11
The In point has been defined.

Note: Remember, you can slowly scan through your footage by using the J, K, L, and spacebar keys to navigate the source tape, using the Shuttle and Jog controls, or even typing the exact timecode you want to start at in the Current Timecode field so the tape will automatically shuttle to that point.

3. Play or fast-forward through the footage to find the last frame you want to capture and click the Set Out Point button (O). A timecode value now appears in the Current Out Point field (see Figure 3.12).

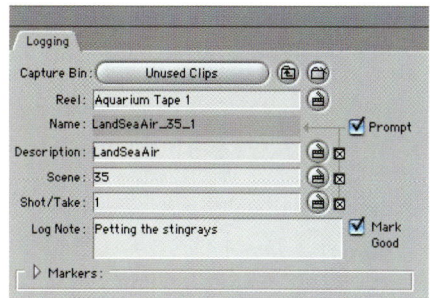

Figure 3.12
The Out point has been defined.

4. If you change your mind, you can reset the In or Out points anytime by repeating steps 2 and/or 3.
5. Click the Clip button in the Capture area.

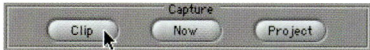

6. The Log Clip dialog box appears, enabling you to name the clip, as well as write an optional Log Note. Use a Log Note if you have something more involved to say about the clip, such as the audio is too loud, the shot is overexposed, or there's a really nifty part with a dancing bear you want to use.

7. Click OK. Final Cut Express automatically shuttles the tape to the In point that you set and begins capturing, stopping at the Out point. You will see the Capture Preview window as the clip is recaptured. Press the Escape key anytime to interrupt the capturing process.

When capturing is done, the clip will appear in the Browser, in the designated capture bin (see Figure 3.13). Repeat steps 1–7 until you've brought in all the clips you need.

Figure 3.13
The new clip is placed in the Browser and automatically opened in the Viewer.

Tips on Capturing

When you review your source tapes and decide which parts to bring into Final Cut Express as individual clips, you'll be making some very important decisions that will affect how you edit your project.

There are two main styles of capturing:

- Taking in long clips that cover a lot of shots and dividing them later
- Taking in shorter, refined clips from the start

Both methods are valid, and which method you choose will depend on your project. If you have a lot of footage from, say, a vacation, you might want to take in long clips, so that one clip can have footage from numerous places. This is done if you're not sure when capturing which parts of the footage you're going to want to use. Later, while editing, you can go through the long clip and choose the selects you want. These clips would be given more general names, for example, Beach Footage. This method will also take up more hard-disk space because you're probably going to be taking in a lot of footage that won't end up in your final movie. Typically, you would use the Capture Now method to take in a long clip.

If you are pretty organized from the get-go, you might want to decide to take in shorter, specific clips. You would take in an individual clip that is one specific scene or shot (say of a child building a sand castle, or a shot of a building). You would name each clip a specific title pertaining to the shot you bring in and then organize these shorter clips into bins. This method can help you find specific shots quicker and also will take up less hard-disk space. You would use the Capture Clip method for this kind of capturing. You can also set your capture bin while capturing each clip to automatically organize your clips as they are captured.

Using Capture Project

If, in the course of editing your movie, you decide to delete the space-hogging media files to clear up space, the project file still remembers the sequence of edits, including all the information about your clips and trims, but now can't access the actual video media file itself. When this happens, the clips are *offline*, as indicated by a red slash over the clip icon (see Figure 3.14). This means Final Cut Express has a clip that it can't find the source media file for. The program knows what tape it came from, what its timecode In and Out points were, and even how it was used in your edit. It just doesn't know where the video footage is itself.

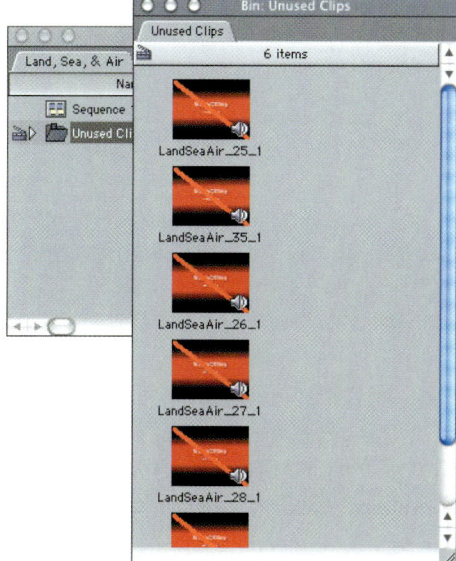

Figure 3.14
Offline clips are indicated with a red slash.

The solution to bringing this media back to the clips is to use the Capture Project function. When you click the Project button in the Capture area, Final Cut Express will recapture all the clips in the currently opened project file.

To recapture the clips for a project, follow these steps:

1. Open the project with offline clips that you want to recapture and open the Capture window (⌘+8).
2. Click the Project button in the Capture area.
3. Check your settings in the Capture Project dialog box (see Figure 3.15) and then click OK.
   - From the Capture list box, choose whether to capture all of the lost items (clips) in the project or just a particular clip.
   - Click the Add Handles check box to select it; this sets extra time before and after the In and Out points of the clips. Then enter the length of the handles. In this example, we set 5-second handles.
   - Choose the Capture Preset type. Generally, you will not need to change this.
   - At the bottom of the dialog box, make sure you have enough disk space left to capture.

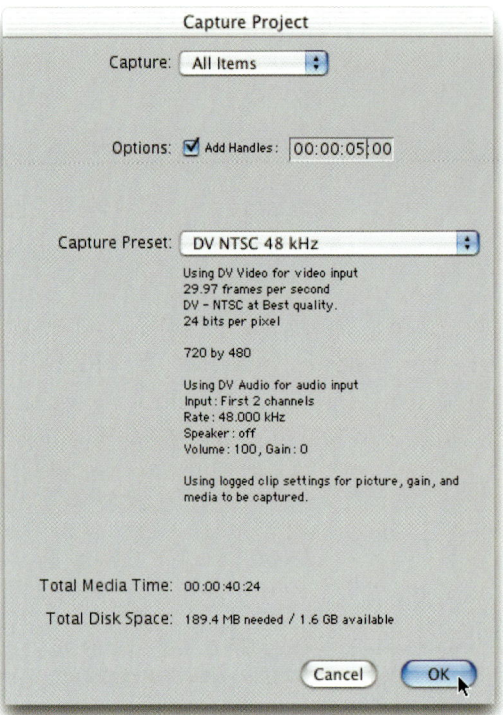

Figure 3.15
The Capture Project dialog box

4. In the Insert Reel dialog box (see Figure 3.16), you will see a list of clips to be recaptured. Check the list and make sure that you have the tapes ready; then click Continue.

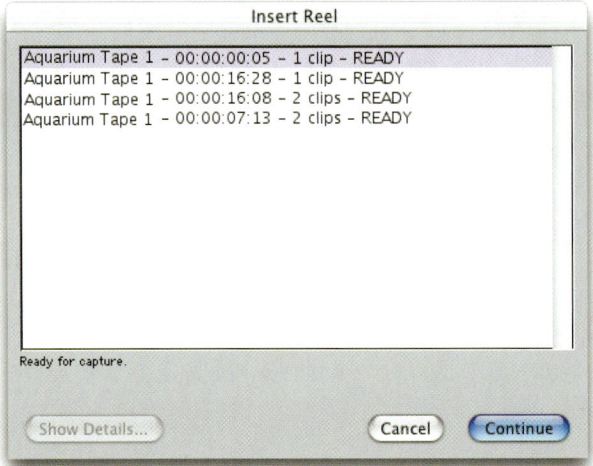

Figure 3.16
The Insert Reel dialog box

5. You will see Capture Preview window as the clip(s) are recaptured. Press the Escape key anytime to interrupt the capturing process. After finishing, the Insert Reel dialog box will reappear, displaying the status of the capture.
6. Click Finish, and the clip now appears online (without the red slash).

When the process is done, Final Cut Express will reconnect the media to your clips, and voilá, your clips are not offline anymore—they are "online"—and you're back in business.

Importing Clips

Not all clips that you use in an editing project will need to be captured. If a media file is coming from the Web, from a file on a DVD-ROM (like this book's tutorial) or CD-ROM, or from a track on an audio CD, you will need to *import* the files rather than capture them. This is also the case for still images such as JPEGs and Photoshop files, audio files such as wave files, QuickTime movies, or movie files created in After Effects. You can think of *importing* as bringing in the files that already exist on a hard disk or CD, whereas *capturing* is the process of bringing video from tape into the computer world.

Using Import to Get Media Files

If a media file already exists on your hard disk, but isn't in your Final Cut Express project, you'll need to import the file into Final Cut Express. If the file is on a CD, CD-ROM, or DVD-ROM, you should copy it from the disc onto your hard disk first (place it wherever you are storing your other Final Cut Express media files), and then import it from your hard disk. Importing enables you to use files saved in most of the common formats:

Audio	MP3, AIFF, WAV	
Video	MOV	
Still	JPEG, TIFF, PNG, GIF, PSD, BMP, EPS, PDF	

Importing Files

To import a single file into the current project, follow these steps:

1. Choose File > Import > Files (⌘+I).
2. In the Choose a File dialog box, find the file you want to import and select it (see Figure 3.17). You can use the Show menu to gray out files that are not of the type you are looking for. Choose the option Standard Files to view only files that Final Cut Express believes it can import. Choose All Files to view files even if Final Cut Express does not believe it can import them (it often can).
3. Click the Choose button to import this file into your current open project. The single file then appears in the Browser.

> **Note:** If you are using Apple iTunes and are hooked up to the Internet, you can have the names of most popular albums with their track names automatically entered for a CD. Place the CD in your drive, open iTunes, and choose Advanced > Get CD Track Names. After churning for a few seconds, all of the names will be automatically supplied. Now when you import the audio file, it will already be named.

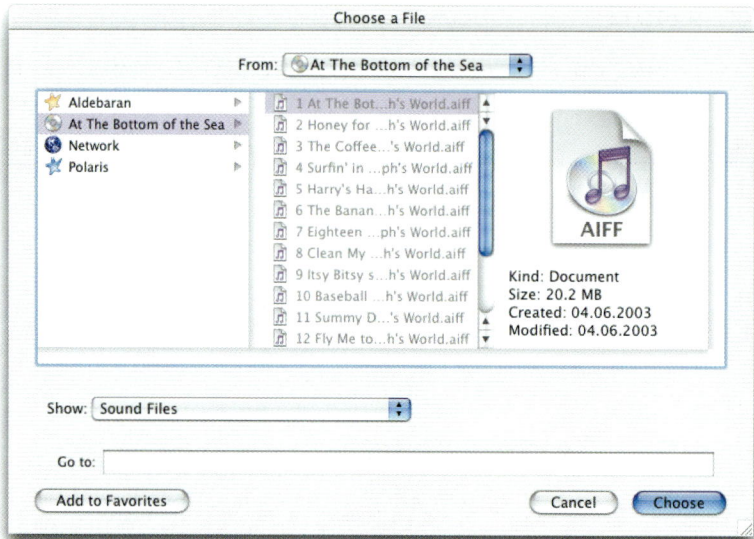

Figure 3.17
A file is being imported from an audio CD. The Show menu has been set to Sound Files so that only audio files can be selected.

Importing Folders

To import a folder of files into the current project, follow these steps:

1. Choose File > Import > Folder.

 Note: You can also Control+click in any blank area of the Browser window and choose Import Files or Import Folders from the contextual menu.

2. In the Choose A Folder dialog box (see Figure 3.18), find the file or folder you want to import and select it.
3. Click the Choose button to import this folder and all files within it into your current open project. A new bin is created using the originating folder's name and containing all of the media clips.

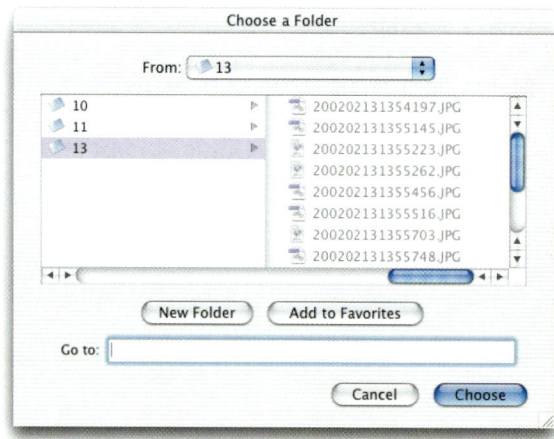

Figure 3.18
A folder of images being imported from the hard disk

Dragging and Dropping Media Files

Although the Import command is an easy way to bring different media files into a project, there is an even easier way: you can simply drag and drop image files directly from your Finder (folders or the Desktop) or even from other applications such as iPhoto into your project through the Browser, Timeline, Viewer, or Canvas.

- To add content from the Finder, with Final Cut Express showing, open the folder with your source material by using the Mac OS X finder. Click and drag one or more files into the Browser, Timeline, Viewer, or Canvas (see Figure 3.19).

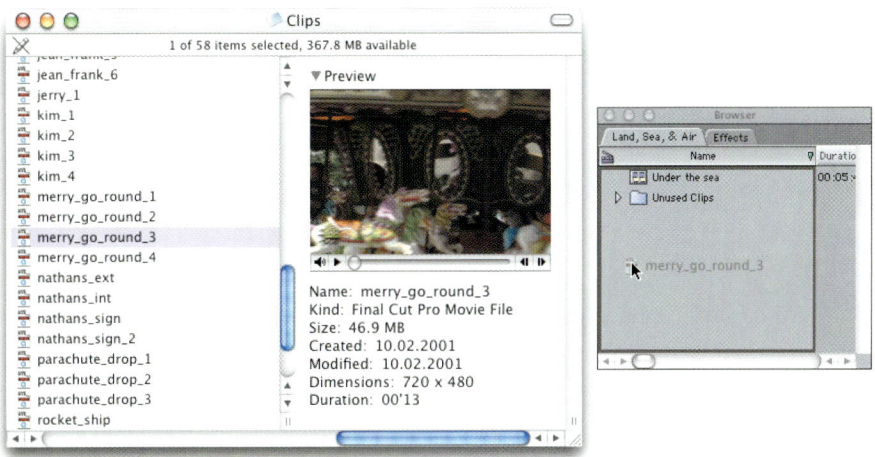

Figure 3.19 A video file is being dragged from a DVD into the project Browser.

- To add content from iPhoto, with Final Cut Express showing, open iPhoto, locate the image or images, and click and drag them from iPhoto into the Browser, Timeline, Viewer, or Canvas (see Figure 3.20).

Figure 3.20 A still image is being dragged from iPhoto into the Timeline.

The real trick with dragging and dropping media files is getting around Final Cut Express's expansive interface. With all of those windows, it can be quite a juggling act to get the windows for the source material and for Final Cut Express to the front of the screen at the same time. Remember, though, that you need to see only part of the Final Cut Express window in order to drag and drop files into it.

Organizing Your Project

After you've captured your clips, you will want to organize them in a fashion that enables you to quickly and easily find the clips you want. If you're working with a larger project that has many clips, this can save you a countless amount of time. How you organize your clips is going to depend on one major factor: what kind of project are you working on? If you are cutting together a short video or a birthday party, you might need only one or two bins—for example, you might create one bin for shots of the birthday girl and one bin for shots of the presents. If you are editing a documentary, you will want to organize your footage by interviews, themes, and B-roll. (*B-roll* is footage that is shot to provide illustration or visual flair over primary footage such as an interview.) If you are editing a short horror movie, then you'll want to create a bin for each scene, and maybe even sub-bins of different shots and takes within each scene.

The Browser's project tab works in a very similar way to Mac's own operating system. Clips are organized in a network of folders called bins, and you can drag and drop clips to move them from folder to folder. Within each project tab, you can create bins to divide and organize your clips. You can even put bins within bins.

Creating a New Bin

To create a new bin, do one of the following:

- Choose File > New > Bin.
- With the Browser window selected, press ⌘+B.
- Control+click on a blank area of the Browser bin and choose New Bin from the contextual menu.

A new untitled bin then appears in your project tab in your Browser.

 Note: To delete an existing bin, click on the bin and press the Delete key. This will delete the bin and all of its contents.

Organizing with Bins

You can move items (clips, bins, or sequences) around in the Browser to place them in bins to organize them. To move items into a bin or from one bin to another, do one of the following:

- Click and drag a single item to the desired bin.
- Command+click or Shift+click to select multiple items, and then click and drag any of the selected items to move them all into the desired bin (see Figure 3.21).

Figure 3.21
Multiple files being dragged into a bin

- Click the first item in a list of consecutive items you want to select. Shift+click the last item in the list to select that item and all items in between. Then click and drag any of the selected items to move them all into the desired bin.

> **Note:** To move an item or items to the top level of the project (out of all bins) while in list view mode, follow the instructions for selecting the clips, but drag them into the header bar.

Organizational Tips

If you are putting together a video with dozens of different clips, organization can not only save you time, but aggravation as well. Here are a few tips we have found useful:

- Create different bins for different subject matters. Let's say you want to make a bin to house all shots from a scene at the penguin house at the zoo. You'd create and name a new bin, say, "Penguin House Clips" and then drag all the penguin-related clips into that bin.

- Create different bins for different media types—for example, create a bin to house your audio track files so they don't get mixed up with the video clips.

- When working with a lot of clips and a more complicated project, use the Browser's list view rather than the default icon view. To change this, choose View > Browser Items > As List. The list view lets you quickly see all your clips in alphabetical order and the properties of those clips at a glance.

- Name your clips and bins something logical and orderly—for example, use prefixes such as *int* for interviews so that you can alphabetically group all interview clips together.

Setting Properties of a Clip or Sequence

Every clip and sequence in a project has several attributes that can be set for it beyond its name. You can change the properties or information about a clip or sequence with the click of your mouse.

Control+click a clip or sequence icon in a project file in your Browser and choose Item Properties from the contextual menu. The Item Properties window appears (see Figure 3.22). Change the properties as desired and then click OK after you finish.

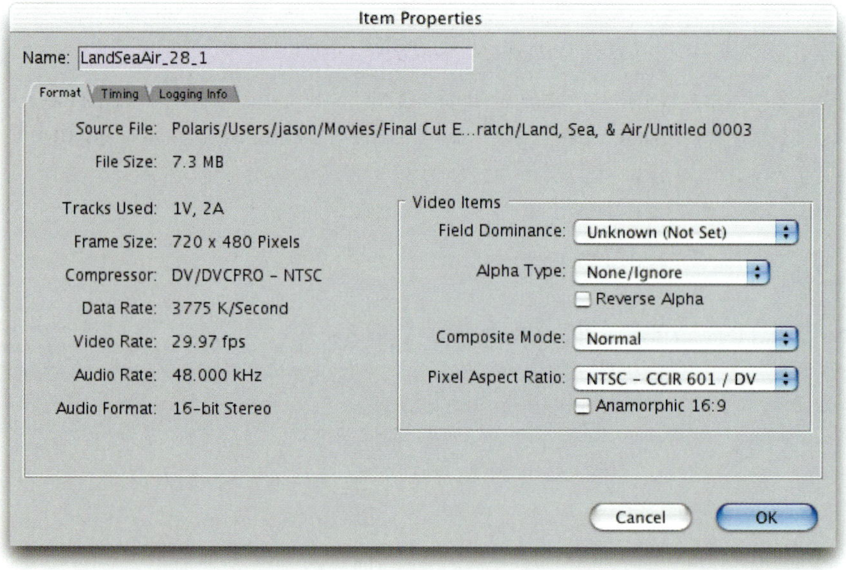

Figure 3.22 The Item Properties dialog box

The Item Properties dialog box has three tabs:

Format This tab gives you a general rundown on the clip or sequence at a glance. If you are dealing with a clip, it will tell you where on the hard disk the clip is saved, its file size, frame size, and so forth. You can also change its properties, such as field dominance or alpha channels (↳ Chapter 7, "Adding Video Effects").

Timing This tab shows you the length of the source media file and the length of the current trimmed clip made from that media file. You can type in new timecode values to trim the clip differently.

Logging Info If you didn't enter this logging information when you first logged the clip, you can do so now. You can review or fill in the Reel number, the shot/take information, and so forth.

Movie Night!

Traffic

Director: Steven Soderberg

Editor: Stephen Mirrione

Traffic, a multilayered film about the illegal drug trade in the United States, mixes a number of separate stories to look at the larger picture of how drugs move from their source to dealer to user. Starring Michael Douglas and Don Cheadle among an ensemble cast, the film intercuts the multiple plots to create tension and drama larger than each individual storyline.

The editing of *Traffic* is a good lesson in how an editor can cut between scenes that have only a thematic relationship without confusing the viewer's sense of time and space. *Traffic* is also noteworthy for its inventive use of color filters on the image—a cool blue for action in Washington D.C., a burning yellow for scenes in Mexico. And these effects aren't just at the fingertips of Hollywood filmmakers; they can be achieved with Final Cut Express's color correction filter, too. *Traffic*'s editing style was noted as a factor in its success, and the film even received the 2000 Academy Award for Best Editing, for what that's worth.

Editing Basics

This chapter introduces you to the fun part—the creative part—of Final Cut Express: editing. Putting together the film clips into a motion picture is what Final Cut Express is all about. For the first three chapters, you've looked at how to set up your system, bring in your footage, and organize your workstation and clips. Now you'll see how all of that preparation pays off. In this chapter, you'll look at the basics of moving clips around in the interface and how to start ordering them into an edited movie.

Chapter Contents
Bringing clips into the Timeline
Creating and using sequences
Setting a clip's In and Out points
Using multiple tracks

Navigating the Timeline

The Timeline is your working space, the creative window where you try different ways of cutting your clips together. To aid you in making the perfect cut, the Timeline offers several tools to let you view or tag certain parts of your cut for efficient editing.

> **On the DVD: Chapter 4**
>
> Starting in this chapter, you will be using the files you moved to your hard disk from the companion DVD. Open the project file Land, Sea, & Air in Final Cut Express. Although there is no sequence for this chapter (as there will be for Chapters 5–10), you will be practicing creating a sequence called Chapter 4 in the project and bringing clips into the sequence from the Unused Clips bin.

Changing Your View

Within the Timeline, you can adjust your view or perspective quickly by scrolling from side to side, zooming in, and zooming out.

To shuttle backward and forward along the length of your sequence in the Timeline, use the scroll bar at the base of the Timeline. This scroll bar can also be used to change the apparent width of tracks by clicking and dragging at either edge.

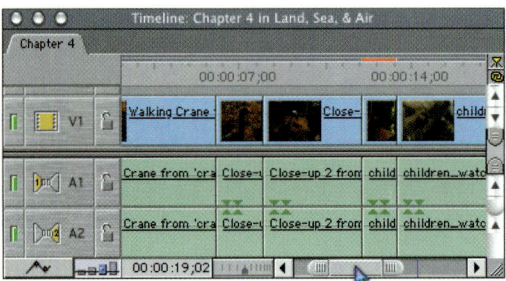

To zoom in to a specific part of the Timeline, use the Zoom (magnifying glass) tool (press Z) to click the Timeline or type ⌘++. (⌘D+plus). This is useful to perform detailed edits on a clip.

To zoom out to get a look at the bigger picture, use the Zoom (magnifying glass) tool 🔍 (press ZZ) to click the Timeline or type ⌘+- (⌘+minus).

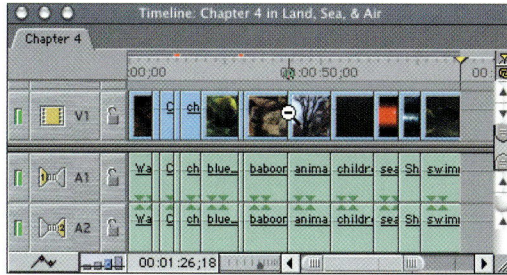

To jump to a specific magnification in the Timeline, choose View > Level and then choose a magnification.

> **Note:** You can also zoom in and out of the Timeline by using the magnification slider found at the base of the Timeline, just to the left of the scroll bar, or by using the tabs on the left and right sides of the scroll handle itself. By dragging these, you can zoom in or zoom out quickly.

> **Note:** All of the zooming methods mentioned here for the Timeline work only if the Timeline is the active window. If the Canvas or the Viewer is the active window, one of those will be zoomed instead.

Setting In and Out Points in the Timeline

Although you can use In and Out points to trim a clip and show only a specific segment of footage, you can also add In and Out points into the Timeline itself. Adding In and Out points into the Timeline is useful for accomplishing a number of tasks, including these:

- Designating the place where you want a clip to be edited into the Timeline
- Setting parameters for printing to video or exporting part of a sequence
- Setting limits of a voice-over recording

In and Out points in the Timeline are also useful whenever you create an edit by using the Canvas window's Edit Overlay options—the clip will default to fit between the In and Out points set in the Timeline. However, the In/Out points will be reset automatically after the edit is made. If no In/Out points are set, the clip will default to the position of the playhead and fill as much space as needed for the entire clip.

To set In and Out points in the Timeline, follow these steps:

1. Make sure that the Timeline is the active window.
2. Place the playhead at the location where you want the In point to appear and press I. An In marker is added in the scrub bar at the top of the Timeline.

3. Place the playhead at the frame in the Timeline where you want the Out point to appear and press O. An Out marker is added in the scrub bar at the top of the Timeline (see Figure 4.1).

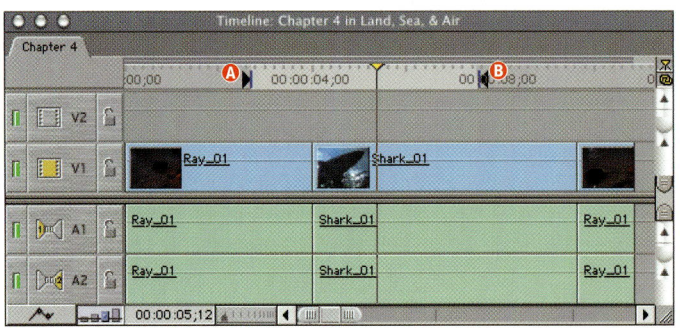

Figure 4.1
The In point (**A**) and Out point (**B**) have been set for the Timeline.

As in the Viewer, you can drag the In/Out points in the Timeline to adjust them.

Using the Mark Menu for the Viewer or Timeline

In addition to setting In/Out points, the Mark menu includes several other options that can be used in either the Viewer or the Timeline (to set In/Out points for an individual clip), or in the Timeline alone (to set In/Out points in the Timeline only). Which window the Mark menu affects depends on which is the active window. For more information on markers, see the next section "Working with Markers".

The options that can affect either window are as follows (keyboard commands are in parentheses):

Mark > Mark In (press I)   Sets the In point to the timecode currently under the playhead in the Viewer or the Timeline.

Mark > Mark Out (press O)   Sets the Out point to the timecode currently under the playhead in the Viewer or the Timeline.

Mark > Mark Split > Video In (Control+I), Video Out (Control+O), Audio In (Option+⌘+I), Audio Out (Option+⌘+O)   Enables you to set In and Out points for audio and video separately by choosing one of the options in the submenu.

Mark > Mark Clip (press X)   Sets the In/Out points to the beginning or end of the clip or gap currently under the playhead in the Viewer or the Timeline.

The following menu options apply only when you are working in the Timeline and you have a clip selected:

Mark > Mark To Markers (Control+A)   With markers set in the Timeline (Mark > Markers > Add), this option sets In/Out points to the two markers that the playhead is between. If markers have not been set on one side or the other, the default is the very beginning or very end of the footage in the Timeline.

Mark > Mark Selection (Shift+A)   Sets In/Out points around currently selected clips in the Timeline.

Mark > Select In To Out (Option+A)   Selects all clips between the In/Out points in the Timeline.

Mark > Clear In To Out, In, Out, Split (Option+X, Option+I, Option+O)   Removes the In/Out points from the Timeline as indicated.

Working with Markers

Markers do what they say: they mark a specific frame or area of a clip or a sequence so that you can make notes about that point, create a mark point to snap to, or just provide a reference for timing of the clip's content.

Adding Markers

Markers can be added to either a clip or to the Timeline itself (so that they don't correspond to a particular clip) in order to add notes to specific points within the video. You can use a marker for a wide variety of purposes, limited only by your imagination. For example, in this book, we have used markers in the Chapters 5–10 sequences to mark where you should move in the Timeline to begin working on a specific exercise for that chapter.

To add a marker to the Timeline, follow these steps:

1. Make sure that the Timeline window is active.
2. Put your playhead in the Timeline over the frame to which you want to add the marker (see Figure 4.2).
3. If you want to add the marker to a specific clip, select that clip in the Timeline. Otherwise, make sure no clips are selected.

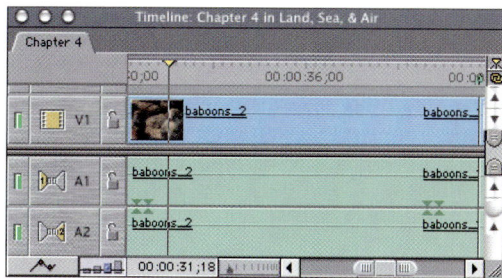

Figure 4.2
The playhead set for the new marker to be placed

4. To add the marker at this point in the Timeline, do one of the following:
   - Press M.
   - Choose Mark > Markers > Add.
   - Click the Add Marker button in the Canvas.

   If you want to name the marker, add notes, or extend the marker over multiple frames, press the M key twice (MM) or double-click the Add Marker button when adding the marker. This opens the Edit Marker dialog box (see Figure 4.3). In this dialog, you can specify the marker's name and duration to create a marker that spreads over several frames. Click the OK button when you finish.

Figure 4.3
The Edit Marker dialog box

A green marker appears in the Timeline's ruler. While the playhead is over the marker in the Timeline, you will also notice the name of the marker being displayed in the Canvas (see Figure 4.4). If you've selected a clip, then the marker will appear on that clip and stay on the clip unless you delete it. Now that your marker is placed, you can use it as a visual guide or as a reference point.

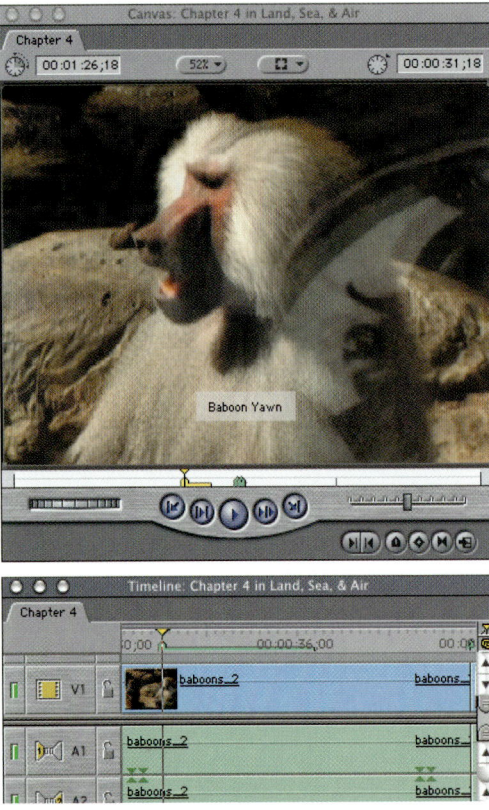

Figure 4.4
The new marker in the Timeline with its name displayed in the Canvas

  Note: If Snapping is on (press N), any clip will snap to set markers.

Editing and Deleting Markers

After a marker has been set (whether it was initially edited or not), it can be edited anytime to change the name, comments, position, and duration. In addition, markers can be permanently deleted when no longer needed. To edit or delete a marker in the Timeline, place the playhead on the marker (the marker's name should appear in the Canvas) and do one of the following:

To edit the marker, choose Mark > Markers > Edit (press M) or click the Marker button in the Canvas. Type the information in the Edit Marker dialog box and click OK. You can change the marker's name, comments, and duration.

To move the marker, move the playhead to the right of the marker to the new desired position and choose Mark > Markers > Reposition [Shift+accent grave (`)]. The marker to the immediate left of this position will be repositioned here. You can, of course, also reposition the marker by using the Edit Marker dialog box.

To extend the duration of a marker, move the playhead to the right of the marker to the desired duration and choose Mark > Markers > Extend (Option+plus`). The marker to the immediate left of this position will now have its duration set to this point. You can, of course, also set the duration of the marker by using the Edit Marker dialog box.

To delete the marker, choose Mark > Markers > Delete (⌘ +`). [Shift+accent grave (`)] or open the Edit Marker dialog box and click the Delete button.

To delete all markers in the current sequence, choose Mark > Markers > Delete All [Control+accent grave (`)].

Navigating Markers in the Timeline

After you start using markers in your work routine, you might not be able to stop (see Figure 4.5). Markers can be indispensable for helping you keep large projects organized. But after you get more than two in a sequence, they can become hard to navigate directly by using the scrub bar in the Timeline.

Figure 4.5
Markers in the Canvas

To make navigation easier, you can use menu and keyboard shortcuts to move around the Timeline, jumping from marker to marker:

To move to the next marker in the Timeline, choose Mark > Next > Marker (Shift+M). The playhead will move to the next marker.

To move to the previous marker in the Timeline, choose Mark > Previous > Marker (Option+M). The playhead will move to the previous marker.

To move to a specific marker in the Timeline, Control+click in the ruler of the Timeline and choose from the list of markers in the current sequence located at the bottom of the contextual menu (see Figure 4.6).

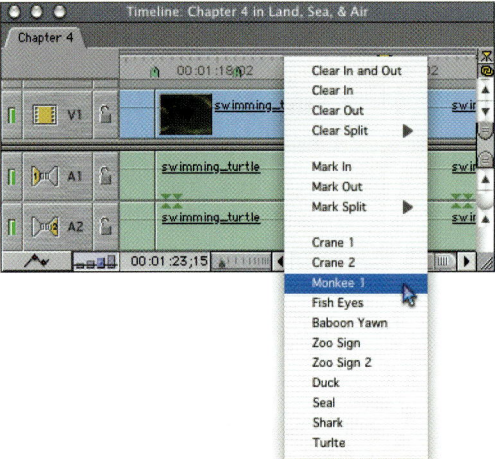

Figure 4.6
The marker contextual menu

 Note: Throughout Chapters 5-10, we reference markers to move to within a sequence in order for you to use clips for that exercise. The most efficient way to do this is to use the contextual menu.

Using Sequences

The Timeline is Final Cut Express' most used window, but it would be useless without the sequences inside it. A *sequence* is a collection of media clips edited together on a series of video and audio tracks. Sequences are viewed and edited in the Timeline. When a sequence is open in the Timeline, it appears under a tab that has the name of the sequence on it. When you have multiple sequences open in the Timeline, multiple tabs appear, and you can move between sequences by clicking the tab of the sequence you want to open. In this section, you'll look briefly at how to create and open sequences.

Creating a New Sequence

A single project can have multiple sequences. For example, if you are editing a narrative and you want to edit each scene separately, you can create a sequence for each scene. You can then later put all the sequences together as a single long sequence when you are ready to output your project to video or Quicktime movie.

To create a new sequence, select in the Browser the project file in which you want to add a sequence. Then choose File > New > Sequence (⌘+N). The sequence appears in your project file tab in the Browser automatically named Sequence with the next available number (Sequence 1, Sequence 2, Sequence 3, and so forth). If you change the name or delete one of these sequences, the numbering will still continue after the highest value (see Figure 4.7).

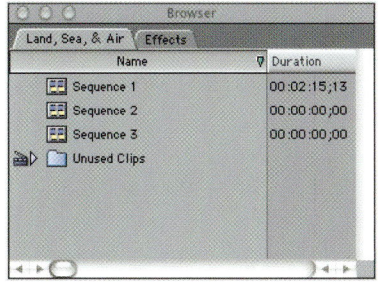

Figure 4.7
Sequences are added in order in the Browser.

Naming and Opening a Sequence

After you create a sequence, you will want to rename the sequence and then open it in the Timeline to begin editing clips.

To name the new sequence (or rename any sequence), click the name (not the icon) of the sequence in the Browser and then click it again without moving the mouse (do not double-click). The current name is selected, and you can begin typing the new name (see Figure 4.8). For this exercise, we are naming the new sequence Chapter 4.

Figure 4.8
The sequence name has been selected and replaced with something more descriptive.

To open the sequence in the Timeline (rather than just selecting the name), double-click the name or sequence icon. The sequence opens with a tab giving its name at the top (see Figure 4.9). With a sequence open, you're ready to bring in clips.

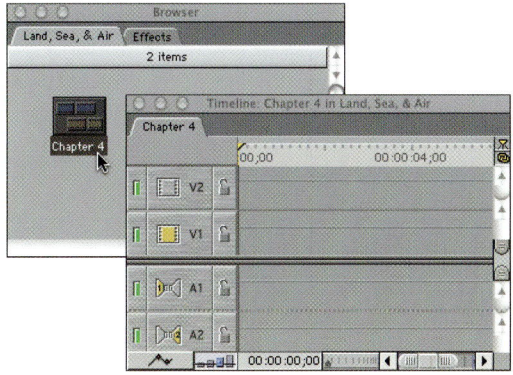

Figure 4.9
The new sequence has been opened in the Timeline and is ready for you to begin adding clips.

Getting Started with Clips

Your freshly captured clips are in the Browser, organized in the appropriately labeled bins within your project file tab. You've also got a sequence in your project file, ready to house your edited clips. But your clips are not going to make themselves into a movie just sitting there in the Browser. You need to get them out into the world. To do so, Final Cut Express gives you a number of ways to bring clips from the Browser or the Viewer into the Timeline to begin editing. However, before you start cutting, you will want to work on each clip on its own to trim it before it is ready to fall in line.

Setting In and Out Points in the Viewer

One of the great advantages of digital video editing is that it is *nondestructive* to the actual media files. Unlike editing physical film, where you would literally cut parts of the clip to trim it to the desired length, with DV you need simply tell the clip where to begin (In point) and where to end (Out point). The program will then show only that portion of the clip, hiding the trimmed portion. If later while editing you change your mind, you merely change the In and/or Out points, and the "hidden" footage will be revealed. This process is called *trimming*—it trims back the source clip to create a shorter sub-clip (see Figure 4.10). Creating sub-clips is discussed later in this chapter.

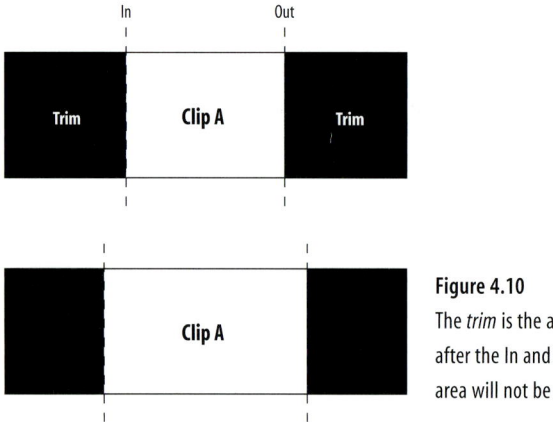

Figure 4.10
The *trim* is the area before and after the In and Out points; this area will not be shown.

    The Viewer window is where you review and prepare individual clips before editing them into the Timeline—enabling you to watch the video, listen to the audio, or preview a still image, and then make necessary cuts or changes to it before adding it into a sequence. The first of these changes will be to trim the clip by adjusting the In and Out points to define the precise portion of the media to be used.

 Note: Later in the book, you will also look at how to use the Viewer to edit audio (Chapter 8), create motion graphics such as cropping and drop shadows, and add special effects (Chapter 7).

To set a clip's In and Out points, follow these steps:

1. In the Browser, double-click the clip you want to review. The clip automatically opens in the Viewer window. For this exercise, open the folder called Unused Clips and double-click the clip called Ray_01 (see Figure 4.11).

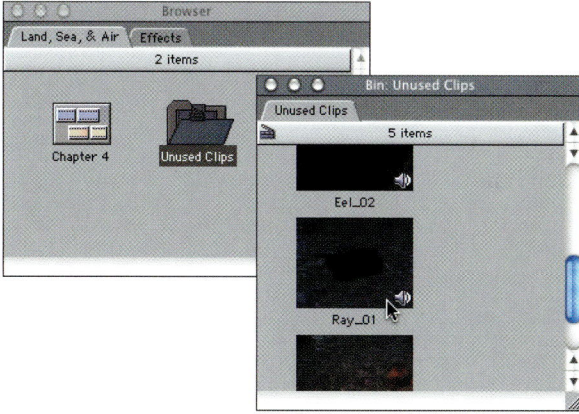

Figure 4.11
Double-click a clip to open it in the Viewer.

2. Use the J/K/L navigating keys or the VCR-style buttons and shuttles on the Viewer to move through the footage on the clip. Notice the white scrub bar under the monitor. A small playhead moves back and forth over the scrub bar showing you where you are in the clip. You can also manually scrub back and forth by clicking and dragging on the scrub bar (see Figure 4.12). After you have reviewed the media in the clip, you'll need to decide what part of it you want to use in your edit.

Figure 4.12
The Viewer is used to set a clip's In and Out points.

Ⓐ VCR controls
Ⓑ Scrub bar
Ⓒ Playhead

3. Move the playhead to the first frame that you want in your trimmed sub-clip. This will be your In point. For this exercise, set the In point at the timecode setting **2;11**, which stands for 2 seconds, 11 frames.

4. Click the Mark In button on the Viewer (or press I). After doing this, you will notice a new arrowhead icon pointing right at the new In point. The area to the left of this in the clip is shaded gray, indicating that it will not be used (see Figure 4.13).

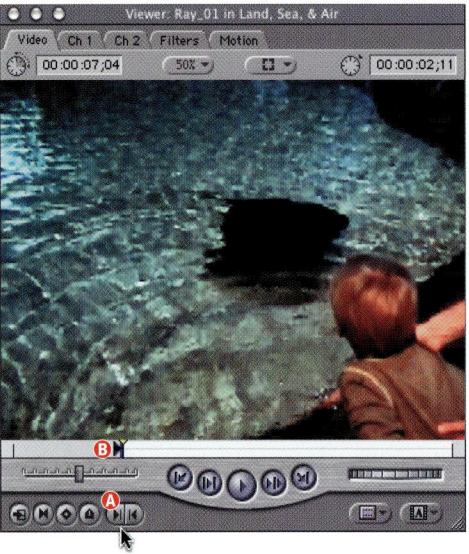

Figure 4.13
The In point has now been set for the clip at 2 seconds, 11 frames.

Ⓐ Mark In button
Ⓑ In point

5. Play through the footage to find the last frame that you want to use. This will be your Out point. For this exercise, set the Out point at **7;17** (timecode value set for 7 seconds, 17 frames).

Note: Remember that although it is important to set the In and Out points as close to where you want them to end up in the final piece as possible, you can change these points anytime if you change your mind. So, for now, close is close enough. Later, you can adjust the points by several seconds or even a few frames so that the clip fits just right with the surrounding clips.

6. Click the Mark Out button on the Viewer (or press O). After doing this, you will notice a new arrowhead icon pointing left at the new Out point. The area to the right of this in the clip is shaded gray, indicating that it will not be used (see Figure 4.14).

You can redefine the In and Out points by repeating the preceding steps or, more simply, by clicking the In or Out point and dragging it left or right. You have now trimmed your clip by setting In and Out points. Every time you use this clip now, the media will use these In and Out points.

In addition to the methods already explained, you can quickly set the In and Out points to the beginning and end of the clip by simply clicking the Mark Clip button (or press X) (see Figure 4.15).

Figure 4.14

The Out point has now been set for the clip at 7 seconds, 17 frames.

Ⓐ Mark Out button
Ⓑ Out point

Figure 4.15

The Mark Clip button snaps the In/Out points to the beginning and end of the clip.

Ⓐ Mark Clip button
Ⓑ In point
Ⓒ Out point

After your clip is trimmed, it's ready to be brought into the Timeline to be laid in with other clips.

Bringing Clips into the Timeline

One of the strengths of Final Cut Express is that it allows for multiple methods that perform the same task. Typically an action or function can be accomplished with the mouse, with a keyboard shortcut key, or with a top menu option. This permits editors to work in the way that suits them best and enables their personal style to flourish. Some editors work visually and tend to use the mouse to drag and drop. Others are more keyboard based and type in their edits. Either way is fine—you should let your own personal thought process navigate you through Final Cut Express's interface.

After you have trimmed your clip in the Viewer and it's ready to be brought into the Timeline, you have a couple options on how to bring it in. The easiest and least precise way is to just drag it into the Timeline. There is also a more sophisticated method involving the Edit Overlay window, which we will start with first.

Dragging Clips Directly into the Timeline

When you drag a clip directly into the Timeline, skipping the Edit Overlay window, you can still decide whether you want to edit it in as an insert or overwrite. After trimming or otherwise editing the clip, you can add it into the Timeline by following these steps:

1. Click the center of the monitor image of the Viewer and drag toward the Timeline (without releasing the mouse button). A ghost clip appears under your cursor as you drag. Carrying on from the previous exercise, begin dragging the clip Ray_01 from the Viewer into the Timeline (see Figure 4.16). Alternatively, you can click and drag the clip directly from the Browser window.

Figure 4.16
As you drag a clip from the Viewer, you will see a transparent "ghost" version.

Note: If you haven't added In and Out points, the entire clip will be edited into the Timeline.

2. Drag the clip down into the Timeline. When you drag the clip over the video track of the open sequence, a dark ghost clip appears in the sequence tracks. Notice the small horizontal divide in each track—about one-third of the way

down from the top of the track. This lets you choose between either an overwrite and insert style edit by doing one of the following:

- Drag the cursor onto the top third of the track to perform an insert edit. The cursor will change to a sideways arrow (see Figure 4.17).

Figure 4.17 Drag the clip into the top third of one of the video tracks for an insert edit.

- Drag the cursor onto the bottom two-thirds of the track— the cursor will change to an arrow pointing down—to perform an overwrite edit (see Figure 4.18).

Figure 4.18 Drag the clip into the bottom two-thirds of the video track to perform an overwrite edit.

3. When you have found the spot where you want to drop the clip, release the mouse button. The clip falls in line onto the video and audio tracks if it contains an audio portion (see Figure 4.19).

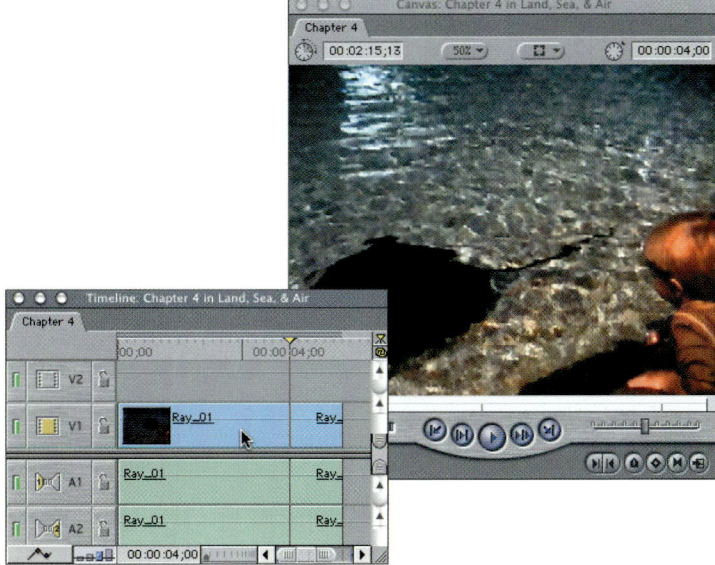

Figure 4.19 The clip is now in the Timeline with a preview in the Canvas.

Your clip is now in the Timeline and is ready to have other clips added before or after it. Repeat these steps with other clips, laying them out beside each other to create an edited piece. Remember that you will now use the Canvas to view the clips in the Timeline. However, if you double-click a clip in the Timeline, it will open in the Viewer to be edited. In that case, you can edit only this particular instance of the clip, and not the original clip in the Browser.

> **Opening Clips from the Browser or Timeline: What's the Difference?**
>
> You can load clips into the Viewer for editing from either the Browser or the Timeline simply by double-clicking the clip. However, when you open the clip from the Browser and trim the clip, the clip in the Browser will hold onto these trims until you change them; existing versions of the clip in the Timeline will remain unaffected. Conversely, opening the clip from the Timeline will enable you to make changes to only that particular instance of the clip, leaving all other instances (including the version in the Browser) unaffected. This enables you to use and reuse the same footage as many times as you want, but with different In/Out points, different effects, and different filters.

Adding Clips by Using the Canvas

Although dragging a clip directly into the Timeline is a cheap and fast way of editing, the Edit Overlay window (part of the Canvas) offers more precision. When you use the Edit Overlay window, the clip will be edited into an existing clip within your sequence at the current location of your Timeline's playhead. To edit the clip into a sequence by using the Edit Overlay window, follow these steps:

1. Place the playhead in the Timeline at the desired time or over the desired clip for the edit. As with the scrub bar in the Viewer, you can click and drag to move the playhead quickly and then use the arrow keys to move frame-by-frame. For this exercise, place the playhead at 4 seconds, which is toward the end of the clip Ray_01 that you added in the previous exercise (see Figure 4.20).

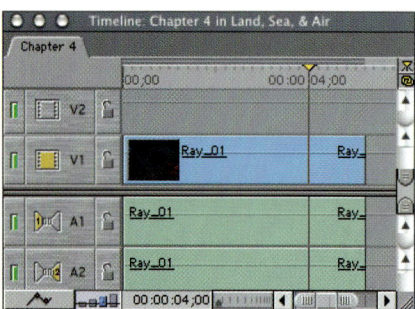

Figure 4.20
The playhead in the Timeline is placed at the desired location for the edit.

2. Open the clip in the Viewer (double-click the clip in the Browser) and check the In and Out points.

3. Now click on the monitor of the Viewer, hold the mouse button down, and begin to drag toward the Canvas window. Alternatively, you can drag the clip directly from the Browser. A ghost clip appears under your cursor, letting you know that

you are dragging the clip. Following from the previous exercise, drag the clip Ray_02 in the Unused Clips bin directly from the Browser toward the Canvas. The In and Out points for this clip have already been set.

4. Drag the clip over the Canvas window. As you do, the Edit Overlay window appears, giving you several editing options. Drag the clip onto the desired editing method, which becomes highlighted when the clip is over it. Each method has a slightly different effect (↝ "The Seven Editing Methods" next), so experiment with each to see how it works, but for now, drag the clip to Insert (see Figure 4.21).

Figure 4.21 The Edit Overlay window with Insert highlighted

> **Note:** Remember that the Canvas window is the monitor for your Timeline, so this is like dropping the clip into the Timeline.

The clip is now inserted into the sequence (see Figure 4.22). Repeat these steps for as many clips as desired.

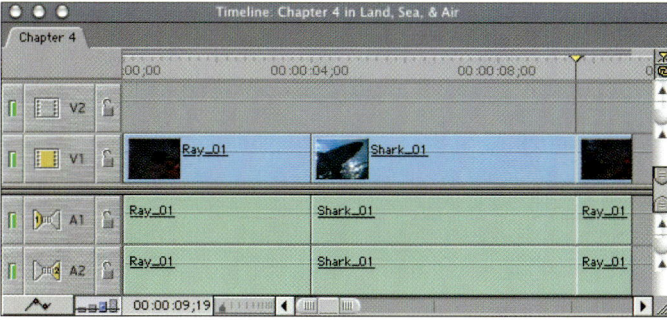

Figure 4.22
Your clip is now in the Timeline.

The Seven Editing Methods

We've just described how to drag and drop your clips onto an edit type; now let's look at the seven Final Cut Express editing methods. As an alternative to drag-and-drop, you can simply place the playhead at the location you want the edit to occur in the Timeline and then press one of the following function keys for the appropriate edit type. The edit will use whatever clip is currently displayed in the Viewer and place it in the Timeline.

Insert Edit (F9) The clip is inserted into the Timeline's open sequence at the point where the playhead lies (or where an In point has been set). If there is any footage under the edit point, it will be split and everything to the right will be pushed over to make room for the incoming clip. The Insert Edit is especially helpful if you've edited a sequence and you forgot to add one shot or want to see how an extra shot in the middle of the sequence will play.

Insert Edit With Transition (Shift+F9) This performs an Insert Edit but with a twist. If the incoming clip is inserted directly following another clip, Final Cut Express will automatically add a transition between the two. The default transition is a Cross Dissolve (⤴ Chapter 6, "Adding Transitions," for information on transitions and setting the default transition).

Overwrite Edit (F10) Like the Insert Edit, this edit also places the clip into the Timeline's open sequence at the point of the playhead or an In point. But instead of pushing footage over to make room, an Overwrite Edit drops the clips on top of whatever is already there, erasing and covering it up. No footage is moved or shuffled. Overwrite Edits are typically used when laying down long clips and building a rough, long sequence.

Overwrite Edit With Transition (Shift+F10) This performs an Overwrite Edit, but adds the default transition. If the incoming clip is inserted directly following another clip, Final Cut Express will automatically add a transition between the two. The default transition is a Cross Dissolve (⤴ Chapter 6 for information on transitions and setting the default transition).

Replace Edit (F11) This removes a whole clip from the Timeline's open sequence and replaces it with a new clip from the Viewer, taking up exactly the same amount of time as the old replaced clip. Think of this as a special kind of Overwrite that fills in a gap. The location of the playhead in the Timeline is used to determine which clip to replace, and the playhead location in the Viewer tells Final Cut Express what footage to replace the clip with. If there's not enough footage from the Viewer's clip to replace the gap left by the removed clip in the Timeline, you'll get an Insufficient Content For Edit error.

Fit To Fill (Shift+F11) This works like the Replace Edit, but actually changes the speed of the incoming clip. The incoming clip from the Viewer is either sped up or slowed down to make it fit exactly in the space of the clip to be replaced in the Timeline. If the Timeline's playhead is not resting on a clip, but an empty gap, the Fit To Fill edit will fill that gap.

Superimpose This edit puts your incoming clip directly on the video track above your footage in the Timeline, superimposing it over the image below. Superimposing is a technique that enables images to be seen simultaneously, so that the two are blended together. Superimposing uses the same method as Insert or Overwrite—it uses three-point editing to determine the location where the clip will appear.

Moving Clips in the Timeline

After a clip is in the Timeline, it is not stuck there for the rest of eternity. You can move it anytime, and you most likely will as you try various editing patterns and juxtapositions.

To move the clip, click and drag a clip in the Timeline (see Figures 4.23 and 4.24). You can either move the clip to the left (back in time) or to the right (forward in time). As you drag, the change in time from the original position is displayed in a small pop-up next to the clip's original position. Simultaneously, you can drag the clip to any track above or below its current track. If you have Snapping on (press N), then when you drag a clip around the Timeline, it will "snap" to the nearest edit or marker point.

Figure 4.23
The clip before being moved

Figure 4.24
A clip being moved in the Timeline

When you are satisfied with the clip's location, release the mouse button and the clip will be dropped in its new location. Notice that if you drop it over another clip, the dropped clip will overwrite the covered part of underlying clip (not the entire clip), so be careful you don't erase a clip you need (see Figure 4.25). If you make a mistake, there is always Edit > Undo to rescue you.

Figure 4.25
The clip is moved over the top part of the previous clip, deleting it.

Note: If you have Linking on and the video and audio tracks are linked, dragging a clip will drag both the video and audio tracks in sync. If Linking is off (Shift+L), only the individual track you click (that is, just the video or just channel 1 audio) will be moved.

Copying and Pasting Footage with the Clipboard

A major advantage of Final Cut Express over other digital nonlinear editing systems is that it uses the Mac's clipboard in the same way that applications such as Photoshop or Word use the clipboard. The clipboard is a place where you can temporarily place an item—in our case we're dealing with clips and sequences—and then later paste this same item back into the Timeline or Browser.

 Note: Keep in mind that the clipboard can hold only one item at a time, so when you copy an item to the clipboard, that item automatically replaces the previous item.

To copy and paste items in Final Cut Express, follow these steps:

1. Select the item you want to copy or cut to the clipboard. This can be a clip or sequence icon in your Browser, or clips in your open sequence in the Timeline. Use Shift+click or ⌘+click to select multiple items.

2. Do one of the following:
   - Choose Edit > Copy (⌘+C) to copy the selected item(s) to the clipboard. This makes a copy of the item but leaves the original intact in the Timeline.
   - Choose Edit > Cut (⌘+X) to cut the selected item(s). This brings the item into the clipboard and removes it from the Timeline.
   - Control+click the clip (or one of the selected clips) and choose Cut or Copy from the contextual menu (see Figure 4.26).

   The clip is now in the memory. Keep in mind that the clip is copied "as is," along with all the trims and effects that have been added to it.

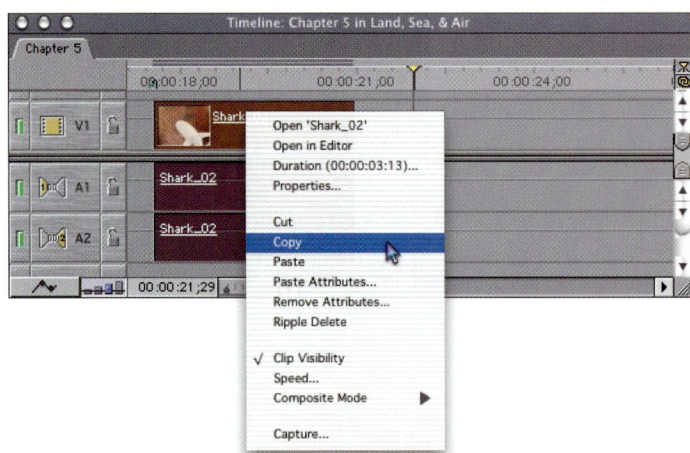

Figure 4.26
A clip being copied in the Timeline

3. Do one of the following:
   - In the Timeline, move the playhead to the location where you want the clip to appear.
   - In the Browser, click to select a bin where you want to place the clip.
4. Choose Edit > Paste (⌘+V). You can also Control+click and choose Paste from the contextual menu. If you have the Timeline highlighted, the item will appear at the current location of your playhead and on the designated target track (see Figure 4.27). If you have a project file in your Browser highlighted, the items will appear in the open bin.

Figure 4.27
A clip has been pasted into the Timeline after the playhead.

Don't worry about filling up your memory with huge video clips. Unlike other programs, such as Photoshop, Final Cut Express is not actually placing the entire video clip into the clipboard memory, only a relatively small reference to the original media file.

Creating Sub-Clips

As mentioned before, a sub-clip is a section of a source clip created by setting In and Out points or markers, enabling you to create one or more independent clips from a single source clip. Sub-clips are especially handy when you need to use several non-sequential pieces from a single clip. Simply create sub-clips for each piece and use these.

Creating Sub-Clips by Using In and Out Points

You can create sub-clips by using the In and Out points set for the clip. To create a sub-clip by using In and Out points, follow these steps:

1. Open the clip from which you want to make a sub-clip in the Viewer by double-clicking the clip in the Timeline, Canvas, or Browser. For this example, double-click the clip called Cranes located in the Unused Clips bin.
2. In the Viewer, set In and Outs points for the clip to define the new sub-clip (see Figure 4.28).

Figure 4.28
In and Out points set to create a sub-clip

3. Choose Modify > Make Sub-Clip (⌘+U). A sub-clip icon appears in the Browser, with the same name as the original clip followed by *Subclip*. You can use the sub-clip just like any other media clip (see Figure 4.29).

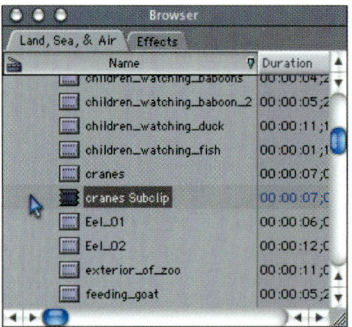

Figure 4.29
The sub-clip in the Browser

You can make as many different sub-clips from the same original clip as you want. Dividing a large clip into many smaller sub-clips enables you to more accurately organize your project.

Creating Sub-Clips by Using Markers

You can also create sub-clips directly from markers set in the clip (👁 "Working with Markers" earlier in this chapter). To create a sub-clip by using markers, follow these steps:

1. Open the clip from which you want to make a sub-clip in the Viewer by double-clicking the clip in the Timeline, Canvas, or Browser. For this example, double-click the clip called Cranes located in the Unused Clips bin.

2. In the Viewer, set markers in the clip. Place the playhead at the location where you want the marker to begin, double-click the Set Marker button, type a name and length of the marker (the length will be used to set the Out point), and then click OK. The marker is now set for the clip (see Figure 4.30). You can set as many markers as you want for a single clip.

Figure 4.30
A marker set for the clip is shown in the Viewer Timeline.

> **Note:** You can also set markers in an individual clip when capturing the clips (⌘ Chapter 3, "Gathering Your Media").

3. In the Browser, expand the clip to view the markers. Click and drag one of the markers from the Browser into the Timeline (see Figure 4.31). The clip is added to your sequence as a sub-clip.

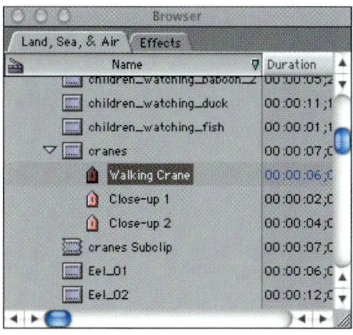

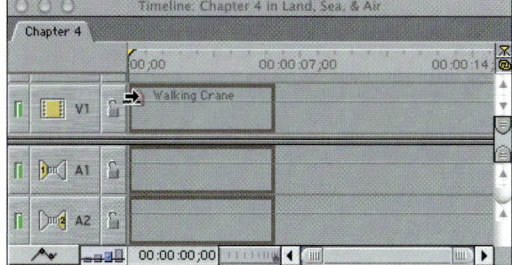

Figure 4.31
A marker being dragged into the Timeline

4. You can drag the sub-clip from the Timeline back into the Browser to create a sub-clip item independent of the originating clip and its markers.

Taking Advantage of Nonlinear Editing

Now that you've started to bring in clips and edit them together, let's look at how you can take full advantage of Final Cut Express's nonlinear editing style. As we've discussed before, *nonlinear* editing means that you can move clips around and change edit points as you work—whenever and however you want.

When you are editing with Final Cut Express, keep in mind that all of your editing decisions can be changed anytime. This will drastically affect the way you work and will let you experiment with your cut. Try changing the timing of your edits, experimenting with how letting a shot last longer or shorter changes the feel of the movie. Some editors like to let clips run long with few edits. This is a good technique if you want your movie to have a more meditative or contemplative rhythm. Other editors prefer to cut rapidly in a "bam-bam" style (and with nonlinear editing this is the more common practice now). Digital nonlinear editing has opened the door to rapid cutting like the kind you see on MTV or in many contemporary Hollywood movies; think of the frantic pace of Baz Luhrmann's film *Moulin Rouge*, a film that could never have been edited in the way it was without digital nonlinear editing. While using Final Cut Express, it's important to remember how the technology you are using doesn't just make things easier; it shapes the way you edit and the way you make your cuts.

That said, you shouldn't always use a million cuts in Final Cut Express just because you can. Although digital nonlinear editing has made an editor's job less frustrating, the flip side is that it has made some editors sloppier. Many films today throw so many edits into the mix that the result can be a mess. Just because you can constantly change your mind and quickly make lots of cuts doesn't mean you should abandon the thought and craft behind the editing. Final Cut Express is a very powerful tool, but the end result still relies on your own vision and skill as an editor.

As you experiment and try out new ways of cutting, take the time to really review and think about the way the edits sculpt your movie. There's a lot to take advantage of with nonlinear editing—and one of the biggest benefits is the ability to try different things. Even if your initial cut looks good, copy it to a new sequence and try it another way to see how it plays. You can create as many sequences as you want to compare and play around with, and you might end up liking one of the alternate takes better than the way you originally envisioned the scene.

Editing with Multiple Tracks

When you start a new sequence, you'll have two video tracks and four audio tracks (one for each left and right stereo pair). However, you are not limited to this default setup. In fact, Final Cut Express gives you the ability to add up to 99 tracks of both audio and video. This may seem excessive, but projects with heavy effects and composite work, or complex audio mixing, can certainly take up an amazing number of track layers.

In this section, you'll look at how to add and delete tracks, and also how to set the target track for editing clips.

> ### Changing Your Mind: Your Friend, the Undo Function
>
> It is the prerogative of all editors to change their minds while working, which is why one of the most commonly used shortcuts in Final Cut Express is the Undo function. This function immediately undoes your last operation, and is invaluable for righting mistakes or back-tracking to try something different. You can undo multiple times to keep back-tracking over numerous steps. You can set the number of allowable undos in your preference window by choosing Final Cut Pro > Preferences. Be warned: the more undos you allow, the more memory this will take up.
>
> - To undo, choose Edit > Undo (⌘+Z). Repeat to undo the previous action.
> - To redo something you just undid, choose Edit > Redo (⌘+Y). Repeat to redo the next action.

Adding Tracks

There are two quick ways to add a single track to the Timeline:

- When you drag a clip into the Timeline, drop the clip one track above the top existing track. A new track will be created automatically (see Figure 4.32).

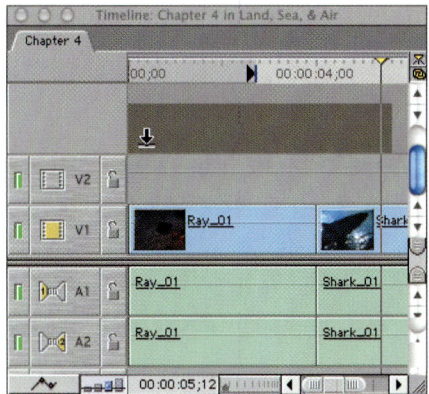

Figure 4.32
The clip is being dragged into a blank area above the topmost track (V2), causing a new track (V3) to be created automatically.

- Control+click either the filmstrip icons or audio icons next to a track and choose Add Track from the contextual menu (see Figure 4.33). The new video track will be added above the existing tracks. Only tracks of the type selected (video or audio) will be added.

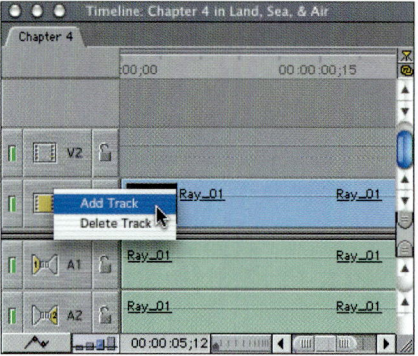

Figure 4.33
The contextual menu enables you to add a single new track.

You might also want to create many tracks at once in preparation for a big project. To add multiple tracks, follow these steps:

1. With the proper sequence open and the Timeline window selected, choose Sequence > Insert Tracks.
2. In the Insert Tracks dialog box (see Figure 4.34), type in the number of video and audio tracks you want to insert and make sure the check box is selected for the type of track you want to add (Audio, Video, or both).

Figure 4.34
The Insert Tracks dialog box with five video tracks being added

3. Now choose where you want the tracks to be added. You can choose from the following options:

   Before Base Track   Inserts tracks under the lowest track for video, and above the highest track for audio.

   After Target Track (or **After Last Target Track** for audio)   Inserts tracks above the current target track for video, and below the current target track for audio.

   After Last Track   Inserts tracks above the highest track for video, and below the lowest track for audio.

4. Click the OK button to create the new tracks.

The tracks are added to the Timeline and are ready for use (see Figure 4.35).

Figure 4.35
Five new video tracks have been added above the previous two video tracks.

Setting Target Tracks

When you edit with multiple tracks, Final Cut Express gives you a way to designate which track you want incoming clips to be edited into. This is called the *target track*. The target track is identified by the yellow filmstrip icon for video on the far left of the sequence, or the yellow speaker icon for audio (see Figure 4.36).

Figure 4.36
The targeted track's filmstrip icon is yellow.

Whether you perform an Insert Edit with the Edit Overlay window, drag a clip in from the Viewer, or copy and paste a clip into the Timeline, the target track will tell the incoming clip which track to appear on.

To set a target track, decide which track you want your incoming clips to appear on. You can choose one video target track and two audio target tracks for stereo clips:

- To set the target track for video, click the film filmstrip icon to the left of the track video number. It will become yellow, showing you that this is the target video track.
- To set the audio track, click the speaker icons to the left of the audio track number. You can set the target track for either the left or right audio of a stereo pair by clicking only on the left or right speaker icon. The selected section will become yellow, so you can select, for example, track A2 for left audio and track A8 for right audio if you want to.

 Note: Even after you have set a target track, you can still deviate from that track if you use the drag-and-drop method (not the Edit Overlay window). However, target tracks will be your default location to drop the incoming clip.

A special tip if you are using the Edit Overlay window: if you don't have any target track set for video, then only the audio of a clip will be edited into your sequence. And vice versa: if you have only a video track set and no audio target tracks, you can edit in video without the audio appearing with it. This is a great trick if you want to bring in only the video image with no sound. Remember, this works only with the Edit Overlay window, not when dragging clips directly into the Timeline.

Deleting Tracks

You can choose to delete certain tracks or get rid of all the empty tracks to keep your sequence neat and tidy. To delete a track, follow these steps:

1. Choose Sequence > Delete Tracks.
2. In the Delete Tracks dialog box, check either the Video Tracks or Audio Tracks check boxes (or both) to designate the kinds of tracks you want to delete (see Figure 4.37).

Figure 4.37
The Delete Tracks dialog box

3. Now select the type of deletion you want to make:

   Current Target Track(s) Deletes the tracks set as the target tracks. This deletes the clips on those tracks.

   All Empty Tracks Deletes all tracks without any clips on them.

   All Empty Tracks At End Of Sequence Deletes only those tracks that are empty and higher than the last track with video media on it and lower than the last track with audio on it.

4. Click the OK button to delete the designated tracks.

> **Note:** You can also delete a single track by Control+clicking the filmstrip icon (video) or speaker icon (audio) to the left of the track and choosing Delete Track from the contextual menu.

Movie Night!

Rashomon, 1950

Director: Akira Kurosawa

Kurosawa's *Rashomon* is a period tale of differing perspectives on the same event. A woman is raped in twelfth century Japan, and the film relates five accounts from five people of what happened. The conflicting versions pose the question of how we determine "truth" and how narratives are told. The film is stylistically theatrical, and one of the versions of the story is told by a ghost!

The editing of the film combines these different takes on the same event and is used to make the viewer question the truthfulness of what is seen. Unlike many films that use editing to make the story seem real, *Rashomon* uses editing to highlight the subjectivity of truth. As an editor, remember that your edits can either create illusions or call attention to the illusion depending on the purpose of your work.

As a side note, Kurosawa is famous for using occasional effect transitions instead of straight cuts. These transitions (such as irising and wipes) are distinctive and also call attention to the editing process. You might be reminded of George Lucas's use of the same kind of wipes in *Star Wars,* and you should. Lucas is a big Kurosawa fan, it's no secret where he got the idea. (👉 Chapter 6 for adding effects transitions such as irises and wipes to your own movies).

Cutting Your Video

5

Trimming is the act of cutting away or adding footage to a particular edit in a clip. When you trim, you are deciding how you want the clip to end and how the next clip should begin. When trimming shots, you have to consider numerous factors: Do these two shots make narrative sense together? Do the rhythm and timing of the shots work? Is this edit awkward or does it cut smoothly from one shot to the next? As you trim and change the Ins and Outs of your edits, you'll be doing two things: technically interacting with Final Cut Express's interface to change the edit points and then reviewing your new cut to see how it works in motion. However, as you work with Final Cut Express's powerful trim tools, such considerations will become less a matter of deliberation as you begin to instinctively create edits that work logically and artistically.

Chapter Contents
Snapping and linking clips
Deleting clips and gaps
Cutting clips with the Razor Blade
Using the Zoom Tool
Trimming with the mouse
Using the Trim Edit window
Using Roll, Ripple, Slip, and Slide edits

Snapping and Linking Clips

Precision when editing is imperative for creating professional videos. Although "close is close enough" when you are simply bringing your raw clips into the Timeline, after you start assembling the clips in a meaningful way, you will need to be meticulous down to fractions of a second.

Two features in Final Cut Express let you quickly move your clips precisely: snapping and linking. Each function can be turned on and off with the click of a button. These small (but important) yellow buttons are located on the Timeline window (see Figure 5.1):

Snapping enables you to make precise edits by constraining where a clip can be edited into the Timeline, forcing its edits to particular points.

Linking enables you to link or unlink video and audio tracks so that they can be trimmed independently.

Figure 5.1
The Snap and Link buttons on the Timeline

Ⓐ Snap toggle   Ⓑ Link toggle

On the DVD: Chapter 5

Open the Final Cut Express project file labeled "Land, Sea, & Air." After this file opens, double-click the Chapter 5 sequence and it will open in the Timeline.

In the sequence there are 9 different sets of clips that have been set up for you to practice the various exercises for this chapter. The instructions will refer to specific markers set in the Timeline to help you find the clip for that exercise. Some exercises will share clips, and some exercises can be performed on any of the clips in the Timeline.

Snapping Tracks into Position

When enabled, snapping forces the clip being worked with to "snap" into position to the nearest adjacent edit, clip, playhead, or marker. So, if you move a clip close to one of these elements while dragging it in the Timeline, the edge of the clip (the edit) automatically jumps to the edge of that element so that they butt together but do not overlap. This is invaluable when you are dragging a clip and want to butt it up exactly against an edit point of another clip. This also will happen with markers in the Timeline, so you can lay down a clip exactly at a marker point.

Turn snapping on by clicking the Snap toggle button so that it is raised and yellow. Click it again to turn snapping off. You can also toggle snapping on and off by pressing the N key or choosing View > Snapping.

Practice dragging the clip Shark_01 around in the Timeline with snapping on and notice how it jumps from edit point to edit point. This way, you know when you drop the clip, it will be snapped to the edit point of another clip, and will not cover up any media or leave a little gap between the clips (see Figure 5.2). Although snapping is great for quickly placing clips in the Timeline in relation to other clips, with snapping off, you can place a clip *exactly* where you want it in the Timeline regardless of the current content.

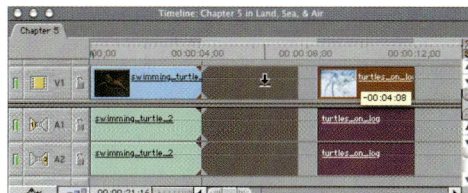 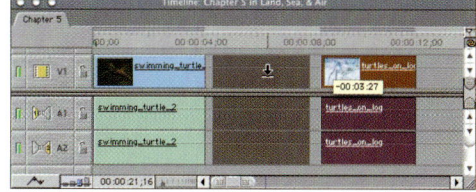

Figure 5.2 Snapping toggled on (left) and toggled off (right)

> **Note:** Because snapping works with the playhead, it's a great trick to place your playhead at the point where you want to drop a clip and then drag the clip nearby. The clip will automatically snap to the playhead's position.

Linking Audio and Video Tracks

When you capture a clip from digital video, it usually comes in with the video and the two audio tracks *linked*. This means that wherever you drag the video, the audio will follow; whenever you trim the video, the audio will be trimmed in the same way; whenever you Razor Blade the video, the audio will be cut in the same place, and so forth. The audio and video function as one clip. When you open the clip into the Viewer by double-clicking it, you'll have access to both video and audio tabs. Basically, they are locked together—they are linked.

Generally, you will want the tracks linked while you are cutting so that the audio and video do not become out of sync. However, sometimes it is necessary to take out the audio tracks, or to assign different In and Out points for the audio and video tracks, or to take either the video or audio track out altogether while leaving the other track. For example, you might want to do a voice-over of particular video footage that has audio recorded with a different video track. To do this, you'll need to turn linking off between the video and audio portions of the clip.

Setting Linking for an Entire Sequence

To turn linking on or off for all clips in the open sequence, first make sure that you do not have any clips selected (click in any empty area of the Timeline), and then click the Link toggle button in the Timeline (right under the snapping toggle). You can also press Shift+L or choose Sequence > Linked Selection. If the clips were linked, you will now see the icon turn into a broken link.

With linking off, you can now move each audio or video track of a clip separately (see Figure 5.3). You can also trim each audio or video track separately (👉 "Trimming Clips" later in this chapter).

Figure 5.3
The audio tracks are being moved independently of their video track.

 Note: Be careful! You can now easily drag a video track out of sync from its corresponding audio track. Nothing is more annoying than a fraction-of-a-second delay between the person on the screen speaking and their lips moving.

Unlinking Specific Audio and Video Clips

To unlink an individual clip so that you can access its audio and video tracks separately, you'll need to first select the clip you want to unlink (make sure that linking is turned on for the Timeline). Because the clip is currently linked, the audio and video tracks should all become highlighted (see Figure 5.4).

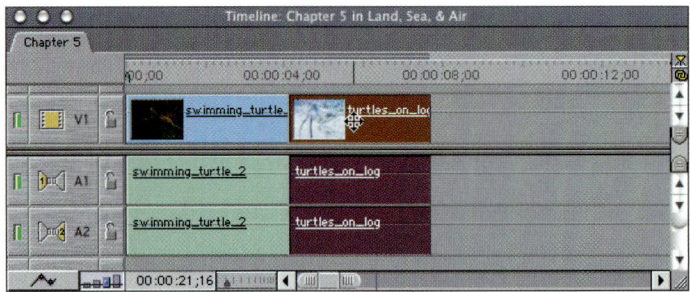

Figure 5.4
The clip selected to be unlinked

Choose Modify > Link (⌘ +L) to unlink the audio from the video (the clip titles in the Timeline will no longer be underlined when unlinked). To deselect the clips, click anywhere in the Timeline. This will enable you to highlight the clips separately. Now you can move the audio and video clips independently, and they will have no effect on each other (see Figure 5.5).

Figure 5.5
The unlinked clip with one of the audio tracks offset by 2:10

When you move an unlinked audio clip independently of its original video clip, a timecode discrepancy box appears over the clips (this is the red box shown in Figure 5.5 reading +/-2:10). This box tells you the number of minutes, seconds, and frames apart the audio and video are from their original sync position.

> **Note:** If you want to move the tracks together again without relinking them, you can simply Shift+click or ⌘+click each track to select them and they will temporarily move together. This is especially useful if you want to move both left and right audio tracks together after they have been unlinked.

Creating a New Link

Linking audio and video clips makes them run in locked sync. It makes any manipulation you do to one clip occur to the other. Although this process can be used to relink audio and video tracks that have been previously unlinked, it can also be used to link video and audio from completely different original sources (see Figure 5.6).

Figure 5.6
The video in one clip has been linked to the audio in another clip.

To link audio and video clips, select the video and audio clip(s) you want to link in the Timeline by Shift+clicking or ⌘+clicking them, and then choose Modify > Link (⌘+L) to link the clips.

You will know that your clips have become linked because the clip names will become underlined in the Timeline. Now, when you select or manipulate the clips, they will act as one linked clip.

Note: You can link a video track to one or two audio tracks, but that's it. You can't link two video tracks together, and you also cannot link two clips that live on the same track.

Using Selection Commands

We've talked about how you can use the mouse to select a clip (or a series of clips). You can also use these shortcuts to help you select the clips you want:

Select All   To select all the clips in an open sequence, choose Edit > Select All (⌘+A). This is especially helpful if you want to move the entire sequence farther down the Timeline.

Deselect All   To deselect all selected clips, choose Edit > Deselect All (⌘+D).

Deleting Clips and Gaps

Selecting clips isn't just used for linking. You can also select clips or empty spaces known as gaps to mark them for deletion. If you want to remove a clip from your sequence, you can easily take it out by selecting and deleting it. Let's look at two ways to remove a clip: the lift delete and the ripple delete. In addition, in this section you'll learn how to remove the empty gap left by a deleted clip.

For this exercise, use the clips after the marker Deleting Clips shown in Figure 5.7, which contains three clips for you to practice with. Practice deleting the middle clip by using Edit > Undo to try different deleting techniques.

Figure 5.7   The original sequence before clips are deleted

Here are the different kinds of delete functions you can use in Final Cut Express:

Lift delete   A lift delete removes the clip, leaving a gap in the sequence where the clip used to be (see Figure 5.8). Remember, you are not deleting any original media when you do this. To perform a lift delete, in the Timeline select the clip and choose Sequence > Lift (or press the Delete key).

Figure 5.8
The clip has been lifted out, leaving a gap.

Ripple delete   A ripple delete takes the clip out of the sequence, but also handily closes up the gap that would have been left in its place (see Figure 5.9). This is a perfect way to remove a clip from a long sequence of clips without creating a space in your montage. To perform a ripple delete, in the Timeline select the clip and choose Sequence > Ripple Delete (or press Shift+Delete).

Figure 5.9
The clip has been ripple deleted, leaving no space.

Gap delete   *Gaps* are the empty spaces between clips. Even though they are empty spaces, you can still highlight a gap just as you can a clip! By doing so, you are selecting the gap and you can then "delete" the gap. Deleting the gap means you close up that space (much like a ripple delete), and all clips to the right of the gap shuffle over to fill the space. It's sort of like sucking out the air between clips and then sucking the clips together.

To perform a gap delete, place the playhead in the Timeline anywhere within the gap (see Figure 5.10) and choose Sequence > Close Gap (Control+G). Alternatively, you can select a gap between two clips by clicking within it and then simply press the Delete key.

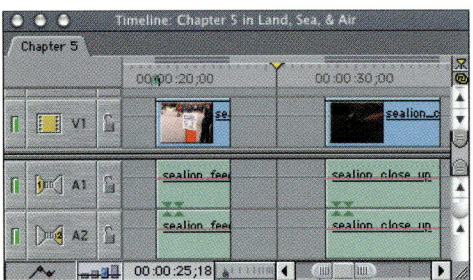

Figure 5.10
The playhead is within the gap to be closed.

Cutting Clips with the Razor Blade

The Razor Blade tool splits a single clip into two clips. This is helpful for quickly lopping off part of a clip you don't want to use or for splitting a clip so that you can use the two parts in different locations. Using the Razor Blade tool does not split up your source media file on your hard disk or even change the clip in the Browser. Instead, it simply affects the specific clip that you razor in the Timeline.

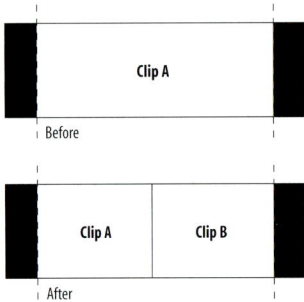

To use the Razor Blade on a clip, follow these steps:

1. Choose the Razor Blade tool from the Tool palette (or press B).
2. Place the Razor Blade over the frame of the clip in the Timeline where you want to make the cut (see Figure 5.11). You might want to place the playhead first on this frame to view the frame. Because the Razor Blade will snap to the playhead, you can use the playhead as a guide for perfect frame accuracy.

Figure 5.11
The Razor Blade poised, ready to cut the clip.

3. Click the mouse to make the cut. The clip instantly splits into two new isolated clips, which can be edited and trimmed independently.

You can now separate the clips and treat them as completely individual clips that can be trimmed, affected, or dragged without relation to the other (see Figure 5.12). Alternatively, you can also create a cut by placing your playhead at the point in the Timeline you want to cut and choosing Sequence > Add Edit (Control+V).

Figure 5.12
The clip after being cut and the right piece moved

If you want to make an incision that cuts through *every* clip at a particular point in the Timeline (across all tracks) use the Razor Blade All tool in the Tool palette (or click BB) and follow the same steps. However, now when you click on the clip, that clip and every clip above and below it in the Timeline will be cut in two.

Getting a Closer Look: The Zoom Tools

The Tool palette has many handy functions, and one tool available to you is the Zoom Tool. This turns your cursor into a tool to zoom in and get a closer look at your edits. When you are making a close trim or want to scroll frame-by-frame through your sequence, you can use the magnifying glass tool to zoom in for a more precise view.

As you might remember from Chapter 4, "Editing Basics," here's how to use the Zoom In and Zoom Out tools:

- Click the Zoom In tool (press Z) to select it from the Tool palette and click on any part of the sequence to zoom in.
- Click the Zoom Out tool (press ZZ) to select it and click in the Timeline to zoom out and get the big picture (see Figure 5.13).

Figure 5.13
The Timeline has been zoomed in.

- While either tool is selected, you can press the Option key to temporarily switch to the other zoom mode.

You can also zoom in and out by pressing ⌘+- and ⌘++ (the hyphen and the plus, respectively). There is also a zoom slider at the bottom of the Timeline directly to the left of the scroll bar.

> ### Reverting to an Older Version of Your Project
>
> There are times when you may decide that you've been headed in the wrong direction with your cuts. In that case, you might want to go back to an older version of your project, before you made changes that you now wish you hadn't. Fortunately, Final Cut Express enables you to do this easily.
>
> Choose File > Revert Project, and the last saved project will load. Final Cut Express will even warn you that you will lose all the changes you've made since the last save.

Making Quick Trims

Quick editing methods allow for you to work almost as fast as your mind can make decisions. This section will look at two ways to make fast edits—with the mouse and with the Extend Edit function.

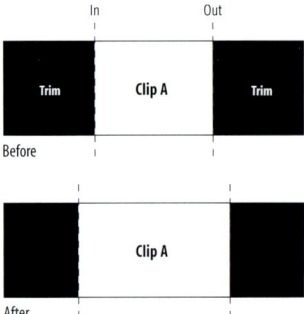

Trimming with the Mouse

The least precise, but often the simplest and most visual, way to start trimming is to use the mouse. As we've said before, Final Cut Express goes out of its way to provide you multiple options to achieve the same task. Using the mouse to trim a clip is for quick trims, and for people who like to lay out their cuts visually on the Timeline.

To trim by using the mouse, follow these steps:

1. Choose the Select tool ▸ from the Tool palette (or press A).
2. Move your cursor over an edit point of a clip in the Timeline. An *edit point* is the line between two clips. The In point is to the left, and the Out point is to the right of this line. Note how the cursor changes from the arrow to a trim icon with two arrows (see Figure 5.14).

Figure 5.14
Edit point in the Timeline

3. Click on the edit point and drag the cursor to the left or right. As you do, the edge of the clip extends or recedes. A pop-up box appears, showing you the number of frames being added (+) or removed (-) and the clip's new duration. As you make your trim, the In point for the clip is shown in the Canvas (see Figure 5.15).

Figure 5.15 A clip being trimmed in the Timeline with the mouse

After you release the mouse, the clip has a new edit point. If snapping is on, the clip's edge will snap to the nearest edit point or playhead.

Extending an Edit

Another quick way to trim the length of a clip, regardless of the clips that come after it or before it, is to use the Extend Edit command. This enables you to select an edit point, place your playhead, and then move that edit point to the playhead.

To use the Extend Edit command, follow these steps:

1. In the Timeline, select the edit point you want to trim. Place the playhead at the position where you want the selected edit point to be moved—this can be either before or after the current edit point (see Figure 5.16).

Figure 5.16
The edit selected with the playhead in the new desired position for the edit

2. Choose Sequence > Extend Edit (press the E key). The edit point moves to the new position if there is enough footage available in the clip to allow it to extend to that point (see Figure 5.17). If there is not enough footage, then nothing happens.

Figure 5.17
The extended edit

Extending an edit can be applied to either end of the clip and in either direction, making it a powerful tool for precise editing.

What Is B-roll?

B-roll is a term that gets knocked around a lot by filmmakers and TV producers, but what is actually meant by this term? Basically, footage can be divided into two main categories:

A-roll is the footage that contains the main action, such as a scene between two characters or talking heads.

B-roll is footage that is used to illustrate, accent, or provide transitions between the A-rolls.

The most common example is the use of B-roll in a documentary. As a talking head interview (the A-roll) tells about an experience of going to a drive-in movie, the image might cut away to scenes of a drive-in theatre (the B-roll). B-roll is often shot loosely so that the editor can use it for lots of purposes. It can also be an editor's savior as it can help cover up awkward edits or jump cuts.

Trimming Clips: Roll, Ripple, Slip, and Slide

After you have your clips in rough position on the Timeline, you are ready to begin trimming them to create your final polished edits. To do this, there are four techniques (each with a separate tool) used to minutely adjust where one clip ends and the next begins: Roll, Ripple, Slip, and Slide. Although they might sound like a series of dance moves from *American Bandstand,* they are actually sophisticated trimming techniques to fine-tune your video clips. At first, it might be difficult to keep Roll and Ripple straight, or to remember what slipping your clip will do, but after a while using these techniques will become second nature. It is unlikely that you will use only one of these edits, although you might begin to favor one over others; instead, you will use them in unison to get the exact edits you desire.

Roll, Ripple, Slip, and Slide edits are all performed by using the trimming tools found in the Tool palette. They are used to modify the In and Out points of clips in your Timeline after the clips have already been laid out. By clicking the appropriate icon in the Tool palette, the mouse cursor will change into that icon and you can start trimming.

The four edits are as follows:

Roll edit The Roll edit enables you to add frames to the end of a clip while subtracting the same number of frames from the clip adjacent to it, maintaining the relative length of the sequence. Roll is used when you are editing two clips that need to stay in their location in the whole sequence, but need different Out and In points.

For example, let's say you have a sequence of clip A (incoming clip) followed by clip B (outgoing clip). By using a Roll edit, you could add five frames to the end of clip A and automatically subtract five frames from the start of clip B. Alternatively, you could subtract five frames from the end of clip A, and then that would add five frames to the start of clip B.

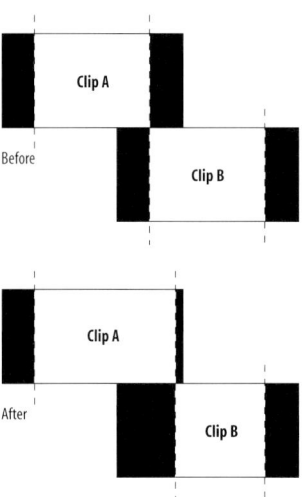

Ripple edit The Ripple enables you to add or subtract frames from a clip without changing the duration or content of the surrounding clips. Instead, it increases or decreases the length of the entire sequence by pushing or pulling the surrounding clips to fit without changing their length. Ripple is used when you want to extend or trim a clip without changing your surrounding clips.

For example, let's say you have a sequence of clip A (incoming clip) followed by clip B (outgoing clip). By using a Ripple edit, you could add 10 frames to the end of clip A, and that would push clip B and all later clips forward 10 frames. Clip B's content and duration will not change, just its location in the Timeline.

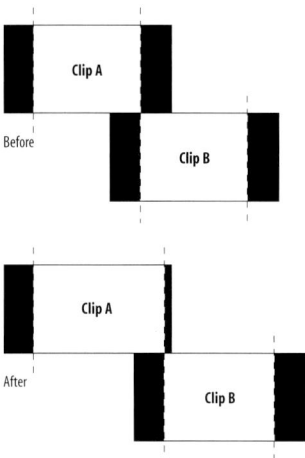

Slip edit The Slip edit keeps the duration and position of a clip, but changes its content by shifting the In and Out points within the source material to show a different section of the original media file. The duration of the overall sequence is unaffected. Slip is used if you want to find a better part of a shot while maintaining its timing in a sequence.

For example, let's say you have a sequence of clips A, B, and C. By using the Slip edit, you can change the In and Out points of clip B (in the middle) without affecting clips A and C or the duration of clip B.

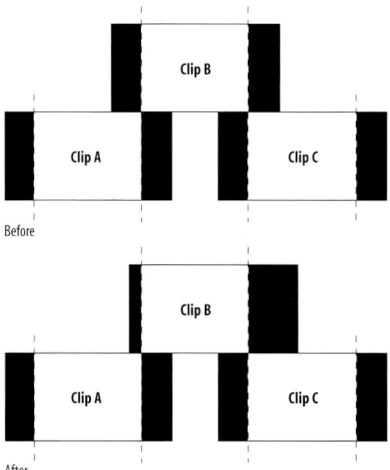

✥ **Slide edit** The Slide edit enables you to move a clip left or right in the Timeline, maintaining the content and duration of that clip, as well as the duration of the overall sequence. The duration of surrounding clips will be changed to fit the new location of the sliding clip. Slide is used when you need to maintain the length of an individual clip and the sequence, but are not concerned about the length of surrounding clips.

For example, let's say you have a sequence of clips A, B, and C. You can use the Slide edit to adjust the position of clip B in the middle without changing its duration or the duration of the overall sequence, by changing the duration of clips A and C.

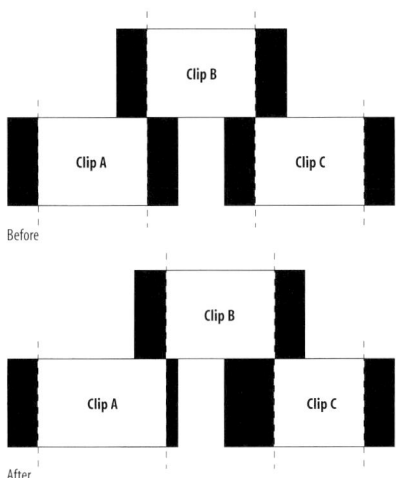

In this section, you'll learn about using the Trim Edit window to make Roll and Ripple edits, and then the specific steps required to use each of the four trimming tools.

Understanding the Trim Edit Window

Although trim edits can be performed directly in the Timeline, Final Cut Express also provides the Trim Edit window for making precise editing decisions for Roll and Ripple edits, letting you see the results of your cutting at a glance. This window shows you both clips simultaneously and lets you make your trims while keeping an eye on the In and Out points of both clips at the same time.

The next two sections explain how to use the Roll and Ripple techniques to trim clips in the Trim Edit window (as well as in the Timeline), but regardless of which editing method you use, the Trim Edit window works the same way, so let's take a look at this important window.

The Trim Edit window (see Figure 5.18) is accessed by double-clicking an edit (the point between any two clips) to select it (see Figure 5.19). The left side of the window controls the *incoming clip* (showing the last frame of the clip to the left of the edit), and the right side controls the *outgoing clip* (showing the first frame of the clip to the right of the edit). The clip or clips that will be trimmed are indicated by a green highlight bar over the top of the monitor.

Figure 5.18 The Trim Edit window

- **A** Outgoing clip and its duration
- **B** Playback controls for outgoing clip
- **C** Selected clip
- **D** Track pop-up menu
- **E** Current sequence timecode
- **F** Incoming clip and its duration
- **G** Playback controls for incoming clip
- **H** Trim controls
- **I** Playback controls for sequence
- **J** Mark In
- **K** Mark Out

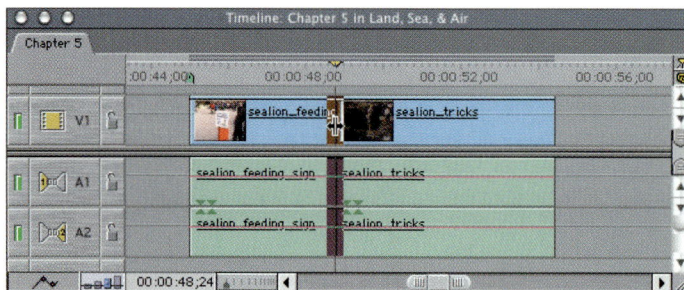

Figure 5.19
An edit selected
in the Timeline

 Note: Selecting an edit can be tricky. You have to double-click the spot precisely between the two clips. Sometimes it helps to magnify your view to get a closer look.

Above each pane is the clip's name and duration; below each is a set of playback controls for that particular clip.

The Track pop-up menu at the top of the Trim Edit window lets you switch between the video and two audio tracks to edit based on their content. This is useful if you are editing a track based on the audio rather than the video portion. Here are some other tools of the Trim Edit window:

Current sequence timecode   This shows the timecode in your sequence at the currently selected edit point.

Selected clip   This indicates which kind of trimming function you are performing. A green bar on either the left or right side means you are performing a Ripple edit. A green bar over both the left and right side means you are performing a Roll edit.

Trim controls   Click to add or subtract frames to your edit in increments of one and five frames.

Playback controls for sequence   These include controls for viewing the clips together: Previous Edit (changes the edit in the Trim Edit window to the edit right before the current one), Play In To Out (plays from the current In point to the current Out point), Play Around Editing Loop (like the Play Around Current function, this plays the edit with a little pre-roll and post-roll), Stop (stops the playhead), and Next Edit (moves the next edit in the Timeline into the Trim Edit window).

Mark In   Click to set a new In point for the incoming clip. To do this, you must place the playhead in the Incoming Clip window at the designated place and then click the In point. If you extend beyond the footage of the digitized media clip in the Browser, it will set the In point at the Media Limit.

Mark Out   Click to set a new Out point for the outgoing clip. To do this, you must place the playhead in the Outgoing Clip window at the designated place and then click the Out point. If you extend beyond the footage of the digitized media clip in the Browser, it will set the Out point at the Media Limit.

Locking Tracks

Sometimes when you are editing, you'll decide to work on specific tracks (for example, only an audio track) and want to leave other tracks unaffected. To keep you from accidentally dragging a clip or selecting the wrong clip, Final Cut Express gives you the option of *locking* tracks, which doesn't allow any manipulation of clips on the locked track.

To lock a track, click the small padlock icon on the far left of the track. The track will appear cross-hatched in the Timeline, showing you that it is locked. To unlock the track, click the padlock again.

The shortcut keys for locking are as follows:

> **F4+track number** locks a video track.
>
> **F5+track number** locks an audio track.
>
> **Shift+F4** locks all video tracks.
>
> **Shift+F5** locks all audio tracks.

Using Roll Edits to Trim

A Roll edit keeps every clip at the same position in the sequence. It adds or subtracts frames from the edit of the incoming clip to make room for the same number of added or subtracted frames from the edit of the outgoing clip. Here you'll learn the steps for using a Roll edit in the Trim Edit window and in the Timeline.

Roll Edits in the Trim Edit Window

To perform a Roll edit in the Trim Edit window, follow these steps:

1. Click the Roll Edit tool to select it in the Tool palette (or press R).
2. With the Roll Edit tool, double-click the edit point you want to trim (see Figure 5.20) to open the Trim Edit window showing the current edit. Because this is a Roll edit, the trim will occur on both sides of the edit point, affecting both clips.

Figure 5.20
An edit selected by the Roll Edit tool

3. In the Trim Edit window, you can choose to roll the edit point between the two clips backward or forward by doing the following:
   - Use the Trim controls to add or subtract one or five frames in the edit (see Figure 5.21). Every time you click the +5 button, for example, the incoming clip will extend five frames and the outgoing clip start will trim back five frames.

   Figure 5.21
   The Trim controls

   - Type plus or minus followed by the number of frames to trim (that is, typing **+36** will add 36 frames). As you type, you will see the number displayed above the clips (see Figure 5.22).

   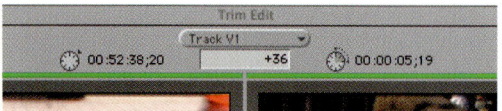

   Figure 5.22
   Typing the roll amount directly

4. You can now preview your newly trimmed edit by clicking the Play Around Edit button (or pressing the spacebar).

5. Repeat steps 3 and 4 to change your edit point until you are satisfied.

After you finish trimming this edit point, close the Trim Edit window by clicking the Close button in the top-left corner or by simply clicking on the Timeline.

Roll Edits in the Timeline

A quick way to make a Roll edit without the Trim Edit window is to simply drag the cursor over the edit point in the Timeline. Follow these steps:

1. Click the Roll Edit tool to select it in the Tool palette (or press R) and make sure the Timeline window is the active window.

2. Do one of the following:
   - Click and drag an edit point to perform a Roll edit. Drag to the left to subtract frames; drag to the right to add frames. A pop-up appears to let you know the number of frames you've added or subtracted (see Figure 5.23). The Canvas shows a split screen of the new last frame of your outgoing clip and the new first frame of your incoming clip.

Figure 5.23
The pop-up shows the number of frames being added or subtracted.

   - Type plus or minus followed by the number of frames to trim (that is, typing -24 will subtract 24 frames). As you type, you will see the number displayed at the top of the Timeline (see Figure 5.24).

Figure 5.24
Typing the roll directly

The new edit points then appear in the Timeline.

Using Ripple Edits to Trim

A Ripple changes the length of one clip while adjusting the subsequent clips to fit the new duration of the trimmed clip. Here you'll learn how to perform a Ripple edit in the Trim Edit window and in the Timeline.

Ripple Edits in the Trim Edit Window

To perform a Ripple edit in the Trim Edit window, follow these steps:

1. Click the Ripple Edit tool to select it in the Tool palette (or press RR). Your cursor is now the Ripple Edit icon.

2. With the Ripple Edit tool, double-click the edit point you want to trim (see Figure 5.25). This opens the Trim Edit window. Because this is a Ripple edit, you need to click the edit to the left or right of the edit point to select an Out point (the left side of the clip) or In point (the right side of the clip).

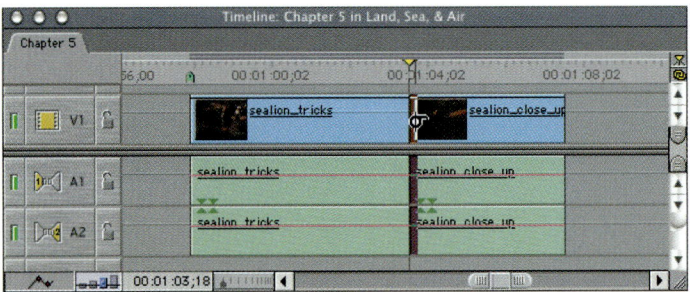

Figure 5.25
An edit selected by the Ripple Edit tool

3. In the Trim Edit window, the edit point of the clip you click is initially selected to be trimmed, indicated by the green bar over the top (see Figure 5.26). You can choose which clip should be trimmed by clicking on the clip's monitor and then do one of the following to trim:

   - Use the Trim controls to add or subtract one or five frames in the edit. Every time you click the +5 button, for example, the selected clip will extend five frames and the other clip start will trim back five frames.

   - Type plus or minus followed by the number of frames to trim (that is, typing **+36** will add 36 frames to the selected clip). As you type, you will see the number displayed above the clips.

4. You can now preview your newly trimmed edit by clicking the Play Around Edit button (or pressing the spacebar).

5. Repeat steps 3 and 4 to change your edit point until you are satisfied.

After you finish trimming this edit point, close the Trim Edit window by clicking the Close button in the top-left corner or by simply clicking on the Timeline.

Figure 5.26 The green bar over the incoming (left) clip indicates that it will be trimmed

Ripple Edits in the Timeline

A quick way to make a Ripple edit without the Trim Edit window is to simply drag the cursor over the edit point in the Timeline. Follow these steps:

1. Click the Ripple Edit tool to select it in the Tool palette (or press RR).
2. Do one of the following:
   - Click and drag an edit point to perform a Ripple edit. Drag to the left to subtract frames; drag to the right to add frames. A pop-up appears to let you know the number of frames you've added or subtracted (see Figure 5.27). The Canvas shows a split screen of the new last frame of your outgoing clip and the new first frame of your incoming clip.

Figure 5.27
The pop-up shows the number of frames being added or subtracted.

- Click the edit point. Type plus or minus followed by the number of frames to trim (that is, typing **-24** will subtract 24 frames). As you type, you will see the number displayed at the top of the Timeline (see Figure 5.28).

Figure 5.28
Typing the ripple directly

The new edit points then appear in the Timeline.

Using Slip Edits to Trim

A Slip edit is a handy trimming technique that lets you keep the clip's location and duration in the sequence constant, but shift, or "slip," the content that appears in the clip. Slip goes back to the original source material and lets you slip back and forth through it to find footage to fill the clip already sitting in the Timeline. Unlike Ripple and Roll, you don't make a Slip edit in the Trim Edit window.

Slipping doesn't affect any surrounding clips or even the duration of the sequence. It affects only the content of the slipped clip. To slip a clip, follow these steps:

1. Click the Slip Edit tool ⊷ (press S) to select it in the Tool palette.

2. Click the mouse on the clip you want to slip and hold down the mouse button. Now drag to the left and right. As you drag, you're shuttling through the footage from the clip's source material—and thus changing the In and Out points set on the original media. A pop-up box appears to let you know the number of frames you've moved the clip forward or backward.

As you slip the clip, the Canvas window shows two screens. The left image is the new first frame (In point) of your clip, and the right image is the new last frame (Out point) of your clip (see Figure 5.29).

3. Release the mouse button to set the clip with these new In and Out points. Now watch the slipped clip in the Canvas to check your work.

Repeat steps 2 and 3 until you're satisfied with your cut.

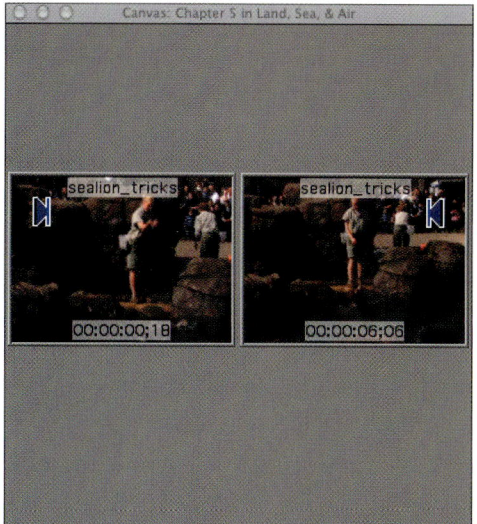

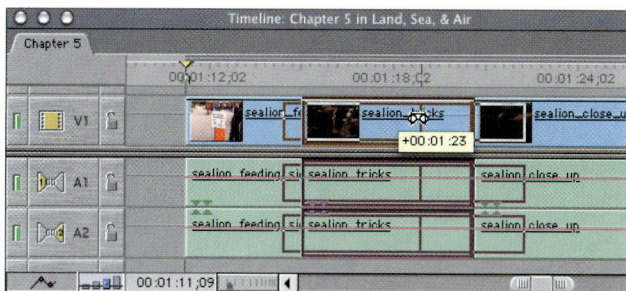

Figure 5.29
The Slip edit shown in the Timeline and in the Canvas

Using Slide Edits to Trim

A Slide edit keeps a clip's duration and media content, but physically moves the clip along the sequence and adjusts the surrounding clips to fit it. Think of the clip literally sliding back and forth along the Timeline. The clips before and after a sliding clip will not move, but their relative In and Out points will change to accommodate the new location of the sliding clip. Slide edits, unlike Ripple and Roll edits, does not use the Trim Edit window.

To slide a clip, follow these steps:

1. Click the Slide Edit tool ⚭ (or press SS) to select it in the Tool palette.
2. Click the mouse on the clip you want to slide and hold down the mouse button. Now drag to the left and right. As you drag, you're sliding the clip back and forth along the Timeline. An outlined ghost clip appears to show you where the clip will land when you drop it.

   As you slide the clip, the Canvas window shows you two screens. The left screen shows the Out point of the clip preceding the sliding clip. The right screen shows the In point of the clip following the sliding clip. This lets you know at a glance what new edit points the surrounding clips will have (see Figure 5.30).

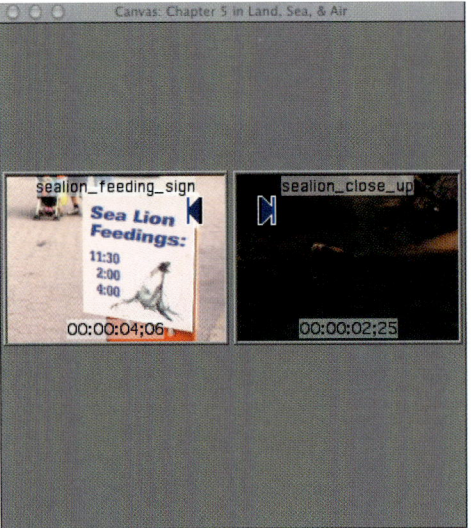

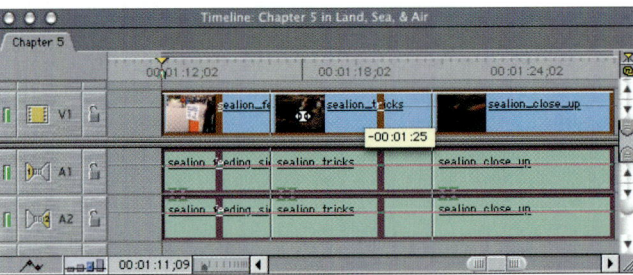

Figure 5.30
The Slide edit shown in the Timeline and in the Canvas

3. Release the mouse button when you have placed the clip where you want it. Now watch the slipped clip in the Canvas to check your work.

Repeat steps 2 and 3 until you're satisfied with your cut. After you finish, your sequence will still be the same length, but the length of the trimmed clip will have changed (see Figure 5.31).

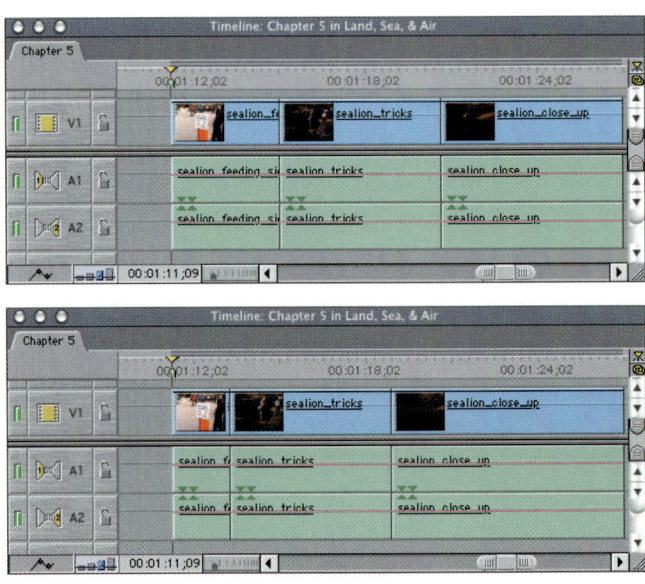

Figure 5.31 The trimmed clips before the slide (top) and after (bottom)

> **Note:** Instead of selecting clips by clicking them, click and drag around a set of clips to select them all. This works in the Timeline and in the Browser (and is the same technique used in your Mac's Finder).

Movie Night!

Stranger Than Paradise, 1984

Director: Jim Jarmusch

It might seem strange to mention Jim Jarmusch's groundbreaking American film in an editing manual because the film itself never juxtaposes two shots. *Stranger Than Paradise* consists of a series of vignettes, but each one is a single shot—one take, no edits. Between each shot, Jarmusch has edited a few seconds of black, so that every cut in the movie is a cut to or cut from black. The effect is unsettling at first as you get used to the movie's style, but after a while the lack of continuity editing makes sense in the world of the film.

The bleakly comedic tale follows Willie, his Hungarian cousin Eva who pays him a surprise visit, and his hipster friend Eddie, as they travel from New York to Cleveland to Florida to avoid boredom, falling into a series of situations of good and bad luck. The editing of *Stranger Than Paradise* is especially important in pointing out that editing does not have to be rapid-fire and doesn't even have to rely on ever juxtaposing shots—editing can be just as powerful when editing is used sparingly. Not only did *Stranger Than Paradise* launch Jim Jarmusch's career, it also sparked American independent filmmaking as we know it today.

Adding Transitions

A straight *cut is an edit that goes directly from one clip to the next. One moment you are looking at clip A and the next moment you are on clip B. This kind of simple break works well in many cases, but can be too abrupt, especially when moving between different scenes.*

An alternative to the straight cut is a transition that takes you from one shot to another. A transition is an effect that uses footage from the outgoing clip and footage from the incoming clip to segue between the clips. The most common type of transition is the ubiquitous cross-dissolve (one shot fades out, the next fades in). You're also probably familiar with a various assortment of wipes and irises, in which one shot literally wipes in front of another. In this chapter, you'll look at how to apply transitions, focusing on the most popular transition, the cross-dissolve.

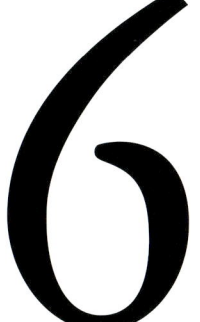

Chapter Contents
Adding a transition
Editing a transition
Creating a fade to black
Using other transitional effects

Adding a Transition

If a straight cut isn't working or isn't right for an edit, you can apply a cross-dissolve to create a smooth transition between two shots. A cross-dissolve does just what it says: it literally dissolves from one image to the next (see Figure 6.1). Cross-dissolves are often used in commercials, industrials, and TV documentaries to make smooth, seamless transitions that would be choppier with a straight cut. In a narrative, cross-dissolves are often used to show the passage of time.

Figure 6.1
The cross-dissolve transition: beginning, middle, and end

In this section, you'll look at how to add a cross-dissolve transition, but this same method can be used for any transition in Final Cut Express (↪ "Using Other Transitional Effects" later in this chapter).

> **On the DVD: Chapter 6**
>
> Open the Final Cut Express project file labeled "Land, Sea, & Air." After this file opens, double-click the Chapter 6 sequence and it will open in the Timeline.
>
> In the sequence there are 2 different sets of clips that have been set up for you to practice the various exercises for this chapter. Each practice clip is then immediately followed by an example of how the finished clip might look. The instructions will refer to specific markers set in the Timeline to help you find the clip for that exercise. Some exercises will share clips, and some exercises can be performed on any of the clips in the Timeline. In addition, there are 10 examples after the marker "other transitions" which show implementations of the transitions discussed in this chapter.

To apply a cross-dissolve, you'll need to have two clips already edited together. You will be applying the transition between these two clips in the Timeline. The clips can either be side by side on the same track, or on two different video tracks. After you have your clips ready, follow these steps:

1. Select the edit point between the two clips, making sure you don't just select one of the clips (see Figure 6.2).

Figure 6.2
Clips selected in the Timeline

2. To add the transition, do one of the following:
- In the Browser, open the Effects tab and choose Video Transitions > Dissolve > Cross Dissolve. Drag the cross dissolve transition icon to the edit point you want to add the cross-dissolve to (see Figure 6.3). You can ignore step 1 if you choose this option.
- Choose Effects > Video Transitions > Dissolve > Cross Dissolve, and a cross-dissolve appears on the edit point. (For this particular transition type, you can also choose Effects > Default Cross Dissolve.)
- Control+click the edit point to bring up the contextual menu. Select Add Transition 'Cross Dissolve' (which is the default transition—see Figure 6.4), and the transition appears on the edit point.

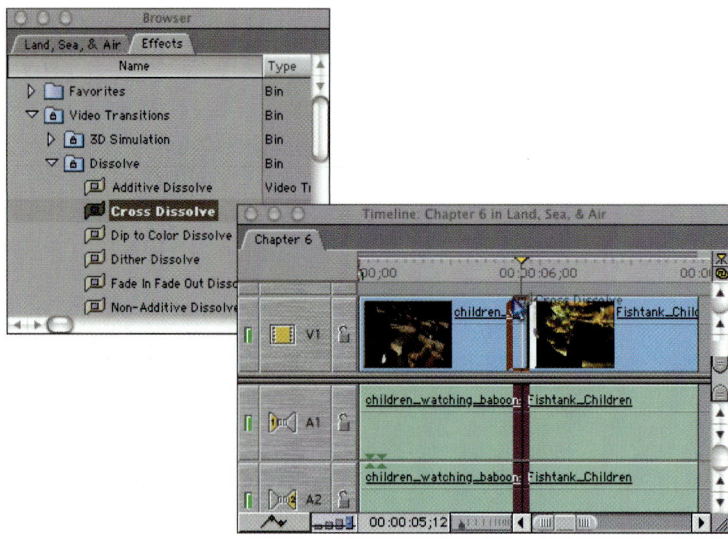

Figure 6.3
Dragging a transition from the Browser into the Timeline

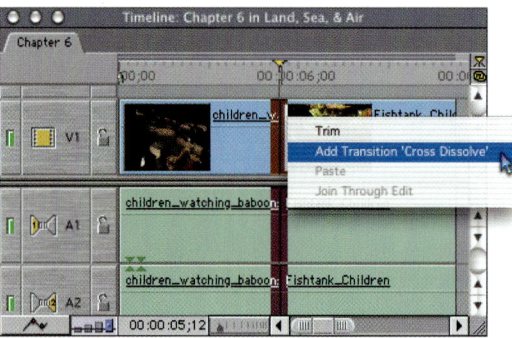

Figure 6.4
The edit contextual menu

When the cross-dissolve appears, it overlaps both clips, showing exactly where one clip begins to fade in and the other clip starts to fade out (see Figure 6.5). If the video clips are linked to audio clips, a dissolve will also appear on the audio tracks. (☞ Chapter 8, "Adding Audio," for creating a cross-dissolve between two audio clips instead of video clips, fading out the sound of one as the other comes in.)

 Note: After a transition has been added, you can remove it by clicking to select it and then pressing Delete. If the clip is linked to audio, it will also delete any parallel audio transition.

Now that you've added the transition, you'll want to watch it to make sure it looks the way you want. However, because you've added an effect, you probably need to render it (this really depends on your computer's memory). The default time of a cross-dissolve is 1 second. To change the timing of a transition, see "Editing a Transition," next.

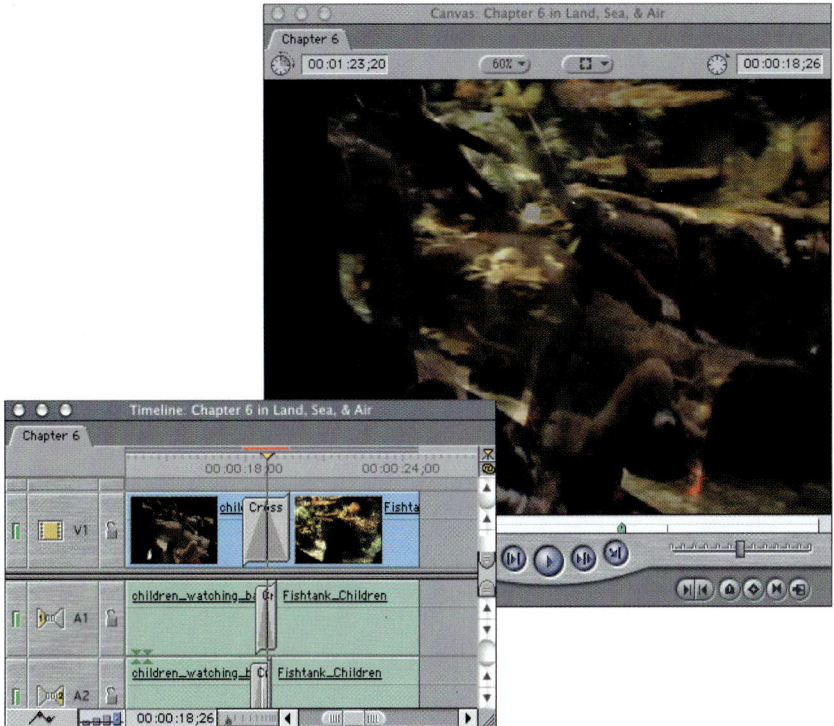

Figure 6.5 The transition added to the Timeline

Editing a Transition

After you've laid down a transition, you aren't stuck with it. Often you'll want to review a transitional effect and make changes to the timing or alignment of the effect. Fortunately, Final Cut Express gives you a number of different ways to alter—to edit— a transitional effect as well as change the alignment of where it begins.

Changing the Transition's Duration in the Timeline

When you place a cross-dissolve, the default is for the transition to be 1 second long. After you've placed the transition, you can change this quickly by using the mouse:

1. Choose the Select tool from the Tool palette (or press A).
2. Put your cursor on the edge of the transition icon in the Timeline.
3. Drag the edge back and forth to lengthen or shorten the transition. A pop-up window shows you how much you are trimming the transition and how long the new duration will be. In addition, you can preview the new In and Out points of the transition in the Canvas (see Figure 6.6).

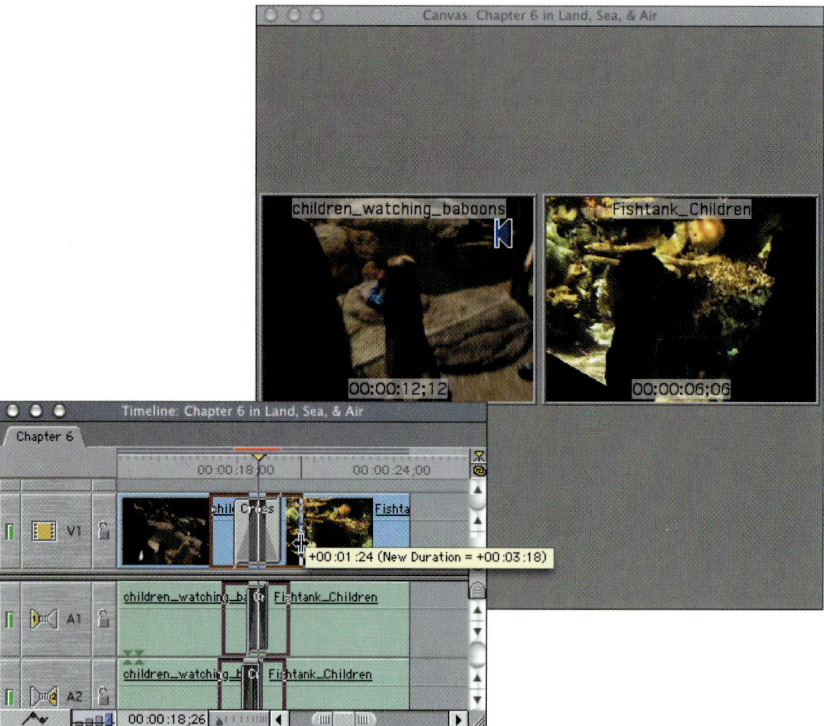

Figure 6.6 Trimming the transition

Anytime you make any changes to the transition, you'll need to re-render it in order to view it in the Canvas unless it is a real-time effect such as a cross-dissolve (☞ "Rendering Effects," later in this chapter). Now review your work and keep changing it until you're happy. You can extend a cross-dissolve as long as you have media in your source media file. If you have a large source file, you can extend a cross-dissolve for a really long time, for a very slow transitional effect.

Changing the Transition's Duration Numerically

If dragging is too imprecise for you, you can precisely enter the duration by typing the exact number of frames you want in the transition.

1. To change the duration, Control+click the transition in the Timeline and select Duration from the contextual menu. The Duration window appears.

2. Type the new duration in timecode format and click OK (see Figure 6.7).

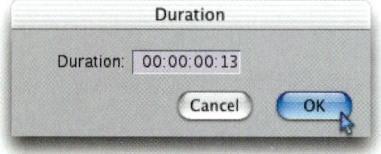

Figure 6.7
Enter the duration for your transition.

The transition grows or shrinks to become the length you typed. Unless you are using a real-time transition (such as a cross-dissolve), you'll now need to render the transition to be able to view it in real time (☞ "Rendering Effects," later in this chapter).

Changing a Transition's Alignment

A transition can be aligned in one of three ways on an edit point: starting at the point of the edit, centered on the edit, or ending on the edit (see Figure 6.8). This indicates where the transition begins and ends in relation to the edit point of the two clips.

Start on Edit

Center on Edit

End on Edit

Figure 6.8 Transition alignments

To change the transition's alignment, click the transition in the Timeline and then press a shortcut key:

End On Edit	Option+1
Center On Edit	Option+2
Start On Edit	Option+3

You can also access the alignment options from the main menu (choose Sequence > Transition Alignment and then select the alignment) or from the contextual menu (Control+click the transition in the Timeline, choose Transition Alignment, and then select the alignment). Your choice of alignment will depend on where you want the transition to take place. If you quickly want the transition between two shots to take place slightly earlier, then changing the alignment to "End on Edit" will set the transition to occur earlier.

The transition now shifts its alignment to this new choice. You'll need to render the transition, which is explained next.

Rendering Effects

Because effects change the appearance of the original video footage, most effects (including transitions) must be rendered before you output your final work, and most must be output before you can even view them in the Canvas. *Rendering* is a process in which the computer takes multiple source footage and effects and computes how the resulting video will look. Depending on the length of the effects in a sequence, rendering can take a few seconds or several minutes. Unrendered video is indicated by a red render line above the clip in the Timeline (see Figure 6.9) and by a blank screen with the word *Unrendered* in the Canvas during playback.

Figure 6.9
The effect is being rendered.

What Are Real-Time and Proxy Effects?

Final Cut Express includes several real-time (RT) effects that can be played back without having to render them first. RT effects are indicated in the Effects Browser by a bold title and in the Timeline by a green (rather than red) render line. RT effects include transitions such as the cross-dissolve and edge wipe.

Proxy effects, represented by a yellow (rather than red) bar in the Timeline, enable you to see an effect close to its finished state, but in a simpler form so you don't have to sit through full rendering. For example, a wipe transition with feathered edges is a proxy effect. It will be seen in real time as a regular hard wipe to give you a feel for the transition, but full rendering will bring in the feathered edge.

 Note: You can view individual frames of the unrendered sequence without rendering by placing the playhead in the clip without playing.

To render effects, do one of the following:

To render a single effect or a selection of effects, select it/them in the Timeline and choose Sequence > Render Selection (⌘+R).

To render all effects in the current sequence, choose Sequence > Render All (Option+R).

To render only real-time effects, choose Sequence > Render RT Effects (Control+R). Only effects with a green bar will be rendered.

To render only proxy effects, choose Sequence > Render Proxy Effects (⌘+Option+P).

A render window then appears, telling you how long the effect will take to render. When the rendering is done, play the sequence back over the effect. You should see a smooth dissolve as one clip fades into the next. You will also notice that the red, green, or yellow render lines in the Timeline have now turned light blue, indicating rendered effects (see Figure 6.10).

Figure 6.10
The effect has now been rendered.

The Matrox Card: Do I Really Have to Wait?

The Matrox card is a device sold separately from Final Cut Express that acts both as a media converter and as a real-time viewer of many effects that require rendering. With the Matrox, you don't have to render effects such as transitions (or scaling, drop shadows, and so forth) to see them play out in real time. This way, you can make faster editing decisions and try out multiple effects quickly before choosing the one you want to use.

However, all of these effects will still need rendering before they can be printed to video or exported into a QuickTime file. The Matrox card simply enables you to view the effects first without rendering. Still, this can be a big help in fast-turnaround, effects-heavy projects. Not all effects will be available for real-time viewing with the Matrox (for example, complicated composite effects such as multilayered filtered clips), but it can still save you a lot of waiting.

Editing with the Transition Edit Window

You can also view and edit the properties of a transition by bringing up the Transitions Edit window (see Figure 6.11). This window launches in the Viewer and gives you a graphic representation of the transition and the two clips (labeled Outgoing Clip and Incoming Clip) and a host of other controls for fine-tuning your transition. The Transition Edit window enables you to quickly alter the duration of your transition, change the alignment, and even trim the transitioning edit.

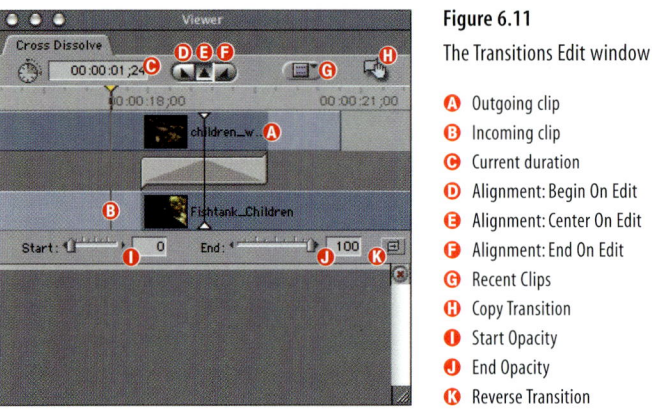

Figure 6.11

The Transitions Edit window

- **A** Outgoing clip
- **B** Incoming clip
- **C** Current duration
- **D** Alignment: Begin On Edit
- **E** Alignment: Center On Edit
- **F** Alignment: End On Edit
- **G** Recent Clips
- **H** Copy Transition
- **I** Start Opacity
- **J** End Opacity
- **K** Reverse Transition

To open the Transitions Edit window, double-click the transition you want to edit, or Control+click it and choose Open 'Cross Dissolve.' The Transition Edit window appears as a tab in the Viewer. To adjust the transition, do the following:

To change the duration of the transition, use the mouse to drag the transition's start and finish points or simply type a new duration, as shown earlier in Figure 6.7. You can also drag the actual clips (as you would in the Timeline) to change the In and Out points (☞ "Trimming in the Transitions Edit Window," next).

To change the alignment of the transition, click one of the alignment buttons.

To modify the opacity (set in percentage) of the transition, slide the Start or End Opacity sliders left or right or type in a percentage value directly. For example, you could set a fade-in to start at 25 percent opacity and end at 75 percent. Most transitions have the outgoing clip go from 100 percent to 0 percent and the incoming clip go from 0 percent to 100 percent. The opacity sliders let you change this. This is rarely done, but can be useful to create a jarring effect.

To reverse the transition (for example, to change a wipe that goes from left to right, to instead go from right to left), click the Reverse Transition button.

To copy the current transition you are working on to a different edit point in the Timeline, click the grab hand icon and hold the mouse button down to pick up the transition. Now drag the transition to the desired edit point in the Timeline and drop it. This transition will now be used at that edit point. This copying is a great way to keep transitions consistent between clips.

The Recent Clips pop-up menu enables you to bring up a clip that you have recently worked on.

After you finish, simply click in the Timeline, and the changes you made will be reflected in the transition. However, as with all changes to a transition, you will have to re-render in order for the changes to show up in your film unless you are using a real-time effect such as a cross-dissolve.

Trimming in the Transition Edit Window

You can perform a Ripple or Roll edit (☞ Chapter 5, "Cutting Your Video") directly in the Transitions window, keeping the transition between the two clips. A Roll edit changes the location of a transition, moving it forward or backward across the two clips. Begin with the Transitions window open and then do the following:

To perform a Roll edit, place the cursor in the graphic representation of the transition itself until it turns into the Roll Edit cursor, and drag the transition to the desired point (see Figure 6.12).

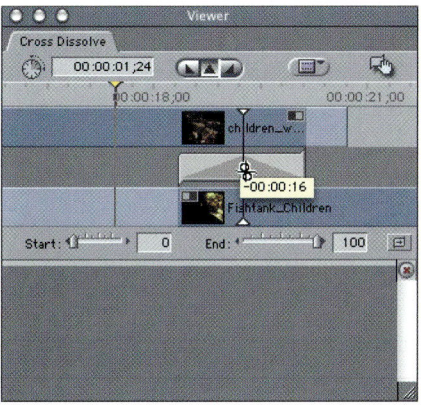

Figure 6.12
Roll edit in the Transition Edit window

To perform a Ripple edit, place the cursor either at the end of the outgoing clip or at the start of the incoming clip, depending on which clip you want to trim. The cursor turns into the Ripple Edit cursor. Now drag the clip to the point where you want it (see Figure 6.13).

Figure 6.13
Ripple edit in the Transition Edit window

As with all changes to a transition, you will need to render or re-render the changed transition in order for it to appear in the Canvas.

Creating a Quick Fade to Black

A common question among Final Cut Express users is how to make a clip fade to black. Because there is no Fade To Black effect, this can be confusing at first, but all it takes is a well-placed cross-dissolve.

To create a fade to black, prepare the clip to which you want to add a fade up to or a fade down from black. Make sure the edit point of the fade (In point for fade up, or Out point for fade down) is *not* adjacent to any other clip.

Add a cross-dissolve to the edit point, as described at the start of this chapter. Render the cross-dissolve ("Rendering Effects" earlier). Because you've placed the dissolve on a clip where no other clip is touching it, the clip automatically dissolves to the default black background (see Figure 6.14).

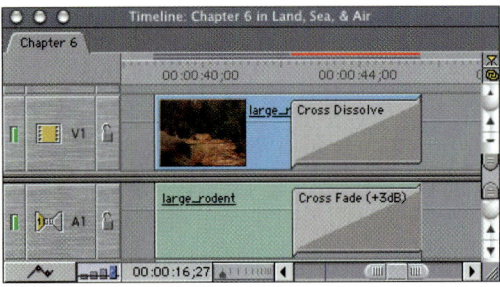

Figure 6.14
The transition is added at the end of the clip over "blank" space.

Although this transition works fine, you can also use the Fade In Fade Out dissolve also located in the Browser's Video Transitions > Dissolve folder. This effect can also be used between two clips to create a dip to black where the outgoing clip fades to black and then the incoming clip fades from black.

You can now edit this fade transition as you would any other transition.

When Should You Use a Transition?

Many editors feel very strongly about transitions. Some editors refuse to ever use them, citing them as lazy and easy covers for bad edits. Other editors revel in the smooth and seamless rhythm they give to a piece. The choice is really up to you, your own style, and the type of project you are working on.

TV commercials and documentaries uses transitions all the time, and one reason for this is that it is a relatively passive medium. Transitions do make edits less jarring and make the viewing process more comfortable. Feature films and sitcoms use transitions less often, because narrative scenes have plot and character to hold them together and keep people interested. In general, we suggest you use a transition when you feel like you have a good reason for it. Avoid throwing a cross-dissolve on every cut because it makes things easier for you. It's often worth the extra time to make a really great straight cut work.

Using Other Transitional Effects

The cross-dissolve is by far the most common transition used in TV and movies, and therefore is Final Cut Express's most common transition. You could edit your whole life and never need any other transitional effect. However, sometimes an editing job calls for flashier or "fancier" effects. Final Cut Express is chock full of all sorts of transitions, but be warned. Just because you have access to them doesn't mean you have to use them. Honestly, many of these transitions are pretty hokey and shouldn't be seen this side of a late night cable access show.

That said, some of these can be fun or useful. We encourage you to open the Effects bin in your Browser and experiment with the effects in the Video Transitions bin. Any of these effects can be applied and rendered just like the cross-dissolve. Let's look at a few of the more involved transitional effects that come with Final Cut Express:

3-D Simulation: Cube Spin   This creates a three-dimensional cube with your clips playing on two adjacent sides of the cube. As the transition occurs, the cube spins so that the face with your incoming clip fills the screen.

Dissolve: Fade In Fade Out dissolve   This provides a quick and easy way to create a dip to black between two clips. This creates a fade to black at the Out point of clip A and a fade up from black at the In point of clip B. This transition is often used to suggest the passing of time and saves you the hassle of manually inserting fade transitions with cross-dissolves.

Dissolve: Ripple dissolve This one simulates ripples on the screen as if the surface were water and a rock had been thrown into the middle. Although not a common transition, this one might be good for flashbacks or for transitions between water scenes.

Page Peel A silly but common effect, often used in kids' shows. The outgoing clip is literally peeled off like a piece of paper stuck to the incoming clip, which is revealed behind it.

QuickTime: Explode This transition literally blows up the outgoing clip like a balloon to reveal the incoming clip in the center. The effect creates a curved, fish-eyed distortion over the outgoing image.

QuickTime: Zoom The outgoing clip diminishes in size as the incoming clip grows from a tiny dot to fill the whole screen. This effect is a typical MTV-style transition that is usually accompanied by a sound effect to highlight the growing and shrinking.

Iris: Star iris The incoming clip is revealed through a matte of a star pattern that grows to fill the screen. Also common on kids' shows, local TV commercials, and disco videos.

Stretch: Squeeze The outgoing clip is squeezed into nothingness, and the incoming clip wipes in from either side—this is another standard TV effect but it tends to look goofy.

Wipe: Edge wipe The common edge wipe looks like your outgoing clip is being scraped over by your incoming clip. The effect looks like a swish of a windshield wiper.

Wipe: Jaws wipe Everybody's favorite Spielberg baddie makes an appearance here as a transition. Like a standard wipe, in which the outgoing clip is covered by a sliding wipe of the new clip, this one makes things more interesting by having the edge of the wipe shaped like shark teeth instead of a flat edge. Your challenge is to find an edit that needs this kind of effect.

Movie Night!

The Cabinet of Dr. Caligari, 1919

Director: Robert Wiene

Many silent movies displayed an amazing array of transitional effects that showed the pioneers of moviemaking experimenting with the newfound art form of film. Early cinema incorporated all sorts of tricks, and the cross-dissolve, iris, wipe, double exposure, and other transitional devices came out of the this era.

The Cabinet of Dr. Caligari was an international success when it was released in 1919 and became one of the first foreign hits in the United States. The twisted story of a doctor who travels around with a mysterious and murderous sleepwalker contains many optical effects and irises. An iris effect starts with only one thing in the frame visible surrounded by black, and then pulls back to reveal the whole frame. These transitional devices are disjointed and make the story dreamlike and surreal. The sets themselves are highly stylized and theatrical pieces, with unreal angles and exaggerated perspectives. In fact, by the end of the movie, it's left to the viewer to decide whether the entire movie has been a fever dream.

Adding Video Effects

The raw footage that comes directly from your digital videotape might be exactly the way you want it: the colors are beautiful, the exposure is perfect, the saturation is lush. If that is true, then you are a very lucky person (and can skip this chapter).

More than likely, though, you'll need to do a little or a lot of tweaking to the video to make it "pop," to correct for something that isn't quite right, or to make the image a little more stylized than the naturalistic raw stock. You might also want to manipulate your footage, adding special effects for a variety of purposes. This chapter introduces the controls in Final Cut Express for changing the way your image looks.

Chapter Contents
Adding effects with filters
Adding special effects
Correcting color
Cropping and distorting the image
Working with composite modes

Adding Effects with Filters

A *filter* is a set of attributes that you add to a clip in order to change its appearance. A filter is a type of effect, like transitions and motion effects. Many software filters attempt to mimic the physical "filters" and distortions filmmakers might place on their camera lens or use when printing optically, but now you can play around with them digitally while preserving your original footage. There are numerous filters that you can add to a clip in order to control its color, contrast, and other aspects of the clip's appearance when played back.

> **On the DVD: Chapter 7**
>
> Open the Final Cut Express project file labeled Land, Sea, & Air. After this file opens, double-click the Chapter 7 sequence, and it will open in the Timeline.
>
> This chapter has 10 clips for you to play around with when working with the exercises; each is followed immediately by one or more examples of what the final results might look like. In addition, the final marker in this sequence, named Composite Mode, includes clips set to show all of the different composite modes available in Final Cut Express. Keep in mind that when you look at these for the first time, the effects (including motion and composite mode changes) will not be rendered (↝ the "Rendering Effects" section in Chapter 6, "Adding Transitions").

Regardless of the filter that you are adding to create an effect in your clip, the process is pretty much the same, although each filter will have different controls. In this section, you will look at how to add a filter, using the Desaturate filter as an example. The rest of this section covers some of the more important filters you will use to control your images, focusing on how to correct for footage that is too dark, too light, or wrongly color balanced.

Adding a Filter: Desaturate

In Final Cut Express, a filter is a type of effect (along with other effects such as transitions, slugs, and so forth) that changes the image by altering the image information based on the filter's parameters. For example, the Desaturate filter takes the color information of a clip (see Figure 7.1) and discards it, so that only grayscale information is left and the clip will play in black-and-white (see Figure 7.2).

You can add as many filters as you want to a single clip, allowing you flexibility and great diversity in the resulting looks. In addition, most filters have controls that enable you to set how the filter interacts with the clip, further increasing your range of potential effects. For example, Desaturate not only enables you to completely remove the color information, but instead to partially remove the color information, creating a washed-out effect (see Figure 7.3). In fact, the Desaturate filter also enables you to increase the saturation to increase color values (see Figure 7.4).

Figure 7.1
The original full-color image

Figure 7.2
The desaturated black-and-white version

Figure 7.3
A partially desaturated washed-out version

Figure 7.4
A saturated version

To use the Desaturate filter, or any other filter, follow these steps:

1. In the Canvas, Timeline, or Browser, double-click the clip to which you want to add a filter. This opens the clip in the Viewer. For this exercise, open the clip marked Desaturate (the clip after it shows the final results).

Note: If you choose your clip from the Timeline or Canvas, the filter will affect only that instance of the clip. If you choose a clip from the Browser, however, the filter will affect all future (although not currently existing) uses of the clip from the Browser.

2. In the Browser, open the Effects tab. Choose Video Filters, and then select the filter type and filter you want to apply to a clip. For this exercise, choose Image Control > Desaturate.

3. Drag the icon for the chosen filter onto the clip in the Viewer window (see Figure 7.5). This adds controls for that filter type to the clip in the Filters tab. (Alternatively, you can also perform this same function by choosing Effects > Video Filters > Image Control > Desaturate.)

Figure 7.5
The Desaturate filter added in the Viewer

4. If you opened the clip in the Viewer you can instantly preview the changes made by this filter in the Canvas while you are making the changes in the Viewer. To do this, place the playhead over a representative frame of the affected clip in the Timeline. As you make changes to the clip in the Viewer, you will then be able to preview the changes in the Canvas, so it is important to pick a frame that will best represent the entire clip.

5. Click the Filters tab in the Viewer window (see Figure 7.6) to view the filter controls for this clip.

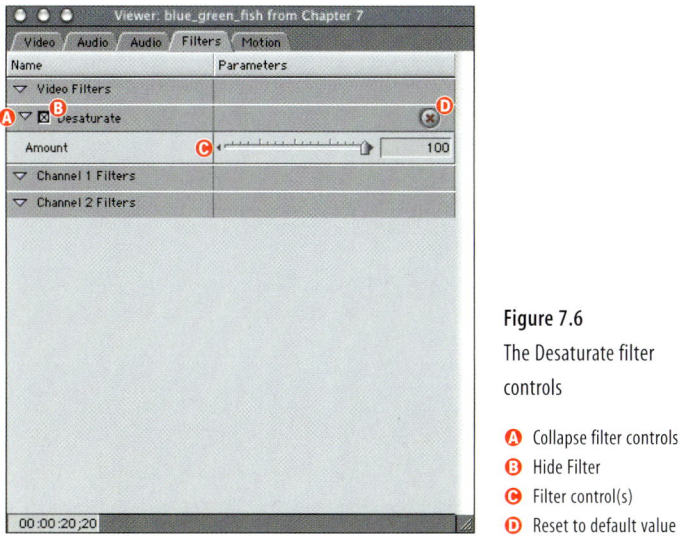

Figure 7.6
The Desaturate filter controls

Ⓐ Collapse filter controls
Ⓑ Hide Filter
Ⓒ Filter control(s)
Ⓓ Reset to default value

Note: As you'll see in the following sections, most of the filters you can apply are not simple on/off toggles; instead you'll control their application by using sliders, entering numeric values, and so on. In the case of Desaturate, you can control the percentage of desaturation.

6. Adjust the filter controls to get the precise results you want. For the Desaturate filter, there is only a single control to set the amount of saturation (increased color) or desaturation. You can set the saturation in the following ways:
   - Move the slider to the left (from the center) to increase the saturation. The value in the box to the right will display negative values from 0 to -100 for increased saturation.
   - Move the slider to the right (from the center) to decrease the saturation (desaturate). The value in the box to the right will display positive values from 0 to 100 for decreased saturation.
   - Return the slider to the center so that the value in the box reads 0 to leave the saturation unaffected.
   - Type a value (from -100 to 100) in the box to the right of the slider to numerically set the saturation.

After you finish adjusting the filter, you can return to the Timeline and play the clip in context.

Adding Multiple Filters

You can add multiple filters (even the same filter more than once for increased effect) to a single clip. Each filter will appear in the Filters tab of the viewer, in a collapsible list in hierarchal order. It's extremely important to know that the order of the filters in the Filters tab will affect the look of the clip. If you have Desaturate before (above) a red tint, the clip will still be tinted red. If Desaturate comes after (below) the red tint, the clip will be black-and-white.

For this exercise, you can practice with the clip marked Multiple Filters, which has several filters applied to it.

- To turn a particular filter on or off, click its check box in the Name column of the effect listing. Turning on and off a filter means you'll have to re-render it when you turn it on again.
- To delete a filter from a clip, select the filter by clicking its name and then press Delete.
- To reorder filters, simply click a clip title and drag it up or down (see Figure 7.7). The filters are applied from the top down, so filters higher in the list will affect those beneath.

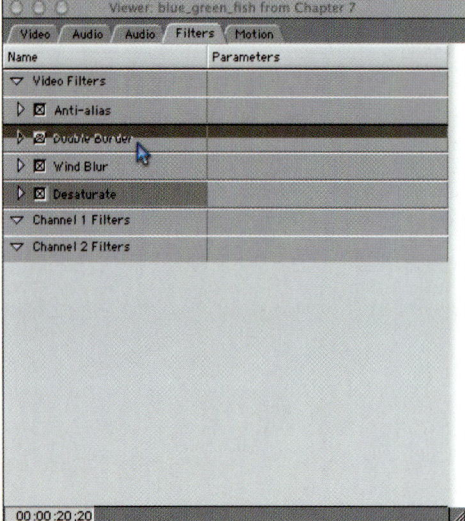

Figure 7.7
The Desaturate filter is being moved up.

If you step through the clip frame-by-frame using the left/right arrow keys, you will see the effect of the filter(s) on each individual frame, but, like all effects, filters have to be rendered before they will be visible when you play back the clip in the Viewer. After you finish, you will need to render the filter (⌘+R or select Sequence > Render Selection, ↻ "Rendering Effects" in Chapter 6) to view the finished piece in real time in the Canvas.

Managing Filter Effects

All filters can be copied from one clip to another or saved for quick access later in the editing process. This is extremely useful when you've modified a filter or group of filters to fit a specific look. You might have these filters on one clip and want to apply exactly the same filters and settings to more clips, or maybe even to all the clips in your sequence.

Copying Filter Effects

Just as you can copy clips, you can easily copy filters (along with the current settings) from one clip to another. To copy and paste filters, follow these steps:

1. In the Canvas, Timeline, or Browser, double-click the clip that has the filter or filters you want to copy (the source clip) to open it in the Viewer.

2. Open the source clip's Filters tab in the Viewer window. Select the effect or effects you want to copy by clicking the name of the effect (see Figure 7.8). The clip's Name column darkens when it is highlighted. You can use ⌘+click or Shift+click to select multiple clips.

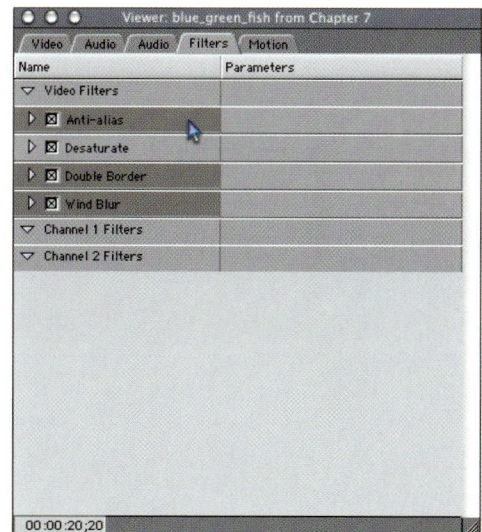

Figure 7.8
Three filters selected (highlighted) in the list

3. Holding down the mouse, drag the effect and drop it in the target clip in the Timeline or Browser. If you want multiple clips to contain this effect, highlight them all in the Timeline or Browser and drag the effect(s) from the Viewer to the highlighted clips in the Timeline or Browser.

Now you'll need to render the clips with the new effects (&⤴ "Rendering Effects" in Chapter 6).

> **Note:** As an alternative, you can also use the ⌘+X or ⌘+C function to cut or copy a selected filter, and then use ⌘+V to paste that filter into the Viewer's Filters tab.

Storing Your Favorite Filter Effects

After you have customized a filter's settings and plan to reuse these settings later, you can store the filter as a *favorite* in the Effects tab of the Browser. This way, you can easily find your customized filter and apply it to any clip where it is needed.

To store a customized filter, follow these steps:

1. The clip whose effect(s) you want to store needs to be open in the Viewer, so double-click it in the Browser, the Canvas, or the Timeline. The clip then opens in the Viewer.

2. Open the Effects tab of the Browser and open the Favorites bin.

3. In the Viewer, open the clip's Filters tab and locate the effect you want to store as a favorite. Drag this effect into the Favorites bin in the Effects tab of the Browser (see Figure 7.9). This effect, with all the settings you have made intact, is now stored as a favorite. You can rename the effect by clicking its name in the Browser's Favorites bin.

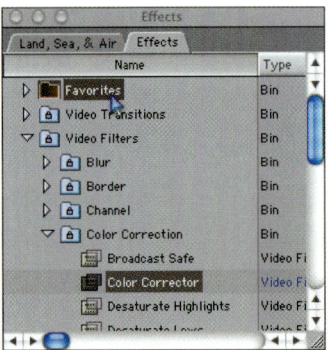

Figure 7.9
The Color Corrector filter is being dragged into the Favorites bin.

To copy a stored effect to a new clip, simply drag the effect from the Browser's Favorites bin and drop it in a clip in the Timeline or the Viewer.

Adding Special Effects

Final Cut Express not only is an editing platform, but also acts as a postproduction facility for adding special effects. Although you're not going to be able to make *The Matrix* with only Final Cut Express, you can come up with some professional-looking, dazzling, and unusual visual effects. In this section, you'll look at a few techniques that will stylize or enhance your footage, using raw video imagery as the basis for digitally created special effects.

For the exercise in this section, move to the clip with the marker Special Effects (the two clips after it shows the final results) as shown in Figure 7.10.

Figure 7.10
The unaltered clip

Inverting Your Images

Channel effects enable you to control and manipulate the color and opacity of a clip. Channels are combined to create the final appearance of the clip. The primary channels in video are the Red, Green, and Blue (RGB) channels which define the relative amounts of those colors in the image. You can also include an Alpha channel, which maps the image's opacity—where parts of the image show through images underneath it—or a UV channel which simulates ultra violet lighting.

One of the most common Channel filters, which we'll use here as an example, is Invert. This creates a perfect negative image of the images in the clip (like a photographic negative). You can even choose which channels to invert. Invert can be used either for abstracting video imagery to create striking shapes and tones for title sequences or backdrops, or for creating a flash negative image often used to highlight a photograph being taken. Negative imagery is also often used in dream or traumatic flashback sequences, because it can insinuate the "opposite" or reverse of what we see, suggesting a dark or hidden side. It also makes a keen effect for a megalomaniacal robot's laser gun blast!

To use the Invert filter, follow these steps:

1. In the Canvas, Timeline, or Browser, double-click the clip that you want to work with; this opens it in the Viewer.

2. Add the Video Filters > Channel > Invert filter to the clip you want to reverse the colors in (☞ "Adding Effects with Filters" earlier in this chapter).

3. In the Viewer window, open the Filters tab for your clip (see Figure 7.11). You will see the Invert filter listed.

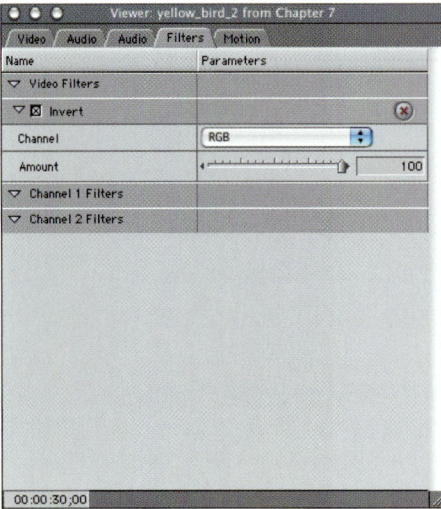

Figure 7.11
The Invert filter controls

4. Adjust the slider or type a number (0 to 100) to set the amount of inversion you want to apply to the clip. A full inversion (100) will create a pure negative image. Other choices are as follows:
   - 0 will not alter the clip.
   - From 1 to 50, the color manipulation affects midtones until it is completely grey at 50.
   - From 50 to 100, the color begins to invert from midtones to full-tones by 100.

5. You need to select the color channel (or channels) to apply the inversion to. For this exercise, choose an inversion of 100 in the combined RGB (Red/Green/Blue) channel for that true negative feel (see Figure 7.12). Another interesting option is to invert in the UV channel for an interesting faded effect (see Figure 7.13).

You can preview your changes in the Canvas if your playhead in the Timeline is over the clip. After you set your inversion the way you want it, render the clip (☞ "Rendering Effects" in Chapter 6) and play it back in the Timeline. If you don't like the results, simply open the clip in the Viewer again, play around with your settings, and then re-render the clip.

Figure 7.12
Inversion in the combined color channels (RGB)

Figure 7.13
Inversion in the UV channels

Distorting the Image

The Distort folder contains filters that enable you to manipulate your footage in some fairly complex ways. In this section, we focus on the Fisheye filter. Fisheye is a Distort effect that mimics the fish-eye lens of a camera, which bulges the center of an image outward. Fish-eye lenses are most commonly used in shots showing the point of view of someone looking through a peephole in a door.

1. In the Canvas, Timeline, or Browser, double-click the clip that you want to work with; this opens it in the Viewer.
2. Add the Video Filters > Distort > Fisheye filter to the clip you want to distort ("Adding Effects with Filters" earlier in this chapter).
3. In the Viewer window, open the Filters tab for your clip (see Figure 7.14). You will see the Fisheye filter listed.

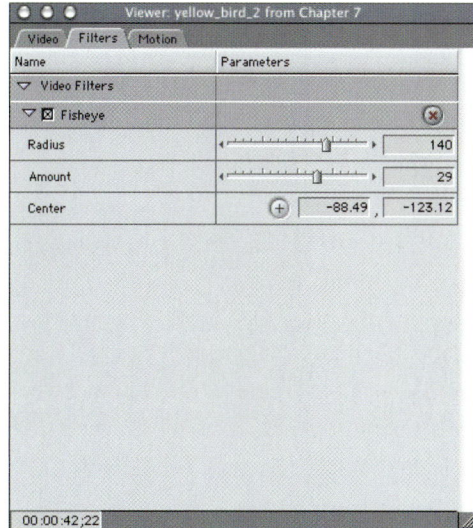

Figure 7.14
The Fisheye filter controls

4. Use the Amount slider control to adjust the "bulbousness" of the bulge and use the Radius slider to adjust the radius of the bulge as it appears on the image. You can also adjust the center of the bulge by using the Select Center tool and clicking a new center point in the Canvas (not in the Viewer) or by typing in new coordinates. The Radius controls range from 0 to 200, whereas the Amount controls range from –100 to 100.

After you have the Fisheye looking as you want it, render the clip and play it back in the Timeline (see Figure 7.15). See how the distortion changes as the image changes and moves. If you are unsatisfied with the results, simply open the clip in the Viewer again, play around with your settings, and then re-render the clip.

Figure 7.15
The Fisheye filter

Blurring the Image

The most common reasons to blur an image are to create an out-of-focus shot from an original shot in focus or to soften a scene that is a little too hard edged. The latter reason is used especially when working with facial close-ups. Final Cut Express offers several types of blurs you can use to simulate motion or soft focus in various ways, but the most common blur, Gaussian blur, is used to help quickly "touch up" your footage. Often a close-up will accentuate pores and lines on the face, and a very minimal Gaussian blur will smooth these out.

 Note: *Gaussian blur* is named after the German mathematician Carl Friedrich Gauss, whose calculations for the distribution of curves are used to produce the blur.

To blur an image, follow these steps:

1. In the Canvas, Timeline, or Browser, double-click the clip to which you want to apply the Blur filter; this opens the clip in the Viewer.
2. Add the Video Filters > Blur > Gaussian Blur filter to the clip you want to blur ("Adding Effects with Filters" earlier in this chapter).
3. In the Viewer window, open the Filters tab for your clip (see Figure 7.16). You should now see the Gaussian Blur effect listed.

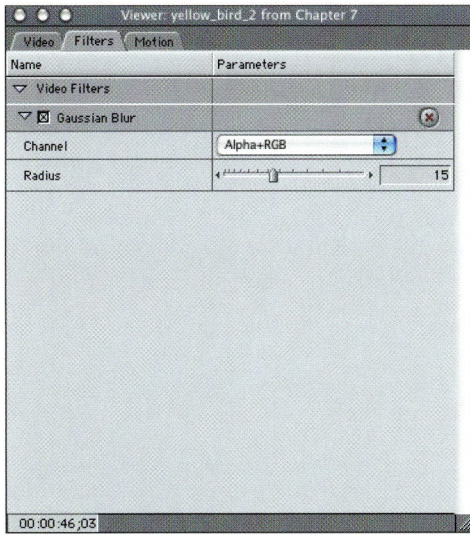

Figure 7.16
The Gaussian Blur filter controls

4. Set a Radius by using the sliding scale, ranging from 0 to 100. This sets how blurry the image will become; as the numerical value increases, the image becomes blurrier. (Radius values refer to the math involved in calculating the blurring, so don't get confused about the immediate circular connotation.) Notice that, as with other variable effects, you can either drag the scale with the mouse or type a numeric value. Slide the scale to the right or type in a higher number. The image in the Canvas becomes blurry.

5. You can also isolate a channel in the video image to blur. Access the pop-up menu to choose which channel(s) you want blur: Alpha+RGB will blur the entire image, or you can choose to blur only the Alpha (transparent) channel or only the Red, Green, or Blue colors; or you can choose to blur based on luminance so that the brighter (more white) a color is, the more blur is applied to it.

After you finish, render the clip and view it in motion in the Canvas window (see Figure 7.17). You'll see that a small amount of Gaussian blur is barely noticeable by itself, but your emotional response to the image does change as it softens. Adding a lot of blur makes the images a mass of unrecognizable forms. By using the Gaussian Blur filter, you can make any piece of footage into an abstract plane of color and movement. If you are creating an abstract image, such as a background for a title, you will often use the Gaussian Blur filter in conjunction with other filters and color effects.

> **Note:** Remember, you can add as many effects and filters to a single clip as you want, but this can start to get unwieldy after about six to eight effects.

Figure 7.17
The blurred image

Changing the Perspective

The Perspective folder contains a number of filters that change the apparent spatial position of the clip. These perspective-shifting effects can aid you when the raw footage is not in the right spot or you want to create an unusual special effect. Changing the perspective, especially if you are using the Basic 3-D and Curl filters, can create fairly complex special effects that you can use to jazz up a promotional or educational video or to create imagery for an experimental video. The other perspective filters—Flop, Mirror, and Rotate—are helpful in changing the placement of a shot or flipping the image to reverse the composition.

In this example, we'll use Mirror, which creates a reflected split image of one side of your clip. Drag the Mirror filter into your clip in the Viewer window. Then follow these steps:

1. In the Canvas, Timeline, or Browser, double-click the clip that you want to work with; this opens it in the Viewer.

2. Add the Video Filters > Perspective > Mirror filter to the clip you want to blur (&⌒ "Adding Effects with Filters" earlier in this chapter).

3. In the Viewer window, open the Filters tab for your clip (see Figure 7.18). You will see the Mirror filter that you added to the clip.

4. Set the orientation of the mirror axis line by adjusting the center with the Reflection Center crosshair and coordinates, either by placing the crosshair in the chosen spot in the Canvas or by inserting numerical X, Y coordinates. Use the Reflection Angle to change the angle of the mirror with values from 0 to 360.

 Note: You can add multiple Mirror filters with different axes to create a kaleidoscope effect.

After you finish, render the clip in the Timeline and view it in motion in the Canvas window (see Figure 7.19). If you are unsatisfied with the results, simply open the clip in the Viewer again, play around with your settings, and then re-render the clip.

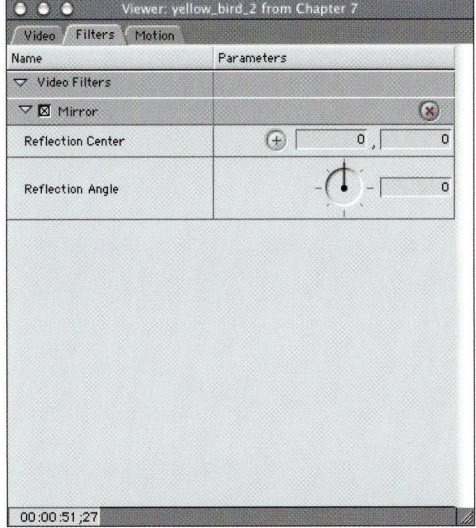

Figure 7.18
The Mirror filter controls

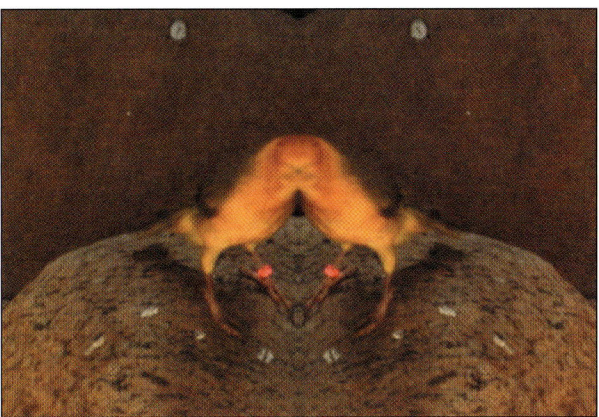

Figure 7.19
The mirrored image

Adding a Border

The Border filter enables you to create either a basic border that surrounds your clip (that is, a solid color around the entire clip) or a beveled border. This can be helpful if you are using the Scale control in the Motion tab to shrink the image and want it to stand out or highlight it as a window. In this example, we'll use the Bevel border, which creates a border that is given a sense of dimension by the illusion that light is shining on it from an angle.

1. In the Canvas, Timeline, or Browser, double-click the clip to which you want to add a Bevel border; this opens the clip in the Viewer.
2. Add the Video Filters > Border > Bevel Border filter to the clip you want to blur (☞ "Adding Effects with Filters" earlier in this chapter).
3. In the Viewer window, open the Filters tab for your clip (see Figure 7.20). You will see the Bevel filter that you added to the clip.

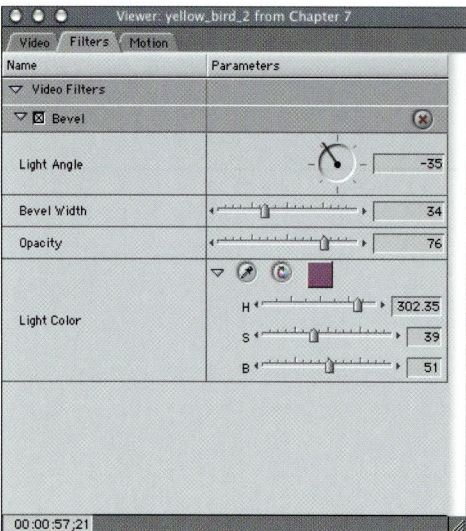

Figure 7.20
The Bevel filter controls

4. Use the slider control to adjust the width of the border (you can do this with either Basic Border or Bevel), from 0 to 100. You can also change the color of the border by double-clicking the color swatch or using the Eyedropper to sample a color from the Canvas window's image (with Bevel, you control the color of the light shining on the border). With Bevel, you can also use the Light Angle control to adjust the perceived angle (0–360) of light shining on the border, and the Opacity slider lets you control the bevel's prominence on the border, by letting the light seem stronger.

You can preview your changes in the Viewer or the Canvas if your playhead in the Timeline is over the clip.

After you set your border (see Figure 7.21), render the clip and play it back in the Timeline. If you don't like the results, simply open the clip in the Viewer again, play around with your settings, and then re-render the clip.

Figure 7.21
The beveled border

Stylizing Your Footage

Creating interplanetary moonscapes, making a dream sequence break from the reality of the narrative, or constructing abstract backgrounds for text or graphic displays—these are all tasks that use filters to stylize your clips. When you stylize a clip, you aren't trying to fix something that is wrong with the footage. You're taking the footage and creating something new that doesn't exist in the real world.

The Stylize folder provides another group of filters that you can use to manipulate images. The example we will use from this set of filters is Solarize, which takes its name from a photographic process performed in the darkroom that involves flashing a print with light while it is developing. The effect dulls the midtones and extremely heightens the shadows and highlights.

> **Note:** The photographer Man Ray is famous for his solarized prints.

The Solarize filter can create beautiful and strange imagery, and gives the image a sense of being otherworldly. You can use it on a landscape shot to create an image that looks like it's out of *Star Trek*, or apply it to an image of a person to create a surreal portrait. To Solarize your video, follow these steps:

1. In the Canvas, Timeline, or Browser, double-click the clip that you want to work with; this opens the clip in the Viewer.
2. Add the Video Filters > Stylize > Solarize filter to the clip you want to stylize (⤺ "Adding Effects with Filters" earlier in this chapter).
3. In the Viewer window, open the Filters tab for your clip (see Figure 7.22). You will see the Fisheye filter listed.

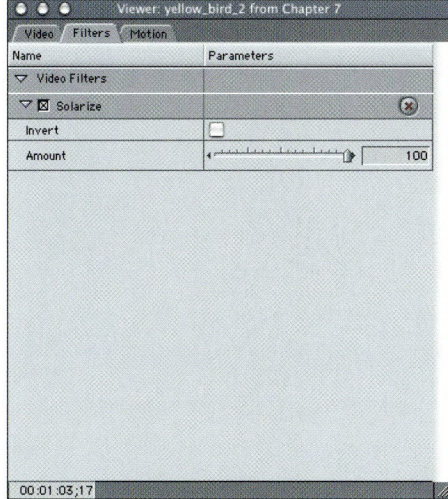

Figure 7.22
The Solarize controls

4. In the Filters tab, set your options:
   - Click to select the Invert check box to invert the image immediately, creating a negative of the solarized image (which might look a lot like the original image) and inverting everything except the whites.

- Adjust the Amount slider control to vary the degree to which the image is solarized. Values range from 0 to 100, with 0 applying no effect, and 100 applying full effect.

You can preview your changes in the Viewer or in the Canvas if your playhead in the Timeline is over the clip (see Figure 7.23). After you set your Solarize effect, render the clip and play it back in the Timeline. If you don't like the results, simply open the clip in the Viewer again, play around with your settings, and then re-render the clip.

Figure 7.23
The Solarized clip (top) and the Inverted Solarized clip (bottom)

Working with Color Correction

Color correction, or color enhancement, is a process of taking the raw video footage and adjusting the hue, saturation, and brightness of the image to correct for improper shooting or to create a totally new look. In this section, you'll look at how to use Final Cut Express's Color Corrector filter to fix exposure problems and footage that is incorrectly white balanced.

Brightening or Darkening the Image

Even the best camera operator can accidentally over- or underexpose an image so that it is too dark or too light. It might also be the case that the available light is so poor that there is no choice but to shoot footage that will look less than natural in the final video.

There is a joke common on the film set when something goes wrong—"We'll fix it in post"—meaning that the editor will do all of the work.

Final Cut Express has a tool called the Color Corrector to help you brighten an image without washing it out or to darken an image without losing contrast. To use the Color Corrector, follow these steps:

1. Select the clip that is underexposed (either in the Browser, Timeline, or Canvas) and double-click it to open it in the Viewer (see Figure 7.24). For this exercise, open the clip marked Brighten/Darken (the clip after it shows the final results).

Figure 7.24
The original uncorrected image

2. Choose Effects > Video Filters > Color Correction > Color Corrector, or drag the Color Corrector effect from the Browser's Effects bin and drop it onto the clip.

3. Click the special Color Corrector tab of the clip in the Viewer and you should see the Color Corrector graphic tool window (see Figure 7.25). The bottom half of the window contains sliders for controlling the brightness and contrast of the image. You can control the brightness of the blacks, whites, and midtones separately, giving you maximum control over the image.

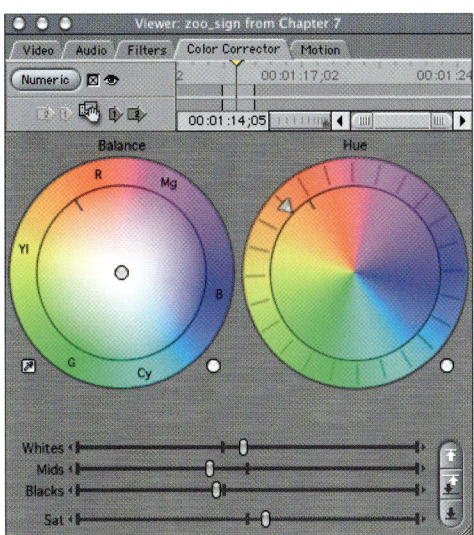

Figure 7.25
The Color Corrector in the Viewer

Note: You can also access advanced color correction controls in the Filters tab or when you press the Numeric button.

4. Now do one of the following:
   - If the footage is overexposed (too light), drag the Mids slider to the left to decrease the brightness of the clip's midtones (see Figure 7.26). This will darken the image without greatly affecting the blackest and whitest parts of the image. It should bring some more detail to the image. Bring up the blacks by dragging the Blacks slider to the right. This will harden the blacks in the image.

Figure 7.26
The darkened version of the image

   - If the footage is underexposed (too dark), first click the Auto Contrast button to give the image strong contrast—that is, to increase the difference between the blacks and whites. Now bring up the brightness of the clip's midtones by dragging the Mids slider to the right (see Figure 7.27). This will lighten the image without greatly affecting the blackest and whitest parts of the image. Doing this might wash out the image's blacks a bit, so you might want to bring up the blacks with the Blacks slider by dragging it to the right.

Figure 7.27
The lightened version of the image

5. You can click the check box next to the eye icon (at the top of the window) to hide the filter and go back and forth between a before and after view of the corrected clip. In this example, the clip is too dark and needs to have the contrast adjusted as well as the midtones.

After you finish, you will need to render the filter (⌘+R or choose Sequence > Render Selection, ⟿ "Rendering Effects" in Chapter 6) to view the finished piece in real time in the Canvas.

> ### Using Brightness and Contrast
>
> Changing the Brightness and Contrast is often the first method an editor tries to correct or manipulate the image. The Brightness and Contrast controls are often used together and so come within the same filter. Remember that you can use these tools not only to "fix" actual problems such as exposure in the footage, but also to add a degree of stylization that gives the image a new and interesting look.
>
> Brightness is presented as a sliding scale that can increase the brightness of the image all the way to white or decrease it to black.
>
> Contrast controls the difference between the blackest and the whitest portion of your image. By increasing contrast, you are making the blacks "blacker" and the whites "whiter," giving your image fewer midtone colors and making the image appear sharper. Decreasing contrast, on the other hand, increases the number of midtone colors, making the image more gray and washed out in appearance.
>
> Like all other effects, Brightness and Contrast appear in the Filters tab of the Viewer when you've dragged the effect into the clip. It is here that you can perform your manipulations of the clip currently being displayed in the Viewer.

Fixing Poor White Balance

White balancing enables you to set your camera so that it adjusts for the "color temperature" of the current lighting condition, correcting for too much blue (too cool) or too much orange (too hot). Most DV cameras have default settings for two types of light: daylight and tungsten. Daylight, of course, is outdoor light with the sun as its main source and appears slightly bluer, whereas tungsten is used for most indoor lighting conditions (except for fluorescent lights) and has an orange tinge.

You might encounter two clips that were shot in the same place with the same lighting, but the camera's white balance was accidentally changed between takes so that one clip is more orange than the other. Or you might get footage that was shot outdoors but was incorrectly white balanced for tungsten, so that everything looks blue.

You will need to use your knowledge of daylight and tungsten to try to correct or change the image. You can use the Color Corrector filter to correct for these mistakes. It can also be helpful to desaturate the images a little to make the color differences less pronounced if you are trying to match shots. No matter what you do, it will take some trial and error, but keeping in mind how color temperature works with scenes lit by daylight and tungsten can be helpful when correcting your image.

> ### Daylight or Tungsten While Filming?
>
> Daylight has a much bluer color temperature, whereas tungsten (most indoor lights excluding fluorescent) has an orange color temperature. Setting the white balance on the DV camera corrects for these differences. Setting the white balance for daylight (usually a sun icon) makes the blue light of daylight seem a pure white on the video image, and setting the white balance for tungsten (usually a lightbulb icon) makes the orange light of light bulbs seem white.

To fix incorrect white balancing, follow these steps:

1. Add the Color Corrector filter to a clip as described in steps 1–3 of the previous section and open the filter controls in the Viewer. For this exercise, open the clip marked White Point (the clip after it shows the final results).

2. Click the Eyedropper tool to select it (see Figure 7.28) and move to the Canvas window. You should have the playhead in the Timeline over the clip you are working with so you can see its image in the Canvas monitor.

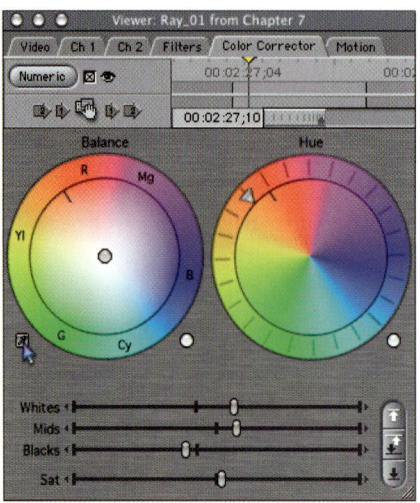

Figure 7.28
The Eyedropper tool being selected

3. Now find a part of the image that you know should be white, but is either orange or blue because of the improper white balancing, and click it with the Eyedropper tool (see Figure 7.29). This can be a cloud, a white wall, a T-shirt, anything that you know should be white.

   Clicking an area causes the clip to be adjust its colors based on the selected color being white instead of its original color (see Figure 7.30). The colors in the image should now appear much closer to the correct colors of the real-life objects they were taken from.

> **Note:** To reset the color balance to its default setting, click the small button at the bottom right of the Color Balance wheel.

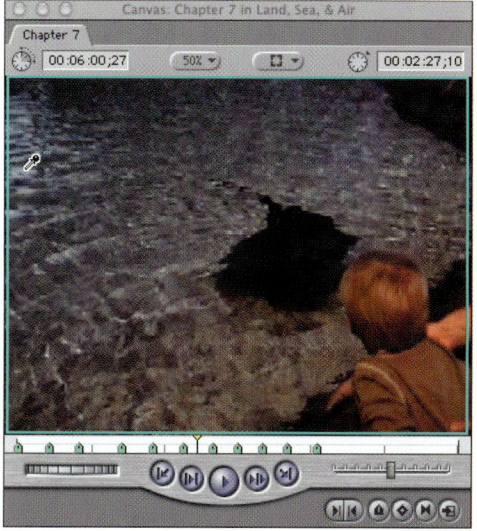

Figure 7.29
The original clip with the white point being selected

Figure 7.30
The white-balance adjusted version

4. If this does not look right, just click another area to try again. Click the check box next to the eye to turn the filter on and off and to see a before and after view of the corrected clip until you are happy with the corrected clip.

After you are satisfied with the white-balance correction, select and render your clips in the Timeline so that you can view the results in real time in the Canvas (⌘+R or choose Sequence > Render Selection, ↩ "Rendering Effects" in Chapter 6).

Manipulating the Image with Motion Controls

The Motion tab, located in the Viewer, houses controls that are used to change the physical properties of the clip (see Figure 7.31). Although these do not add motion per se to the image, they are used to manipulate the image's overall shape, size, orientation, and opacity, and to add a drop shadow. We'll use the clip shown in Figure 7.32 to demonstrate.

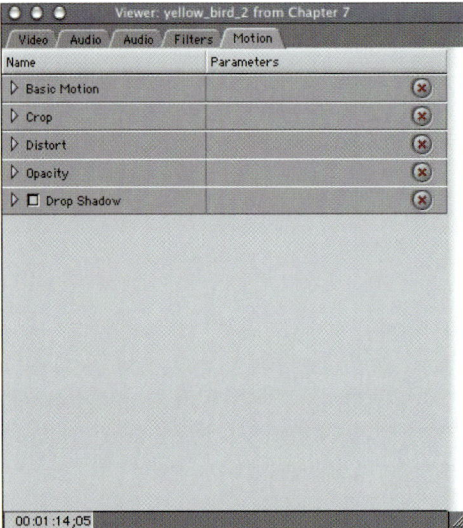

Figure 7.31
The Motion tab in the Viewer

Figure 7.32
The original image

Changing Size, Position, and Orientation

At the top of the Motion tab are the Basic Motion controls, which can be used to change the size and rotation of the clip in relation to the viewing area. Basic Motion functions do not alter the content or aspect ratio of an image; they only resize the image or move its position. To change the size, position, and/or rotation of the clip, follow these steps:

1. Starting from the Canvas, Browser, or Timeline, open your clip in the Viewer by double-clicking it or dragging it to the Viewer. Remember, if you choose a clip from the Viewer or Timeline, changes made will affect only that instance of the clip. For this exercise, open the clip marked Change Size (the clip after it shows the final results).

2. Open the clip's Motion tab in the Viewer. If the Basic Motion control is not open, click its drop-down arrow to the left of its name to open the window (see Figure 7.33).

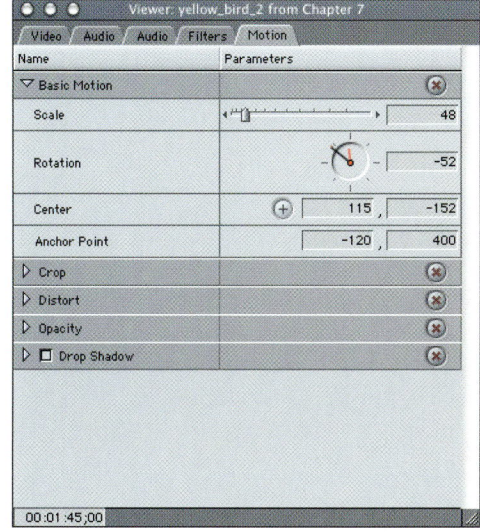

Figure 7.33
The Basic Motion controls

3. Adjust the controls until the clip is the size, position, and orientation you desire. You can see the changes in the Canvas if the playhead in the Timeline is over the clip being changed. You can set the following controls:

   Scale This is where you can increase or decrease the size of the image while maintaining the same proportions. The default setting is 100 percent, the size at which the clip was captured. Use the slider or type a percentage (0 to 1000) to increase (greater than 100) or decrease (less than 100) the size of the clip. Experiment with this; here, we reduced the image size by 48 percent.

Note: Keep in mind that as you increase the size of the image, your clip will become less sharp and more pixilated.

Rotation This control lets you spin the clip around the anchor point. Click the dial or type a value in degrees (-8640 to 8640) in the input field. Although realistically you can rotate the image only between −360 to 360, if you are using keyframes to create a spinning image, you can exceed 360 and have the image rotate multiple times in either direction. The small red dial shows you the number of times the clip has been given a full rotation forward or backward. In this image, we rotated −52 (👁 Chapter 9, "Adding Titles," for an in-depth look at the Wireframe mode, which will let you look at your clip as a geometric figure).

Center This places the center of the clip at a specific coordinate location (measured in pixels) on the Canvas. You can think of the Canvas as a giant grid with X and Y axes whose origin (0,0) is at the center. Therefore, you can divide the screen's dimensions by 2 to find the edge position (+ or -). For example, if the screen's width is 720 pixels, then the far right edge would be at 360 pixels and the far left edge would be at −360 pixels. You can position an object off of the screen by exceeding these values.

There are two ways to specify a center point. If you are doing precise movements with your clip, it's best to type exact coordinates into the input fields—do the math and get your clip exactly where you want it—between −10000 and 10000. If you can be looser with the placement, you can place the clip visually. Click the centering control (the crosshair in the Viewer) to select it and then click the point of the Canvas (not the Viewer) that you want to be the new center point. In this picture, we set the center point to 115, −152.

Anchor Point   This defines the point within the clip used to center as the center point of the image in rotation and to position the center point. The default is 0,0 and is the true center of the clip. You can change it to any other point on the clip by typing in new X and Y coordinates with values between −10000 and 10000.

This control is most helpful for changing how the clip will be rotated or spun when movement is added with keyframes, basically changing the point of the clip's own axes that it rotates on. You will notice a change in the clip only when you rotate it, because the anchor point doesn't change the clip's placement in the frame, only its internal rotation point. For this example, we reset the center of the clip to −120, 400.

You can play with these settings, and then, as with all effects, render the clip to watch it in motion, make changes, re-render, watch, make changes, re-render... you get the idea (⌘+R or choose Sequence > Render Selection, ↩ "Rendering Effects" in Chapter 6).

Cropping the Image

Cropping enables you to cut off parts of the image from any of its four sides. By using the Crop control, you can create thin strips of video or widescreen effects, and you can use the effect to shave off video noise or borders that might be on the very perimeter of your clips. Cropping can also be used in conjunction with the Scale setting.

If you need to shave off the top of an image because, for example, the boom mike is in the shot, you can crop off the top with the Crop control. However, this will leave a black bar at the top of the screen. To get rid of this, increase the size of the image with the Scale control by a small percentage until the image is big enough to fill the screen again. Unfortunately, doing this will degrade the quality of the image by adding unwanted visual artifacts.

To crop an image, follow these steps:

1. Open the clip you want to crop by double-clicking it in or dragging it from the Canvas, Browser, or Timeline. For this exercise, open the clip marked Cropping (the clip after it shows the final results).

2. In the Viewer, open the Crop controls in the Motion tab (see Figure 7.34).

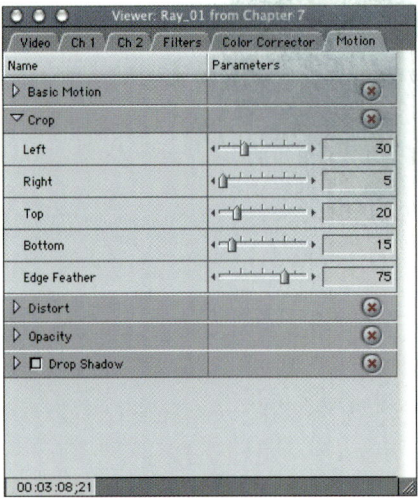

Figure 7.34
The Crop controls

3. Use the slider or type values (0 to 100) to indicate the distance to trim each of the edges of the clip in pixels. This distance is measured from the left, right, top, or bottom edge, enabling you to set each independently. For this exercise, set the edges to 30, 5, 20, and 15 (see Figure 7.35).

 Note: You can press the Tab key to jump between different entry fields.

Figure 7.35
The cropped image

4. Use the slider or type a value (0 to 100) for the Edge Feather setting to soften the hard edge of a clip into a gradated border fading into the background color or image(s) beneath it. Unlike cropping the edges, you can set the feather value only for all four sides simultaneously. For this exercise, use a value of 75 (see Figure 7.36).

Figure 7.36
The feathered edges

Make sure you've got the playhead in the Timeline on the clip you are cropping so you can preview your work in the Canvas window. After you are satisfied with the changes, render the clip and view it in the Canvas window (⌘+R or choose Sequence > Render Selection, ↪ "Rendering Effects" in Chapter 6).

Distorting the Image

Distorting an image enables you to change the coordinates of all four corners of the clip to create a new skewed image. This enables you to pull and stretch the image into any kind of four-sided shape, shaping the image to fit your new parameters. You can also use the Aspect Ratio control to squeeze the image horizontally or vertically.

To distort an image, follow these steps:

1. Open the clip you want to distort by double-clicking it in the Canvas, Browser, or Timeline. For this example, move to the clip marked Distorting in the Timeline.

2. Open the Distort controls in the Motion tab (see Figure 7.37).

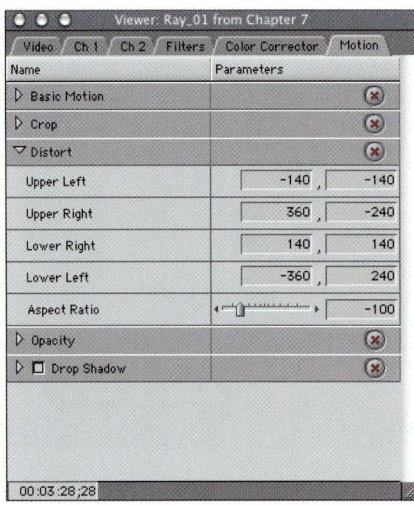

Figure 7.37
The Distort controls

3. Type new values (-10000 to 10000) for the X and Y coordinates for each of the clip's four corners as desired to skew the edges. This pulls or stretches the corners to these new coordinates. Remember, the origin of the X, Y coordinates (0, 0) is at the center of the Canvas or as defined by the center set by Basic Motion. For this exercise, set the upper-left corner to -140, -140 and the lower-right corner to 140, 140 (see Figure 7.38).

Figure 7.38
The skewed image

4. Use the slider or type a new value (-10000 to 10000) for the Aspect Ratio. This enables you to squeeze the image either horizontally or vertically, creating a squashed image. To squeeze the image horizontally, drag the slider to the right or type a value greater than 0. To squeeze the image vertically, drag the slider to the left or type a value that is less than 0. For this exercise, set the Aspect Ratio value to −100 (see Figure 7.39).

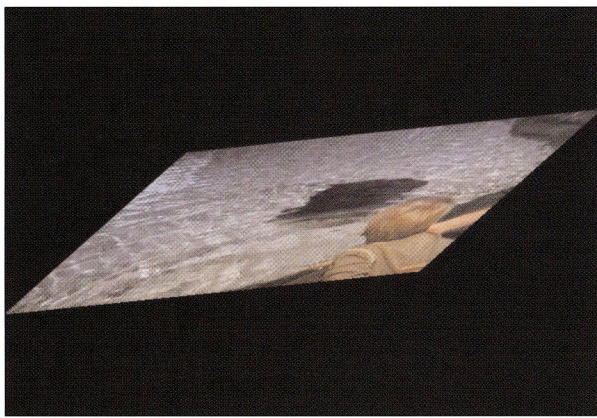

Figure 7.39
The squashed image

Note: The Aspect Ratio setting of 0 is your default ratio as set in Final Cut Express (for NTSC DV, this is 4:3, and PAL is 5:4).

After you have distorted your image to look the way you want, render the clip and watch it in the Canvas (⌘+R or choose Sequence > Render Selection, ↶ "Rendering Effects" in Chapter 6).

Why Would You Want to Distort the Image?

Distorting an image is again something that will be used for many different reasons and situations. As an example, say you want to create a dream sequence. The footage looks okay, but you might want to add a dimension of skewed perspective to make the dream sequence more unreal. By changing the corners and distorting the image so that the footage no longer follows normal rules of perspective, you can create the feeling of a dreamlike world. This effect also can be interesting for experimental purposes, and especially when used with other effects to isolate a single object in the image and distort it in a particular way.

Changing the Opacity

The *opacity* of a clip is a value of how transparent the clip is. When opacity is at 100 percent, nothing can be seen underneath the clip—it is completely opaque. When opacity is at 50 percent, the clip is 50 percent transparent, so any clip underneath will show through.

To change the opacity of a clip, follow these steps:

1. Open the clip you want to change the opacity of by double-clicking it in the Canvas, Browser, or Timeline. You will need to have one clip placed over the top of another clip in a separate video track. For this exercise, choose the clip in the V2 channel marked Opacity (the clip after it shows the final results of the opacity change), as shown in Figure 7.40.

Figure 7.40
One clip stacked on top of another in the Timeline

2. Open the Opacity controls in the Motion tab (see Figure 7.41).

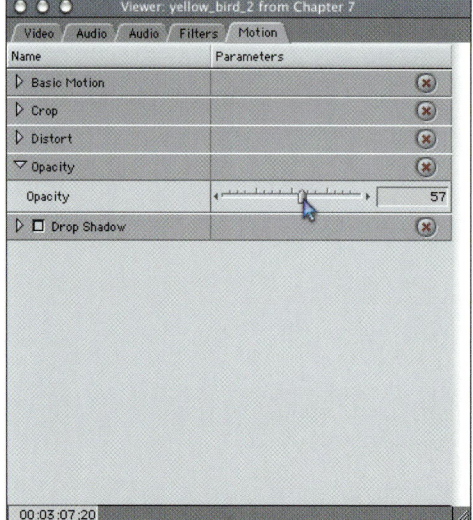

Figure 7.41
The Opacity controls

3. Use the slider or type a value (0 to 100) for the opacity of the clip. A setting of 0 percent makes the clip completely transparent; 100 percent makes the clip completely opaque. For this exercise, set the opacity to 57 percent (see Figure 7.42).

Figure 7.42
The bottom clip shows through the top clip.

After you have changed the opacity of your clip to look the way you want, render the clip and watch it in the Canvas (⌘+R or choose Sequence > Render Selection; ↝ "Rendering Effects" in Chapter 6).

Adding a Drop Shadow

Adding a drop shadow is a common technique used to allow an image to appear as if it is floating over its background by creating the illusion of a shadow underneath. With Final Cut Express, a drop shadow can be added to any clip by setting the options in the Motion tab. However, if the clip is taking up the entire screen, then the drop shadow will not appear, so you will want to crop or resize your clip first (↝ previous sections) before applying the drop shadow.

To apply a drop shadow, follow these steps:

1. Open the clip you want to add a drop shadow to by double-clicking it in the Canvas, Browser, or Timeline. To create an effective drop shadow, you will need to have one clip placed on top of another clip in a separate video track and then crop and move the top clip. For this exercise, choose the clip in the V2 channel marked Drop Shadow (the clip after this one shows the final results with a drop shadow), as shown in Figure 7.43. This clip has already been cropped and moved, ready for you to add the drop shadow.

Figure 7.43
The original clips without the drop shadow

2. In the Motion tab, click the Drop Shadow check box to select it, and then click the arrow at the left to open its controls (see Figure 7.44).

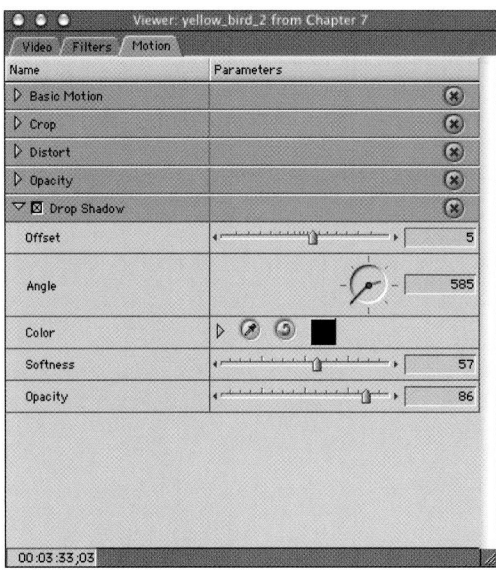

Figure 7.44
The Drop Shadow controls

3. Use the Drop Shadow controls to adjust the position and appearance of the shadow:

   Offset   Use the slider or type a value (from -100 to 100) for the distance in pixels the shadow should appear from the image. For this exercise, we used a slight offset of 5 pixels.

   Angle   Use the dial or a type a value (from -720 to 720) for the angle of the simulated lighting source that is creating the shadow. For this exercise, we used an angle of 585.

   Color   Use the Eyedropper tool or the Hue, Saturation, and Brightness (HSB) controls to set the color of the drop shadow. For most "shadows," this will be black. However, you can experiment with a variety of different colors to get different effects. For example, you might try a white or a very bright color and 0 Offset to create a glow rather than a shadow effect. For this exercise, we stuck with the basic black.

   Softness   Use the slider or type a value (from 0 to 100) to set how soft or hard the edges of the shadow should appear. A value of 0 sets a hard, solid edge, whereas values approaching 100 set increasingly blurred soft edges to the shadow. For this exercise, to get a natural feel, we went with an extremely soft 57.

   Opacity   Use the slider or type a value (from 0 to 100) to set the transparency of the drop shadow. A value of 0 renders the drop shadow completely transparent, whereas values approaching 100 increase the solidity of the shadow. For this exercise, to keep the shadow pronounced but not too dark, we went with 86.

After you have set the desired drop shadow for your clip (see Figure 7.45), render the clip and watch it in the Canvas (⌘ +R or choose Sequence > Render Selection, ↻ "Rendering Effects" in Chapter 6).

Figure 7.45
The clip of the bird is casting a shadow onto the fish.

Working with Composite Modes

Composite modes are settings that control how the layers of your video will interact with each other when they are stacked on top of each other on multiple video tracks (that is, clips on tracks V1, V2, V3, and so forth). The default composite setting is Normal, which makes a clip uniformly transparent across the whole image according to the Opacity percentage setting. Other settings control which parts of an image become transparent based on factors such as color and light.

Composite modes are set within a clip, and they affect only the clip's interaction with other clips *below* it in the Timeline, not the clips above it. If you are an Adobe Photoshop user, you've probably encountered composite modes (which are also referred to as "blend modes" in programs such as Photoshop), and the concept here is the same. They work by taking the opacity and pixel color of the top clip and merging it with the color of the pixels beneath based on the parameters of the mode selected. The exact mathematics can be complicated to explain, but the results can be stunning, and you do not have to understand how they work to get the most out of them.

To change a clip's composite mode, first select the clip whose composite mode you want to control in the Timeline. If there are clips above this one in the Timeline whose opacities are 100 percent, then this clip might not be visible from the Canvas. For this exercise, you can view examples of clips using the various composite modes by moving to the clip marked Composite Modes. The following 12 clips each use a different composite mode.

After you select the target clip, choose the Modify menu or Control+click the clip, and select a mode from the Composite Mode submenu (see Figure 7.46).

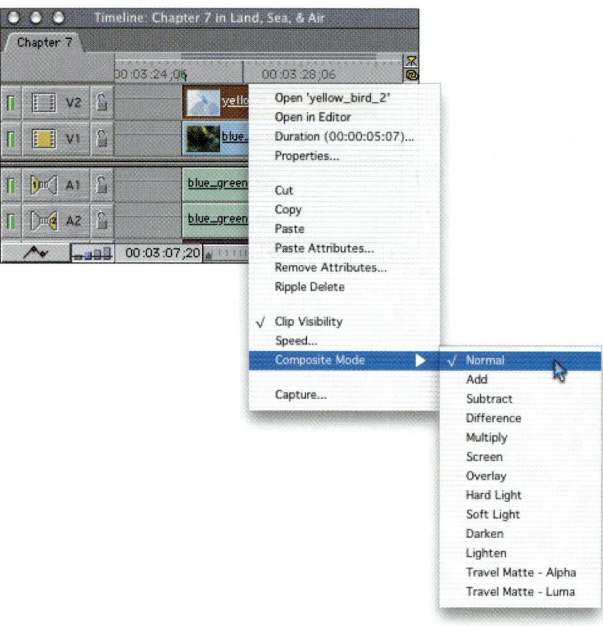

Figure 7.46
The selected clip with the contextual menu

Final Cut Express offers the following composite modes:

Normal The default setting, which applies the selected clip's opacity setting uniformly.

Add Adds the color values of the selected clip and the clip beneath it. The image will appear lighter as it interacts with the image beneath.

Subtract   Subtracts the color values of the selected clip from the clip beneath it. The image will appear darker as it interacts with the image beneath.

Difference   Subtracts the color values of the lower clip from the selected clip; this can create the impression of a photographic negative.

Multiply   Multiplies each pixel's color values in the selected clip with those of the clip beneath it. This will darken lighter images and is helpful to make white parts of the image, such as a bright sky or paper, completely transparent.

Screen   Multiplies the inverse of each pixel's color value in the selected clip with the clip beneath it. This lightens darker images and is useful in making transparent the dark black parts of an image, such as harsh shadows or a black backdrop.

Overlay   Calculates the color value of the pixels of the selected clip and applies either Screen or Multiply. If the color value is greater than 128, Screen mode is used. If the value is less than 128, Multiply mode is used. This will darken the lighter parts of the image and lighten the darker parts.

Hard Light   Adds an effect to mimic the effect of shining a hard light on the clip; this will generally add contrast on the selected clip.

Soft Light   Adds an effect to mimic a soft diffused light, generally reducing contrast on the selected clip.

Darken   Compares each pixel of the selected clip and the clip beneath it, and shows only the darker pixel.

Lighten   Compares each pixel of the selected clip and the clip beneath it, and shows only the lighter one.

Travel Matte (Alpha, Luma) Composites the selected clip with a lower clip that follows the form of a matte placed between them. There must be a matte placed between the two clips (☞ the upcoming "What Are Mattes?" sidebar).

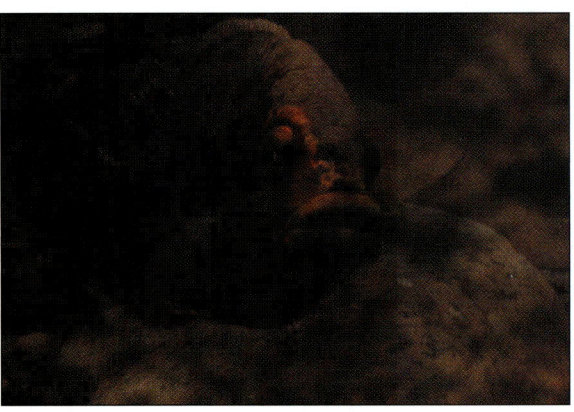

 Note: A single clip in the Timeline can have only one composite mode at a time, but you can overlay clips with different composite modes on different video tracks.

You will see the results of your selection in the Canvas. As usual, you will have to render your clips before you can view the new effect in real time (☞ "Rendering Effects" in Chapter 6). After the effects are rendered, view your work in the Canvas window.

What Are Mattes?

A *matte* is an overlay that blocks out part of the image on a clip. Mattes are often used to obscure parts of the frame or to create a "widescreen" look on footage that was shot at a 3:4 ratio. If you want to add a widescreen matte to your video footage, you can add a Widescreen filter from the Effects > Video Effects > Matte bin in the Browser by dragging it into the clip you want to make widescreen. You can choose standard film aspect ratios such as 1:1.66 or 1:1.85 to give your video a letterbox. Make sure when you add the matte that you don't block off important action or pictures at the top and bottom.

Mattes can also be used more generally to vignette the image or block out something, for example, a boom mike or light. You can use the Image Mask in the Effects > Video Effects > Matte bin to create rectangular, oval, and many other kinds of mattes to lay over your image.

Movie Night!

Fallen Angels, 1995

Director: Wong Kar-Wai

Wong Kar-Wai is a filmmaker whose work grew out of Hong Kong action cinema and has applied that genre's techniques of quick, disorienting cuts and stylized camera work to a series of beautifully crafted, strange, and funny character studies. *Fallen Angels* is made up of two intercut stories. One follows a young man who breaks into other people's businesses when they are closed and then pretends to run them for the confused customers, while the other thread follows a hipster hit man who has an unrequited love affair with his agent, whom he's never met. Mixing existential cool with meditative passages on human connection, Wong Kar-Wai uses a lot of stylized imagery to tell his story. Constantly manipulating the saturation to provide vibrant city colors or stark black-and-white imagery, the film sometimes feels more like a music video than a typical narrative. The film illustrates how stylized footage can contribute to the storytelling, and present characters and themes through unusual visual techniques.

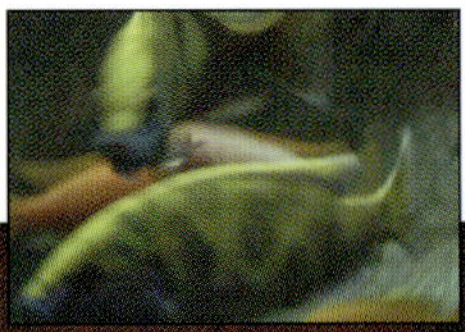

Adding Audio

Video is only a part of the Final Cut Express editing process, even though it often overshadows audio work. The sound of your movie is just as important and can create moods, set the tone, and tell a story in a way that visuals cannot.

In this chapter, you'll look at how audio works in Final Cut Express. You'll learn how to use it with your video image to create seamless edits, split edits between sound and image, get rid of pops or unwanted segments such as pauses and "ums," and bring music in from a CD or other sources (such as a WAV file). Most of your work with audio will be in the Viewer, where you can open the Audio tab to view and change your audio for a particular clip.

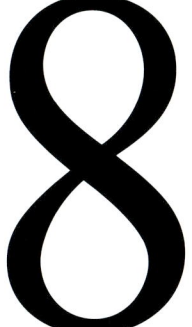

Chapter Contents
Combining and splitting stereo pairs
Adjusting audio levels and spread
Making split edits
Adding audio transitions and pauses
Importing audio
Adding special effects to audio

Combining and Splitting Stereo Pairs

Audio is typically recorded on digital video in two tracks, as a left and a right track in sync with the video image. Both tracks could have the exact same audio information, as is likely with a consumer-grade camera that records with only one microphone. However, if the audio was, for example, recorded with two microphones simultaneously, then one track will have the audio from one microphone and the other track will have audio from the second microphone. Sometimes you might want to separate the original stereo audio from a clip to work with only one audio track. Other times, you might want to create a new stereo pair using two audio tracks from totally different sources. When two audio tracks are a stereo pair, meaning that the two audio tracks are linked together in a stereo combination, four green triangles appear to show the paired nature of the clips (see Figure 8.1).

Figure 8.1

A stereo pair in the Timeline

Ⓐ Left channel
Ⓑ Right channel
Ⓒ Stereo pair clip
Ⓓ Non-stereo-pair clip

It's important to remember that when two audio clips are a stereo pair, they appear as one Audio tab when the clip is opened in the Viewer. When clips are linked but not a stereo pair, they will appear in two separate audio tabs in the Viewer (named Ch 1 and Ch 2).

On the DVD: Chapter 8

Open the Final Cut Express project file labeled Land, Sea, & Air. After this file opens, double-click the Chapter 8 sequence, and it will open in the Timeline. Use the markers set in the Timeline to move among different exercises.

In this chapter, you will be exploring the sound capabilities in Final Cut Express by using several clips with incidental sound recorded while filming outside at a zoo and inside at an aquarium. Although not a voice-over or other strong sound, these clips should provide the rough material you need to practice splitting audio from video, setting sound levels (more commonly known as *volume*), and fixing sound problems by using the common audio filters.

You can change which audio tracks are paired by using the Modify > Stereo Pair toggle. You might want to make a stereo pair out of two tracks that come from different sources, or to re-pair two audio tracks that you previously broke up. If you have two audio tracks that are not already connected in a stereo pair and you want to pair them, follow these steps:

1. Highlight the two clips you want to link as a stereo pair in the Timeline. You can Shift+click or ⌘+click to select audio clips on separate audio tracks. For this example, choose the clip called Fishtank after the marker titled Stereo Pairs.

2. Choose Modify > Stereo Pair. A check mark then appears beside this option. Notice the four triangles appearing in the sound clips in the Timeline indicating that this is now a stereo pair.

The two clips will now operate as single clip and play in stereo over the speakers. They function as a single clip and will be moved and modified as one.

On the other hand, let's say you have two audio clips that are connected as a stereo pair and you want to work with these tracks separately. This is often the case when the left and right channels have different audio on them and you want to isolate one channel's audio without using the other. To do this, you'll need to disable the pairing, effectively freeing up the two tracks to be modified independently.

To do so, highlight the paired clips you want to unlink as a stereo pair in the Timeline; then choose Modify > Stereo Pair. The check mark then disappears beside this option. The two clips will then operate as individual clips. You can highlight them, delete them, move them, and modify them separately from now on.

Common Audio Terms

There are a few terms you need to know to understand audio:

Decibels (dB) This is the measurement of audio levels used by Final Cut Express. It is based on a logarithmic scale that relates to loudness as perceived by the human ear. In Final Cut Express, 1 unit of dB is roughly the smallest change in volume that can be picked up by the human ear.

Gain This number determines how much the audio is amplified. A negative value makes the audio quieter, and a positive value makes the audio louder. Too much gain can distort the audio.

Spread This value determines how the audio signal is "spread" over the left and right stereo speakers. A value of −1 means the signal goes completely to the left speaker; a value of 1 means that the signal goes completely to the right speaker. Mono audio is set at a 0 spread, which sends the audio equally to both tracks. However, if you are working with stereo clips, typically the left channel is set to a −1 spread and the right channel is set to a 1 spread.

Waveform This is a graphic depiction of sound, which illustrates the frequency of the audio. The waveform shows you the loudest parts of your audio—the highest peaks—as well as the quietest, represented by the lowest crests.

Adjusting Audio Levels and Spread

To look into the "guts" of a clip's audio, you'll need to open the clip in the Viewer and bring up the Audio tab. Here you'll see the waveform monitor as well as controls to change the spread and level of the audio. In this section, you'll look at the Audio tab and learn how to adjust the audio levels of your clip.

Note: It's a good idea to have your audio linked as a stereo pair when doing audio correction. If the tracks are not linked, you will have to work on both tracks individually, which is an unnecessary pain.

To adjust audio levels, follow these steps:

1. Open the clip in the Viewer (by double-clicking it in the Canvas, Timeline, or Viewer). If you click on a video clip that is linked to an audio clip, both Video and Audio tabs will be available in the Viewer. For this example, double-click the clip immediately after the Adjust Audio marker in the Timeline.

2. Click the Audio tab and you will see a graphic representation of the stereo tracks called the waveform. This is where you can view, set In and Out points, and adjust the audio levels for the clip independently of the video (see Figure 8.2).

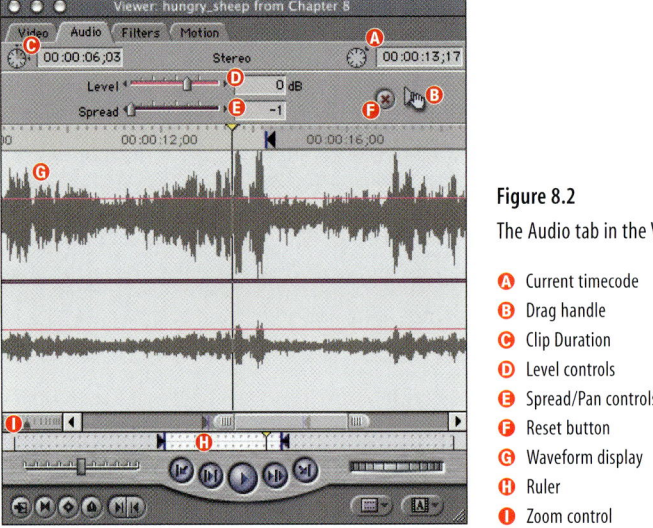

Figure 8.2

The Audio tab in the Viewer

- **A** Current timecode
- **B** Drag handle
- **C** Clip Duration
- **D** Level controls
- **E** Spread/Pan controls
- **F** Reset button
- **G** Waveform display
- **H** Ruler
- **I** Zoom control

The Audio tab includes the following readouts and tools:

Current timecode   This field shows the timecode position of the playhead in the Viewer's Audio tab. Type a value in this field to move to that position or use the + or – keys followed by a number to advance or retreat the playhead a specific number of frames.

Drag handle   Click and drag this icon to copy the clip into the Browser, Timeline, or Canvas. This will bring the video portion of the clip as well as the audio.

Clip duration   This file shows the total duration of the clip between the In and Out points.

Level controls   Drag the slider or type a value (from -60 to 12) to increase or decrease the sound level (volume) of your clip. This value is measured in decibels (dB).

Spread/Pan controls   Drag the slider or type a value (from -1.00 to 1.00) to set the stereo separation between two stereo-linked audio tracks (spread) or the balance between two separate tracks (pan). For spread, at a value of –1 (the default), the left and right channels are fully separated; each one is heard only in the corresponding speaker. As the value approaches 0, the tracks mix together in both speakers, for mono sound. As the value approaches +1, the channels begin to reverse speakers until the left channel is in the right speaker and the right channel is in the left speaker.

Reset button   This button resets the Level and Spread/Pan settings of the clip to default levels.

Waveform display   This is a visual representation of the audio clip in a waveform pattern. This area works as a mini-Timeline just for the audio, where you can use the transport controls to move backward and forward through the clip. Like the Timeline, it has a playhead that specifies what part of the clip you are playing. You can also use the magnifying glass tool in the Tool palette to zoom in on a specific part of the audio for very specific work, such as setting an In or Out point at an exact frame. There is also a sound-level line that you can drag up and down with the mouse to change the level rather than typing in a new level above. This is also the field where you can graphically add and change keyframes with the Keyframe tool in the Tool palette.

Shuttle/Transport/Jog controls   These are the same controls found in the Viewer's Video tab, and used to move through the footage; this time, they pertain to the audio of the clip opened in the Viewer.

Ruler   This is a representation of the entire audio clip, its In and Out points, and the playhead location. You can use this to see your location in the clip, but you should use the waveform display for your real work, because you can zoom in and out and see the waveform graphic.

Zoom control   By dragging the marker in the Zoom control, you can zoom in and out of the waveform display, to get a larger picture of the clip or to go in for detailed work. You can also press ⌘ with the plus (+) or minus (–) key to zoom in and out, centered on the playhead's position.

> **Note:** In addition to these controls, you still have at your command the usual Viewer controls such as Mark Frame, Set In, and Set Out, which now apply to the audio clip.

3. With your clip's Audio tab open in the Viewer, play the audio clip and watch the Audio Meter. If the clip's levels are peaking too high in the meter, you'll want to lower the levels (see Figure 8.3). Typically you don't want the sound level to be higher than –3dB.

Figure 8.3
The audio is in the red zone.

4. To raise or lower the levels, drag the Level slider to the left or right, or type a new dB value directly in the field (remember that you must enter a value between +12dB and –60dB). Alternatively, you can also click and drag the sound-level line in the waveform up or down directly (see Figure 8.4).

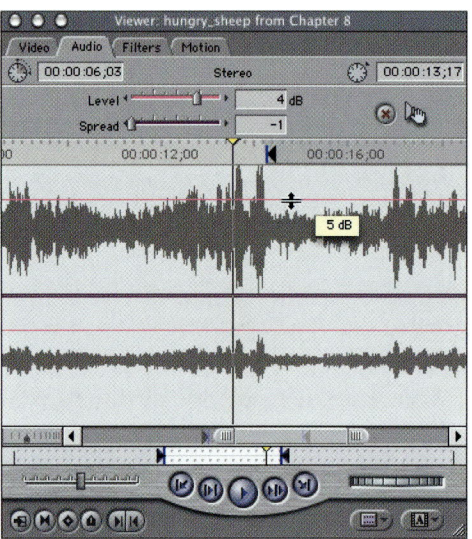

Figure 8.4
Dragging the sound-level line up

5. Play the audio back and check the Audio Meter levels to make sure the audio is peaking at an acceptable level.

Now that the audio levels are set, you should play the whole piece back, listen to the audio as a whole to see how levels play throughout the entire piece, and go back and adjust as necessary.

As we said earlier, if the audio tracks are not a stereo pair, then you will not see the Audio tab, but Ch 1 (channel 1) and Ch 2 (channel 2) tabs representing the two separate audio tracks (see Figure 8.5). The controls in the tabs for both channels are the same as described here for the Audio tab, but you will see only one audio channel waveform, and all adjustments must be made independently to both channels. If the audio tracks are a stereo pair, only one Audio tab will appear that functions for both tracks joined together.

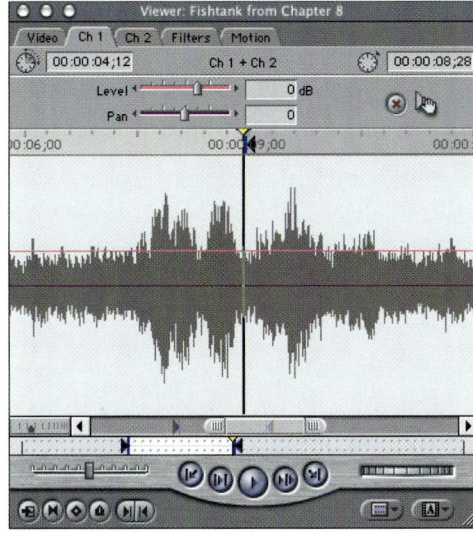

Figure 8.5
The channel 1 and channel 2 tabs in the Viewer

Getting the Best Sound

Most captured or imported clips come into Final Cut Express with a dB level of 0. The actual volume that this level refers to is determined by the way that the sound was recorded and the level at which it was captured.

If the audio is peaking too high in the Audio Meter or if you need to lower the volume so that another clip can be heard, you'll first want to estimate a new dB level and try out the new setting until your ear and the Audio Meter give you the correct level. Play your adjusted clip back and assess whether it's at a good level or it still needs to be adjusted. Keep doing this until you have an appropriate level. Once again, there is no magic formula for this. You'll need to use your ear and good speakers to determine how the audio balances and what sounds good. Between −12dB and −3dB is good for full volume, but of course if you want the audio to be quieter or to serve as background sound to another, you'll want to set it to peak lower.

Using Keyframes to Adjust Audio Levels over Time

So far, you have learned how to adjust the sound levels over an entire clip's length. However, sound is temporal, and the amount you need to adjust the audio levels might change over the course of the clip as the sound conditions change or as you desire different effects. It is definitely not a one-setting-fits-all medium. You might need music to dip down so that a voice-over can be heard or you might need to raise the volume of a specific part of dialog, like a whispered sentence. In these cases, you will need to set different audio levels at different parts of the clip and even gradually increase and decrease these over time. Changes such as these require the use of keyframes.

Keyframing is done with the Pen tool, which is used to set two or more points in your audio clip so that you can adjust the audio levels between them. To add keyframes to an audio clip and adjust levels, follow these steps:

1. Select the clip you want to work with and open it in the Viewer by double-clicking it in the Browser, Timeline, or Canvas. Make sure you have picked either an audio clip or a video clip with an audio clip linked to it. Open the Audio tab (or one of the channel tabs if you are not using linked stereo pairs).

2. Choose the Pen tool from the Tool palette (or press P).

3. Using the scrub bar in the Audio tab, place the playhead on the first frame for which you want to adjust the sound levels. Click on this frame (on the pink Sound-level line) with the Pen tool, and this will mark the point of an audio level change. A keyframe then appears on this frame (see Figure 8.6).

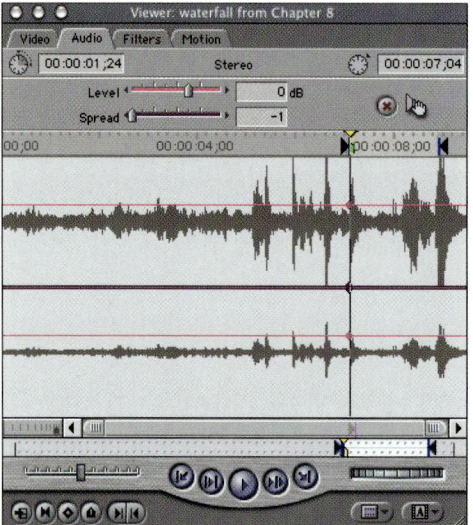

Figure 8.6
A keyframe added to the audio Level line

4. Place the playhead at the point where you want the audio adjustment to end and adjust the audio level by using the slider or by typing a value (do *not* drag the Audio-level line directly up and down at this point). A new keyframe is then automatically inserted at this point with the Audio-level line slanting from the first keyframe, representing a lowering or raising of the volume (see Figure 8.7).

Alternatively, you can click to add another keyframe at this point, and then use any method (including clicking and dragging the keyframe point in the Audio-level line) to adjust the volume.

 Note: To create an instant change in the volume, drag a keyframe directly over or under another keyframe that is located just one frame away.

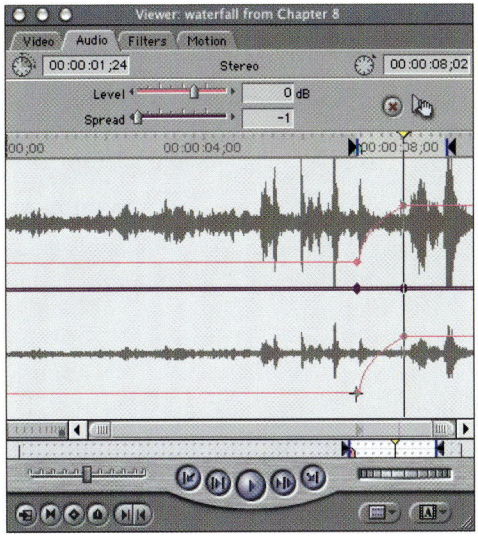

Figure 8.7
The volume is gradually increased over time between the two keyframes.

You can now add more keyframes or adjust the level of existing keyframes by placing the playhead over the keyframe and changing the levels. You will have to add at least two keyframes in order to make changes to the levels over time, but you can add as many keyframes as you want at anytime during the editing process. After a keyframe is set, it works as an anchor point, which you can drag up or down to change the level at that frame.

Adding Keyframes in the Timeline

You can also make quick keyframe changes to your audio in the Timeline with the Pen tool. This is especially useful if you need to make quick changes to check audio levels before fine-tuning your keyframe settings.

To use the Pen tool to make keyframe changes, follow these steps:

1. Make sure that the clip Overlay option is on in the Timeline so that the Audio-levels line is displayed (see Figure 8.8).

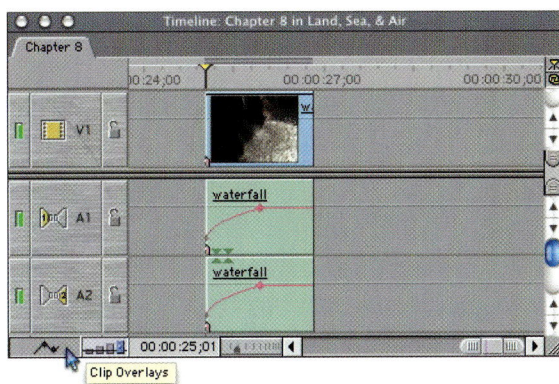

Figure 8.8
With the Overlay option on, you see an Audio-level line in the Timeline including keyframes.

2. Choose the Pen tool from the Tool palette (or press P).

3. Click on the Audio-level line in the Timeline (the pink line running through the audio tracks) of the clip (see Figure 8.9).

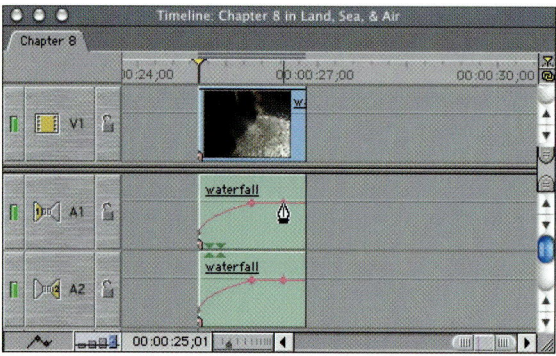

Figure 8.9
Adding a keyframe to the Timeline

4. Click again to set the second keyframe. Each time you click on the Audio-level line with the Pen tool, a keyframe appears.
5. Click and drag between two keyframe points to adjust the level for that portion of the clip or click directly on a keyframe and drag it to create a gradual change in the audio level (see Figure 8.10).

Figure 8.10
The audio levels being adjusted in the Timeline

Keyframes set in the Timeline will also appear if the clip is shown in the Viewer, and vice versa.

 Note: To delete a keyframe, you can Control+click on the keyframe in either the Viewer or the Timeline and choose Clear from the contextual menu. You can also choose the Pen Delete tool (press PP) from the Tool palette and then click the keyframe that you want to delete.

Editing Video and Audio Independently: Split Edits

So far, when we've covered the relationship between sound and image, we've often talked about them as a linked pair: the video track linked to the two audio tracks. These paired clips move together, and when you adjust one, Final Cut Express adjusts the other to match so that they stay in sync. For example, if you apply a Ripple edit to a video track that is linked to audio tracks, the audio portion will likewise be trimmed.

Having linked clips is indispensable for keeping clips synched together. At times, however, you'll want to separate the audio or video of linked clips to work with them independently. That is, you'll want to split the edit points of the clip's audio and video tracks.

In this example, say you have clip A (the outgoing clip) and clip B (the incoming clip). You want the video for clip B to begin over the end of the audio in clip A so that it is heard after you cut to the new video clip.

This enables you to have the beginning of the video in clip B playing over the end of the audio in clip A. This is called *splitting the edit points*, which you can do by following these steps:

1. Locate your two clips in the Timeline (see Figure 8.11). If the clips are linked, turn off Linking ("Snapping and Linking Clips" in Chapter 5, "Cutting Your Video"). You can now drag and manipulate the video and audio of the clip individually. For this example, use the clips immediately after the marker Split Edit.

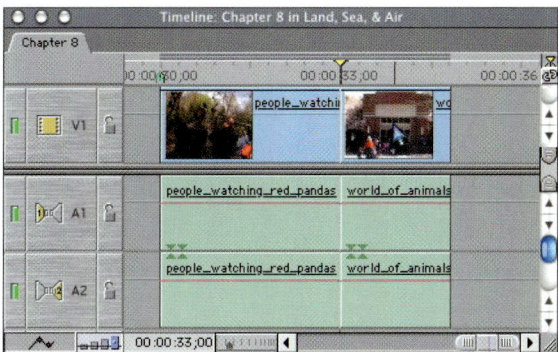

Figure 8.11
Two clips in the Timeline

2. Choose the Roll Edit tool from the Tool palette.
3. Click and drag the edit between the clips in the audio track either to the right or left (see Figure 8.12). The video edit stays put while you move the audio edit independently. What you are doing is "splitting" the edit, creating a cut where the In and Out points of the audio are different from those of the video.

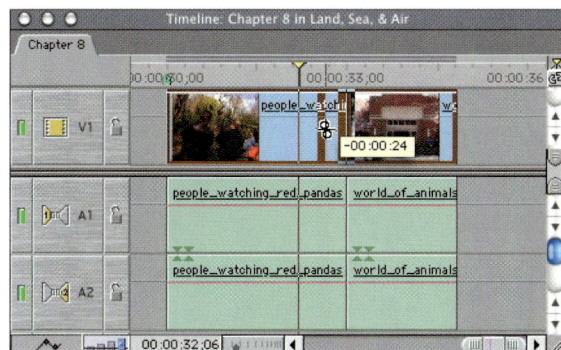

Figure 8.12
Creating a split edit

Play the two clips and keep adjusting until you've made the split edit you want (see Figure 8.13). You can also use the Ripple Edit tool on the video if you want to move the video edit point without adjusting the audio edit point. And don't forget to turn Linking back on when you're finished. Once turned back on, edits will again be applied to both video and audio tracks in sync.

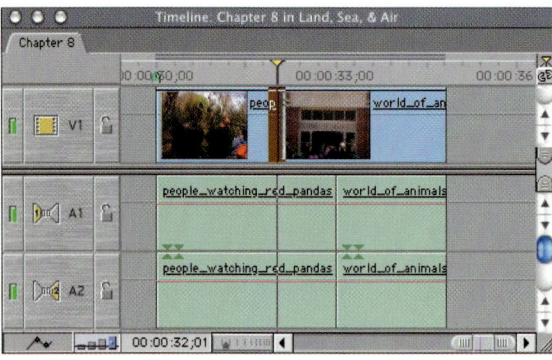

Figure 8.13
The final split edit

Editing Split Edits in the Viewer

If you want to change the location of a split edit, you can use the split In and Out points in the Viewer's ruler bar. This is a quick way to make adjustments to your split edits visually by dragging the In and Out points. If you are making a quick change or want to briefly see how a new edit will look, this is an easy way to adjust the edit points.

Follow these steps to change the location of a split edit:

1. Open the clip in the Viewer by double-clicking it in the Timeline. The split edits are represented in the ruler by half arrows, the top one for video, the bottom one for audio (see Figure 8.14).

Figure 8.14
A split edit in the Viewer

2. Choose the Selection tool, Roll Edit tool or Ripple Edit tool from the Tool palette.

3. Click and drag the Out point. Both video and audio Out points will move together, keeping the same relative distance from each other if they are split (see Figure 8.15). Likewise, if you drag an In point, both audio and video In points will move together, keeping the same distance apart.

Figure 8.15
Dragging the split in the Viewer

Adding Audio Transitions

In Chapter 6, "Adding Transitions," you learned how to add transitions to the video track by using the ever-popular cross-dissolve transition. This transition not only affects the video track of the clip, but also applies a transition to the audio track if the video and audio are linked. However, many times (for example, when using a straight edit) you might want to add an audio transition. Adding an audio transition works very much like adding a video transition, with the difference being that you have significantly fewer choices—only two—and they are located in the Audio Transitions folder.

The two audio transitions are Cross Fade (0dB) and Cross Fade (+3dB). Cross Fade (0dB) has a dip in the levels of audio during the transition; Cross Fade (+3dB) keeps the levels constant during the cross fade. The transition you need to use will depend on the sounds you are mixing. Often, if you are mixing two music tracks together, it is best to have a slight dip in the audio to make a smoother transition between two pieces of music, so you'd use the Cross Fade (0dB). If you're trying to hide a cut between two clips of background sound, you'd use Cross Fade (+3dB) to hide the transition.

To add an audio transition, follow these steps:

1. Make sure your two audio clips are adjacent in the Timeline on the same track, or on two different tracks with an area of overlapping footage. For this example, use the clips marked Audio Transition.

2. Click the Effects tab in the Browser to bring up the Effects menu. Open the Audio Transitions folder and select an audio transition (see Figure 8.16).

Figure 8.16 Audio Transitions in the Effects tab

3. Drag the Cross Fade (+3dB) audio to the edit point between the two clips. Drop the audio transition on the edit point or edge (see Figure 8.17). If you are dropping the audio transition on an edit point between two clips on the same track, you can choose to drop it before the edit point, centered on the edit point, or after the edit point. If you need to add a transition between clips located on separate tracks, drag the transition to the edge of one of the clips and release.

Figure 8.17
The cross-fade audio transformation in the Timeline

Alternatively, you can add audio transitions by using the Effects or contextual menu. Select the edit point between the two clips to which you want to add an audio transition in the Timeline and then do one of the following:

- Choose Effects > Audio Transitions > Cross Fade (0db) or Cross Fade (+3dB). A cross-fade will be added to the selected edit point.

- Control+click the edit point where you want to add an audio transition and choose Add Transition 'Cross Fade (+3dB)' from the pop-up menu (see Figure 8.18). This will apply the default transition (which is initially set to Cross Fade) to this edit point. As with video transitions, the default audio transition can be set in the Browser by Control+clicking the effect.

You can edit the audio transition's length by clicking and dragging its edges or by double-clicking it and entering a new duration in the Duration dialog.

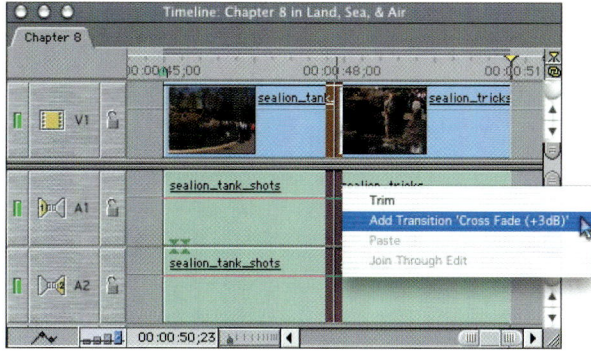

Figure 8.18
The contextual menu selecting the Cross Fade (+3dB) transition

Adding a Pause

If you have a responsible camera operator, there's a good chance they will have recorded sound tone in every location a scene was shot in. This will give you about a minute of "silence" that matches the silence of the space. Silence in an office building sounds very different from silence in a cornfield. It is often helpful to use small clips of this audio to smooth over edits or to fill in gaps in the audio seamlessly. To use sound tone effectively, it's a good idea to create a separate lower audio track all its own for sound tone.

> **Note:** In the world of professional videomaking, the terms used are *room tone* for silence recorded in an interior and *world tone* for silence recorded in an exterior.

For example, if you are cutting an interview voice-over and need to add a few seconds of pause between two statements, you will need to fill this pause with sound tone so that the audio doesn't drop out completely.

Follow these steps to add the pause:

1. Open the sound tone clip in the Viewer and set In and Out points so that the clip lasts a little longer than the audio gap. If the camera operator recorded sound tone, then you should have captured this as a separate clip. If the camera operator did not record sound tone, you can often find a few seconds of quiet somewhere in another clip—usually at the beginning or end of a take—and use this as your tone clip.
2. Drag the audio with sound tone to a free audio track and place it to fill the gap left between your main audio clips. There should be some overlap so the sound tone will merge smoothly with the main audio.

You might need to adjust the sound level or add audio transitions to further smooth the sound tone so that it "disappears" into the mix.

Importing Audio

Final Cut Express can import audio tracks from a compact disc, a data DVD, or audio files from your hard disk (MP3, WAV, AIFF, or other formats). The import creates a new audio clip in the project folder of your Browser. The method is similar to importing other files, such as JPEGs or QuickTime (☞ "Importing Clips" in Chapter 3, "Gathering Your Media"):

1. Put the CD or DVD in your computer's drive or make sure that you have access to the hard disk from which you will be getting the sound file. If you are bringing in material from a CD or DVD, first copy the file to the hard disk of your computer.

2. Choose File > Import > File and find the sound file in the Import dialog box. You can also use the File > Import > Folder option to select a folder to import numerous files at once. Now click OK. In this exercise, use the DVD provided with the book and import the audio file FCE_Tutorials/resources/ExoticFishandLlamas.aiff (see Figure 8.19).

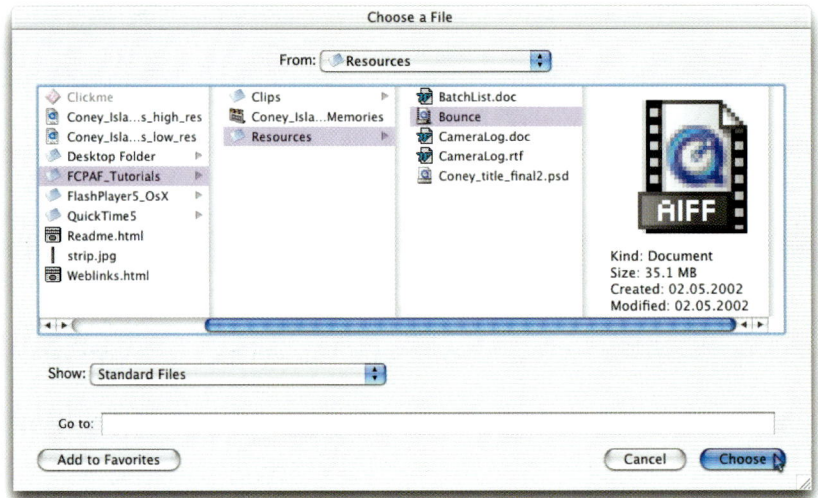

Figure 8.19 The song file being imported

The track(s) will appear as audio clips in your project file in the Browser. You should immediately label each clip by clicking its name and typing a new one. Most clips will be imported with the name of the file from the original source (for audio CDs, this will be the track number from the CD) unless you are hooked up to the Internet and using iTunes, which will automatically gather the song name for each track.

Adding Imported Audio

Once imported, these audio-only clips can be used like any other clip, but can, obviously, be placed only in the audio tracks. To do this, click and drag the clip into the Timeline, choosing one of the following options:

- Add the new audio track to the Timeline (see Figure 8.20). You may want to use keyframes to reduce and then increase the volume of the audio track over the course of the clip playback to bring in music at some points and then fade it into the background for others.

3. The important option to look at is the Type pull-down menu. Here you can select the type of environment you would like your audio to sound as though it is coming from. Choices include Room (Small) and Tunnel.

4. After you've chosen a type of Reverberation environment, play back the audio to hear the difference. Typically, the audio will sound more muffled or tinny as an environmental constraint has been put on the original audio.

> ### Movie Night!
>
> *Blue Velvet*, 1986
>
> Director: David Lynch
>
> David Lynch made a name for himself as a master of the weird and uncanny with early films such as cult-classic *Eraserhead* and *The Elephant Man,* but when *Blue Velvet* was released in 1986, his reputation was cemented. On the surface, the film is a simple teen love story with a Hardy Boys–style mystery, but as the plot unfolds, the innocent trappings of the genre fall away to reveal a twisted and perverse world.
>
> Although he is often mentioned for his sometimes garish and bizarre visuals, Lynch is also a true pioneer of sound design. He usually creates the sound design for his films himself, an unusual additional role for a director to take on. In the opening of *Blue Velvet,* a fifties pop song slowly transforms into the amplified sound of ants scuttling in the grass and the camera descends into a suburban lawn. Low industrial hums are often heard throughout the movie, setting a sonic backdrop of ominous dread. Lynch uses sound with as much skill and attention as other filmmakers use their cameras, and the combination of the visual with the carefully constructed sounds help Lynch do what he is best known for—creating worlds that are strange and surreal, but also make sense with a logic of their own.

Land, Sea, & Air

Adding Titles and Finishing Up

After the editing is done, there is still plenty left to do to finish your video. Not only can you still play around with changing a clip's playback speed, animate clips within the Canvas, add a voice-over, and add your titles, you will also need to combine sequences and organize your clips for final output.

Chapter Contents
Changing your clip's speed and running it in reverse
Creating a freeze-frame
Adding a voice-over
Using keyframes to animate a clip
Adding static or moving titles
Setting item properties
Reconnecting clips to their media files

Changing a Clip's Speed

Although you will generally want your clips to run in real time—that is, so each second lasts for a second—at times you might want to elongate time, shorten time, freeze time, or even reverse the direction of time.

> **On the DVD: Chapter 9**
>
> Open the Final Cut Express project file labeled Land, Sea, & Air. After this file opens, double-click the Chapter 9 sequence, and it will open in the Timeline. Use the markers set in the Timeline to move among different exercises.

Playing a Clip in Slow Motion, Fast Motion, or Reverse

Slow motion is a commonly used effect to create a romantic feel or to heighten a scene of extreme action. Hong Kong action filmmakers often use slow motion to zero in on the acrobatic moves and violence of a film's characters. Slow motion can also easily look silly or hokey, so be wary of overdoing it.

Fast motion is used less often but can be used effectively in slapstick comedies (think Benny Hill) or to create a time-lapse effect.

Reverse motion can be used to create an otherworldly effect—water falling up, people walking backward along the sidewalk, a broken glass coming back together into a whole. It can also be used to change the direction of a camera movement when it isn't evident that the footage is running backward.

To change the speed at which a clip plays, follow these steps:

1. Select the clip in the Timeline that you wish to modify. For this example, choose the clip immediately after the Clip Speed marker (see Figure 9.1).

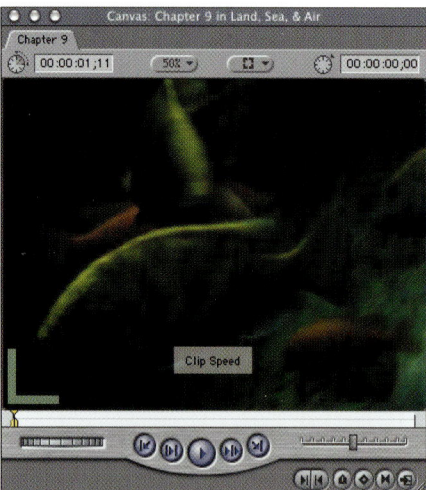

Figure 9.1 The frame to be frozen

2. Choose Modify > Speed (⌘+J).
3. In the Speed dialog box (see Figure 9.2), do the following:

   To change the clip's speed, type a percentage value to indicate the change in speed. Typing a value less than 100 percent will slow down a clip. Typing a value greater than 100 percent will speed it up. You could also type a new duration for the clip, and the clip will speed up or slow down to fit this new duration. The clip will grow or shrink in the Timeline to accommodate the new length.

   To run the clip backward, click the Reverse check box to select it. This causes the clip to play from end to beginning. When you reverse a clip, Final Cut Express literally takes the order of the clip's frames in reverse, so that it plays the last clip first. You can still alter the speed of the clip in reverse.

   To create a smoother transition between frames, select the Frame Blending check box. This will make the speed change less jerky.

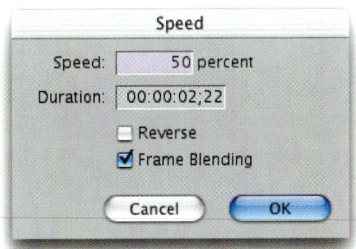

Figure 9.2
The Speed dialog box

4. Click the OK button.

   To watch the changes you made in real time, render your clip (⌘+R) and press the Play button in the Canvas.

Creating a Freeze-Frame

A freeze-frame is a single motionless image—like a photograph—that is taken from a single frame of moving video. Freeze-frames are used all the time as background for titles or elements in a montage.

To make a freeze-frame, follow these steps:

1. Place the playhead in the clip at the exact frame you want to use for the still image. For this exercise, use the clip immediately after the Clip Speed marker again (see Figure 9.3).

Figure 9.3 The frame to be used as a freeze-frame

2. Choose Modify > Make Freeze Frame. A new freeze-frame clip appears in the Viewer window. The freeze-frame's name automatically incorporates the originating sequence's name and the timecode of the frame (see Figure 9.4).

Figure 9.4
The new freeze-frame clip in the Viewer

3. Set the In and Out points for the clip to set the duration of the freeze-frame (👉 "Setting In and Out Points in the Viewer" in Chapter 4, "Editing Basics").

You can now edit the freeze-frame clip directly into your video (👉 "Bringing Clips into the Timeline" in Chapter 4) or drag it into the Browser to add it to your library of clips (see Figure 9.5). Freeze-frames are real-time effect clips, which means that you can view them in real time in the Canvas, but you'll need to render your clip before output (👉 "Rendering Effects" in Chapter 6, "Adding Transitions").

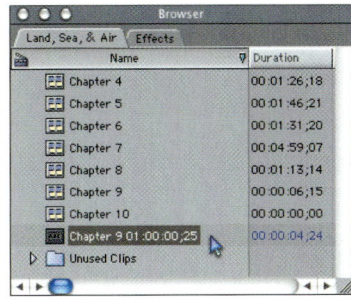

Figure 9.5

The freeze-frame clip has been added to the Browser.

Adding a Voice-Over

You can add voice-overs directly to your film by using your computer microphone. This enables you to record a voice-over in real time as the images play and to have this audio appear directly in your Timeline. To record a voice-over, you'll need a microphone that can input its signal into your computer. This microphone can be built into your computer, plugged into a microphone port, or set up through a USB audio capture device or a PCI audio card.

You can use this function anywhere, but it is especially helpful if you are editing on the fly—say, editing a segment for a quick news broadcast or annotating a clip on a laptop in the field. This way, you don't have to bring the footage back to an audio studio to record and time the voice-over.

To add a voice-over, follow these steps:

1. Choose the target audio track where you want to record (&⎯ "Adding Tracks" in Chapter 4) and place the playhead at the point in the Timeline where you want the voice-over to begin. For this exercise, use the clip immediately after the marker called Voice Over (see Figure 9.6).

Figure 9.6 The voice-over clip will be added immediately after the playhead.

Note: You can also set In and Out points in the Timeline to delineate the exact the area you want to record in ("Setting In and Out Points in the Timeline" in Chapter 4).

2. Choose File > Voice Over to open the Voice Over tab in the Tool Bench window. Make sure your microphone is plugged into your computer's sound-in jack (if you have one).

 Note: Desktop Macs generally have an external microphone plug, whereas PowerBooks have built-in mikes (yes, there is one, but where it is is anybody's guess). If the microphone is set up properly, the Voice Over tab will automatically detect it.

3. In the Voice Over tab (see Figure 9.7), adjust the Input settings as needed, type a name for the voice-over, and press the Record button (Shift+C) to begin recording your message. There will be a 5 second pre-roll before recording begins for you to prepare yourself. Speak clearly into the microphone while watching the sequence play.

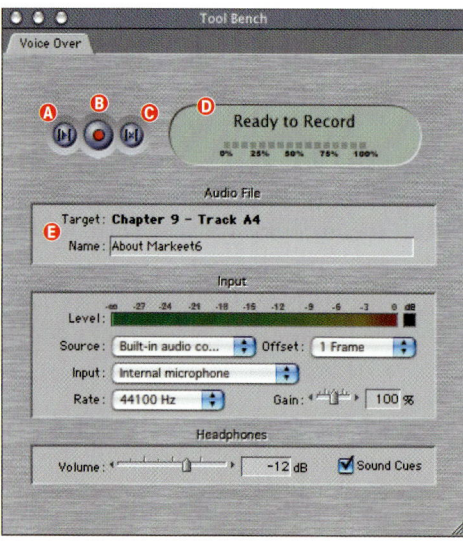

Figure 9.7
The Voice Over tab in the Tool Bench window

A Review
B Record/Stop button
C Discard Last Recording
D Status window
E Audio target track and audio clip name

To add a Voice Over, you need to be familiar with tools of the Voice Over tab (see Figure 9.7). You can adjust the following settings:

Review   Plays the section of the Timeline that you've delineated as the area in which you want to record the voice-over.

Discard Last Recording   Press this button to delete the last audio clip you recorded.

Status window   This window lets you know the status of the recording and shows a time line of how much has been recorded.

Target track This shows which audio track the voice-over will be placed on. This is designated by clicking the 2 audio setting in the target track area.

Name In this field, type a name for the clip.

Input window Here you can set the source information, the input information, the audio sample rate, the gain, and an offset. The offset is used because there might be a couple frame delay in the real-time recording into the microphone and the newly recorded audio clip in the Timeline. USB typically delays one frame; DV cameras typically delay three frames.

Headphones window Use the Volume slider to set the volume for the monitor headphones.

4. After you finish speaking, press the Record button again (Shift+C) to stop recording. There will be a two-second post-roll to add a buffer at the end of your clip.

The voice-over audio clip will appear in your Timeline at the designated point in the designated track (see Figure 9.8). You have built in the post- and pre-roll that you can trim if you need to do some fine-tuning to the clip, such as adding an audio fade.

Figure 9.8
The new voice-over clip in the Timeline

Watch your sequence with the new audio voice-over included. Adjust the volume and other settings to mix the new audio clip into your sequence. If you don't like the voice-over you recorded, click the Discard Last Recording button and then repeat steps 3 and 4.

> **Note:** If you recorded your voice-over with a mono microphone, you will probably want to copy the voice-over onto another audio track and then link the two audio clips as stereo pairs, so that the sound will be played in both speakers (☞ "Combining and Splitting Stereo Pairs" in Chapter 8, "Adding Audio").

Using Keyframes to Animate a Clip

Although Final Cut Express is not, strictly speaking, an animation program, it can be used to move a clip around as it plays, and to change its size and rotation. In Chapter 7, "Adding Video Effects," you looked at how to use keyframes to change the audio level at individual points while the clip is playing. Another way to use keyframes is to create motion within your clip or graphics. To do this, you use keyframes in the Canvas to plot the motion of an individual clip. Keyframing can create complicated movements to animate a title sequence or can be used to fashion more experimental visuals. In this section, you'll learn how to move a clip across the Canvas and then how to alter that movement.

Creating a Motion Path

In the following exercise, you'll add keyframed motion effects to make a clip move across the Canvas; you'll drag the clip in the Canvas window to create a *motion path*. You'll start by resizing the clip so that it is smaller than the Canvas area, giving you room to really move about.

Note: Instead of making your images zip around the screen—which can look silly—it's often better to use slow motion to create subtle movement of a "window" image.

Follow these steps to animate a clip:

1. In the Timeline, double-click the clip for which you want to create a motion path to open it in the Viewer. For this exercise, use the clip immediately after the marker labeled Keyframe Animation (see Figure 9.9).

Figure 9.9
The clip in the Viewer

2. In the Viewer Motion tab, change the Scale to a value less than 100 and the Rotation to a value between -8640 and 8640 ("Changing Size, Position, and Orientation" in Chapter 7). In this example, we used 40 for the scale and –65 for the rotation (see Figure 9.10).

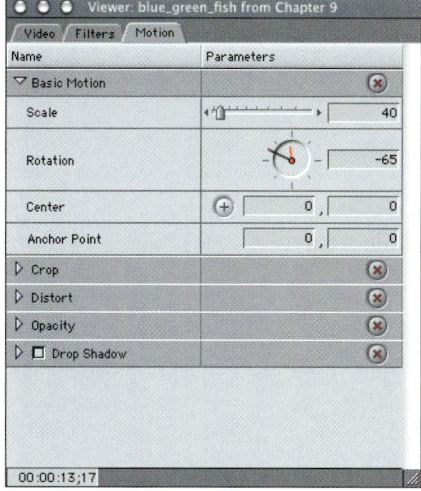

Figure 9.10
Reducing the clip size
in the Motion tab

3. Place the playhead in the Timeline at the beginning of the clip. You will see the first frame of the clip in the Canvas.

4. In the Canvas window, choose Image+Wireframe from the View pop-up menu (see Figure 9.11). Wireframe mode represents all clips in the Canvas as simple boxes, each with an X through it. This enables you to drag the clips around without having to worry about the time it takes to redraw the images as they move.

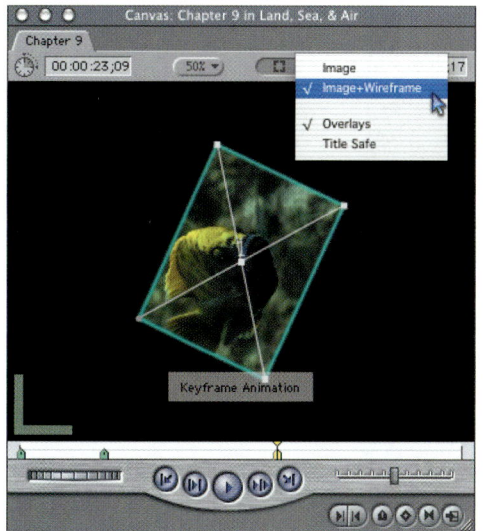

Figure 9.11
The View menu in
the Canvas

5. In the Canvas, click and drag the clip to the exact location in the Canvas frame where you want the clip to start moving from.

6. Click the Add Keyframe button (Control+K) in the Canvas to set the initial keyframe in the movement. Notice that the wireframe over the image turns from gray to green, indicating that a keyframe is present in this frame (see Figure 9.12).

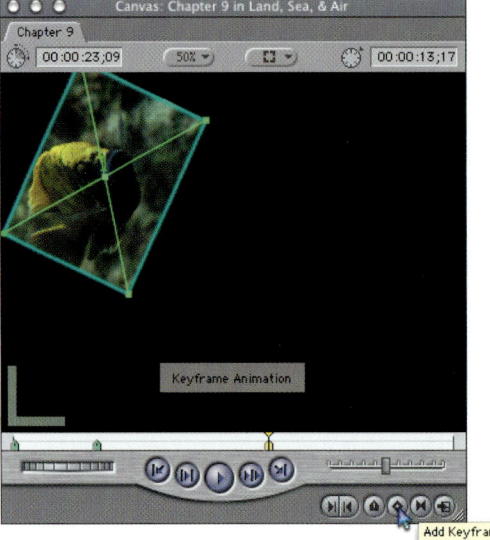

Figure 9.12
The Add Keyframe button

7. Move the playhead to the frame where you want the motion to finish.

8. In the Canvas, click and drag the clip to the final position for the animation. As you drag, a motion path is drawn between the original position and the final position in the animation (see Figure 9.13). A new keyframe is automatically added for this frame (indicated by a green dot on the motion path).

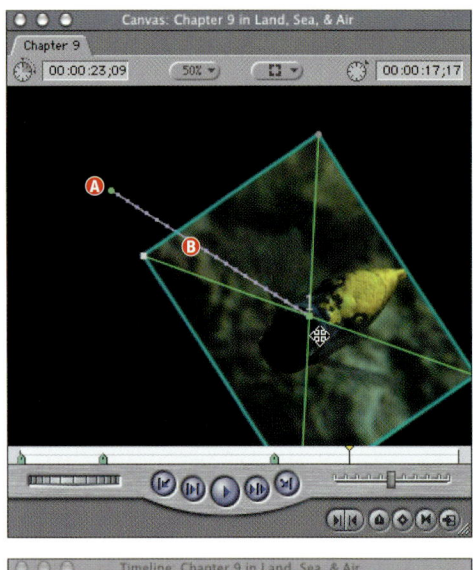

Figure 9.13
Click the clip and drag to a new position.

Ⓐ Keyframes
Ⓑ Motion path

> **Note:** In addition to moving the clip, you can change its rotation and size. You can also change size and rotation for the clip in the Viewer's Motion tab, you can also click directly on a clip in the Canvas to make changes. Click on a corner to resize or on an edge to rotate.

You can now repeat steps 7 and 8, each time automatically adding a new keyframe and giving new direction and movement to the clip from the previous keyframe position (see Figure 9.14). After you finish, render the clip and watch it in the Viewer (☞ "Rendering Effects" in Chapter 6).

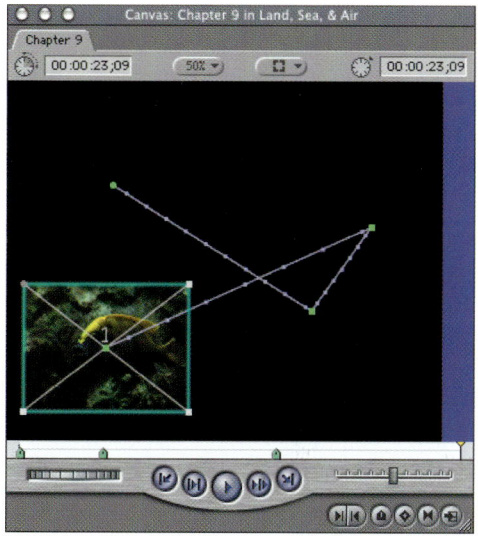

Figure 9.14
Multiple motion paths for a single clip

Editing the Motion Path

After you've "drawn" your motion path in the Canvas window, you can use the Pen tools to edit the paths, adding curves and deleting keyframes. By default, the path between keyframes is a straight line. This, as you know, is the shortest distance between two points, but it's not always the most interesting and it might not give you the desired effect.

To change the shape of the motion path, do one of the following:

To adjust a keyframe's position, choose the Pen tool (press P) and click and drag the keyframe (the green points) to the new position.

To add a new curved anchor point, choose the Pen tool (press P) and click anywhere on the existing motion path. You can also click and drag to reposition the keyframe while you are adding it.

To delete an anchor point, choose the Pen Delete tool (press PP) and click anywhere on the existing motion path. You can also click and drag to reposition the keyframe while you are adding it.

To change a keyframe from a corner keyframe to a curved keyframe, often called smooth or back, choose the Pen Smooth tool (press PPP) and click a keyframe. If you change a keyframe to be smooth, a Bezier curve handlebar will appear on that point, enabling you to change the amount of curvature between that keyframe and surrounding keyframes by moving it around (see Figure 9.15).

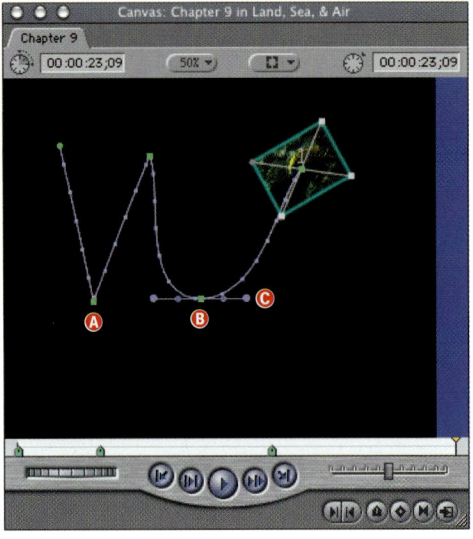

Figure 9.15

Motion path with multiple corner styles

A Corner point
B Bezier curve point
C Bezier curve handlebar

To adjust the curvature of a smooth keyframe, use any of the Pen or Selection tools to click either end of the keyframe's Bezier curve handlebar and move the bar around and/or toward the keyframe. As you move the handlebar, the curve will adjust but remain smooth.

Ideas in Motion

To create a more involved sequence, you can add other clips that are moving at the same time by stacking the clips in different tracks in the Timeline and giving them all separate motion paths. By using these effects in combination with each other, you can have a number of images moving in and out, fashioning a collage of animated imagery.

Be experimental in the effects you mix:

- By adding feathered edges to your clips, you can make them appear to float in the frame for a ghostly effect.

- By changing the offset of a drop shadow as a graphic or a clip moves around the frame, you can create the illusion of a fixed light source.

- By putting a background slug or image behind your other moving clips, you can give them a backdrop to move on that's more interesting than the default solid black background.

- By using Perspective effects such as Curl and Basic 3-D, which are especially geared for use with keyframes, you can create 3-D motion effects from your 2-D clip.

The sky really is the limit here on creating special-effect sequences, so the more you experiment with different moving compositions, the more likely you'll discover something unique.

The only drawback to using a lot of different effects in a sequence is the render time it will take before you can view them in real time. Obviously, the more effects (filters, transitions, motion, opacity, image modes, and so forth) that you use, the more time you will be sitting watching that little line slowly creep across the screen before you can view the fully realized visuals.

Adding Titles

One of the final steps for many editors is to add titles (and credits) at the beginning and end of the movie and to bring in graphic clips from design software such as Photoshop. Titles can be as simple as white letters on black backgrounds or can use elaborate, colorful letters on a moving background of video. The titling of your movie can engage your creativity at least as much as the actual editing, but you should always watch your video carefully to determine the style of titling that best suits this individual work. When you are ready to create a title to use in your sequence, you might want to sketch it out first on paper or have a good mental image in your head. Watch the footage that will come before, after, or under the titles, and try to come up with a creative way to have titles that fit with the visuals.

Final Cut Express offer a plethora of tools for creating titles limited only by your imagination. For all titles, you can specify the standard typographic controls (font, leading, alignment, text color, and so forth) for the text by using the Controls tab in the Viewer (see Figure 9.16). Within this tab, each title type will also have controls unique to it for setting its special properties.

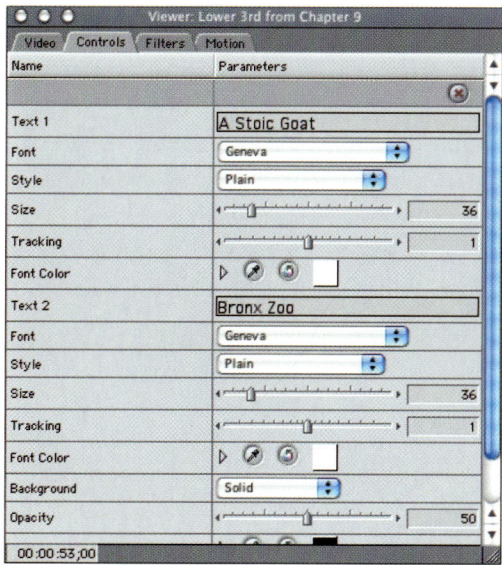

Figure 9.16
The Controls tab in the Viewer

Making Sure Your Title Is "Title Safe"

When you place and size your title graphics, you'll want to make sure that the graphics will appear readable and not cut off on any TV monitor. Because different monitors crop the edges of the image differently, you should use the Title Safe guide to make sure your title graphics will fit the edges of any monitor (the guide is roughly 10 percent smaller than the full frame).

You can bring up a Title Safe guide in either the Viewer or the Canvas. Either choose View > Title Safe to bring up a wireframe box, or choose Title Safe from the View pop-up menu in the Viewer or Canvas window. All text and graphics in your title should appear within this box.

Creating Basic Titles

Basic titles are an easy, yet effective, way to add text to the screen at the beginning of a video, end of a video, or anywhere in between. All basic titles are located in the Video Generators/Text bin of the Effects tab and can be split into two basic categories: static and animated.

Final Cut Express has three static title types and three animated types:

Lower Third   The title is placed as two lines of text in a solid-colored bar across the bottom third of the screen (see Figure 9.17). You can control the color and opacity of the bar. This is especially useful for placing introductory text for a segment, as with a news story.

Figure 9.17
Lower Third Title

Outline Text   The title text has a colored outline around it (see Figure 9.18). You can specify the softness of the outline to create a glow or halo affect. You can also specify a media clip to use in the text, in the outline, or as the backdrop by dragging the image onto the filmstrip or question mark icons in the controls . The text or outline will be used to mask the clip.

Figure 9.18
Outline title

Text The title is simple text (see Figure 9.19)—no frills, no fuss.

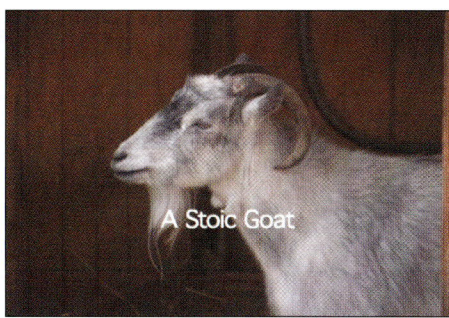

Figure 9.19
Simple Text title

Scrolling Text The title is animated, moving up or down the screen (see Figure 9.20). You typically see scrolling text in the credits at the end of a Hollywood movie, where the text rolls up the screen vertically.

Figure 9.20
The title scrolls down the page

Crawl   The title is animated, moving from left to right or from right to left across the screen like a stock ticker, as often seen on news programs (see Figure 9.21).

Figure 9.21
The title crawls from right to left.

Mind the Gap

If you want your title to appear without video footage under it but you began your video immediately at frame 0, you will have to clear a spot in the footage. To do this, use the All Tracks Forward tool to select all of the tracks after the point where your title will be, and simply drag the clips to the right to create a gap at the beginning of the Timeline. You can now place your title in this new gap.

Typewriter   The title is animated, with each letter of the text appearing one at a time, as if being struck by a typewriter head. This one has already become a cliché because of its use in *The X-Files* (see Figure 9.22).

Figure 9.22
The Truth is…
ahhh, never mind.

To add a basic title to your video, follow these steps:

1. In the Timeline, place the playhead on the frame where you want your title to be placed into your sequence. For this example, place the playhead on the marker labeled Basic Titles, which already contains a video clip in the V1 track. You will be placing the title in the V2 track above it.

2. In the Browser's Effects tab, open the Video Generators/Text bin. Double-click the text effect you want to use, and it will be displayed in the Viewer window (see Figure 9.23). For this example, choose Text.

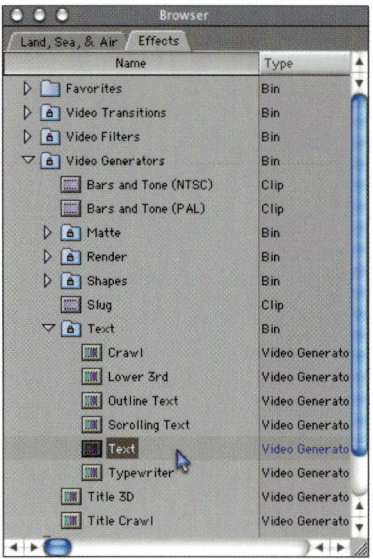

Figure 9.23

The Text bin in the Effects tab

You can also access all of these title options in the Video Generators/Text submenu in the Viewer window (see Figure 9.24). Using this menu will open the specified title type in the Viewer.

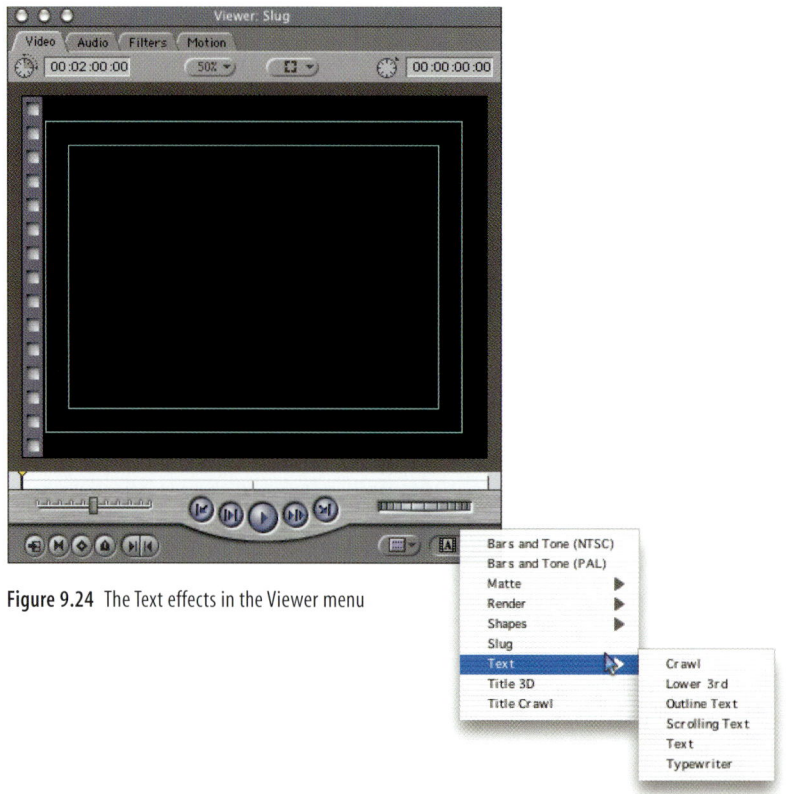

Figure 9.24 The Text effects in the Viewer menu

In the Viewer, you will now see a *generated* clip (a clip created within Final Cut Express, rather than captured or imported from an exterior source) ready to be modified for your title. At first, the message "Sample Text" will appear in the title.

3. Notice that the Viewer has a new tab, located after the Video tab and before the Filters tab, called Controls; click it (see Figure 9.25). This is where you'll make all your adjustments to the title clip.

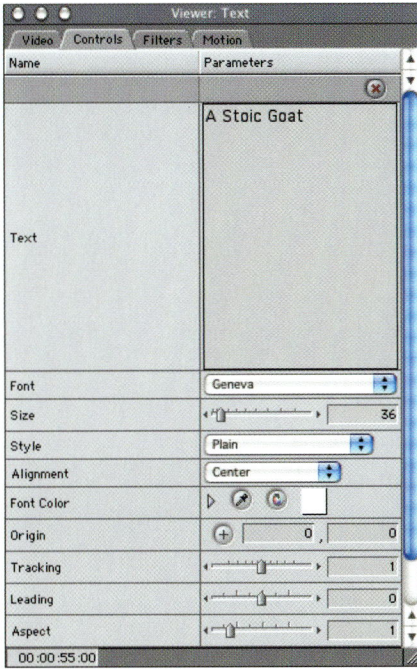

Figure 9.25
The Text title controls

4. Adjust the title controls as desired. The Controls tab enables you to change the text being used in the title sequence. Different effects will have different controls in these areas, but for a simple text title, the controls are as follows:

Text   Type your title text as you want it to appear on the screen.

Font   Choose the font for the text.

Size   Type the point size or use the slider.

Style   Choose styles such as bold, italic, or underline.

Alignment   Choose the type of justification you want. *Justification* means that all your text will be lined up to a left margin or a right margin, or will be centered.

Font Color   Choose the font color. You can double-click the color swatch to open the color wheel window or you can use the dropper icon to select a color from an image in the Canvas. If you know the HSB code for a specific color, you can type the three-number code in the color wheel window.

Origin   Set the coordinates for the center of the title; 0, 0 is the center of the screen. You can type the coordinates or use the crosshair to select the center visually. First select the crosshair and then click within the Canvas window (*not* the Viewer) at the point where you want to center the text. Either have the Timeline's playhead on the clip so you can see the placement in the clip or flip to the Video tab in the Viewer.

Tracking Set the spacing between letters in the text. Fonts have a default spacing that, generally, is optimized for reading when printed. Obviously, for the screen you might need to play around with this spacing or you might want to use the Tracking control to create more distinctive titles by spacing the letters out.

Leading Set the distance between lines of text. The default for text is single-spaced, but you might want to stylize a title by spreading out the lines of text.

5. After you have set all the parameters for your title clip, click the Video tab. Then create In and Out points in the Viewer to limit the title's duration.

 Note: The default length for a title clip is defined in the Preferences window (Final Cut Express > Preferences) in the Still/Freeze Duration window.

6. You can now treat this clip like any other:
   - Drag the clip from the Viewer into the Timeline or to the Edit Overlay window in the Canvas to edit it into the sequence. The clip will appear like any other clip in the Timeline and will run as long as you have set it to run. Place the clip where you want it in the Timeline.
   - Drag the clip into your project tab of the Browser to add it to your clip library.

After you have added the clip to a sequence, though, you will have to render animated titles to see the clip play in real time in the Canvas.

If you drop the title clip with no clips below it in the Timeline, the background will be black by default (see Figure 9.26). If the text is over a video clip, then the text will superimpose over the clip's footage (see Figure 9.27). You will probably want to make sure that the title is legible throughout the entire clip. For example, if the title is white text and you are superimposing it over an image of the sky, you might not be able to read it. To make it pop out, change the text color or add a drop shadow. Once again, any effects or changes that you add will have to be re-rendered before you can view the clip in real time.

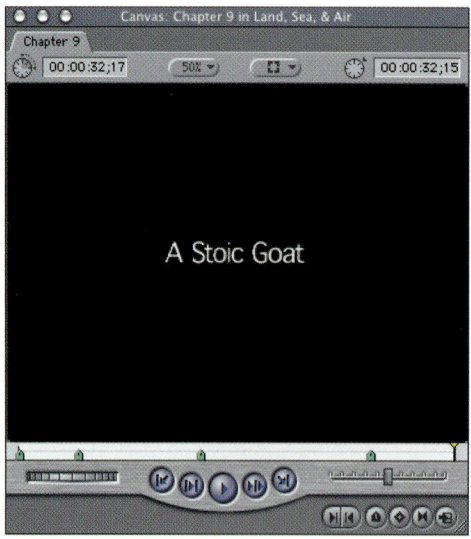

Figure 9.26

The title against the default black background

Figure 9.27
The title against a clip

Customizing a Title Clip

When creating a title card (i.e. a static screen with titles and possibly graphics on it), you'll want to think about the graphic design and the placement of your elements in the title. To do so, you'll be simultaneously adjusting the size, font, alignment, and origin, among other things, to get the title exactly where you want it to be. A good way to do this easily is to open the title in the Viewer and type your text in the Text section of the Controls tab.

After your text is entered and you've set a rough duration for the clip, drag it into the Timeline. Now place your playhead in the Timeline over the title clip. You'll get a preview of the way that your text will look in the Canvas window. With the clip still open in the Viewer, make changes in the Controls tab (you can also use the Motion tab for placement changes).

As you make your changes, such as selecting a new origin point or increasing the font size, you'll see your changes reflected immediately in the Canvas window as long as the playhead rests on the open clip in the Timeline, so you can quickly decide whether they are working. This is especially helpful if you have laid the text over an image and need to size and shape the text to fit in a specific part of the frame.

Using Advanced Title Techniques

In addition to the standard title controls, Final Cut Express also offers advanced effects created by Boris FX (not Apple) that can be installed from your Final Cut Express CD. You have one static and one animated option:

Title 3D The title is text but greatly increases your control over the typography (see Figure 9.28). Whereas the basic Text title effect has a dozen controls, the Boris FX titles have over three dozen controls that enable you to manipulate virtually every aspect of the letterform. You can turn them, stretch them, skew them, pivot them, even tumble them. You can also add up to five drop shadows to the text at the same time to simulate multiple light sources.

Figure 9.28
The 3D title with three (of the possible five) drop shadows showing

Title Crawl The title is animated either horizontally (crawl) or vertically (roll). In addition, you can play around with the edges of the titles to clip them and/or blend them into the background (see Figure 9.29). It offers all the same text tools as the Title 3D effect but does not give as exacting control over the placement of the text.

Figure 9.29
The title crawls from right to left with faded edges.

These titling effects allow for far greater versatility in titling options but might take some getting used to. The Boris FX tools can seem quickly overwhelming with all of their options, but play around with them for a bit and you'll be hooked. Still, if all you want is simple text, these can be overkill and you should probably stick with the effects shown earlier in this chapter.

1. To use the Boris FX titles, first open the Video Generators bin in the Browser's Effects tab. Under the Text folder, you will see the options Title 3D and Title Crawl. Double-click the text effect you want to use, and it will be displayed in the Viewer window. For this example, choose Title 3D.

2. A new generated clip opens in the Viewer for you to manipulate. However, the Title 3D options window immediately appears on top of that. In this window, you will add your title text and format the text as desired.

The Title 3D video generator has a lot of controls, but once you start using it, you will notice that most of these controls are similar to those found in a word processor (see Figure 9.30).

Figure 9.30 The Boris Text Editor
Ⓐ Text area **Ⓑ** Tab **Ⓒ** Font tab **Ⓓ** Paragraph tab **Ⓔ** Fill tab **Ⓕ** Letter Edge tab **Ⓖ** Shadow tab

Text area Type your title text here. To apply a style, the text you want to affect must be selected.

Tab Set tabs in the ruler.

Font styles Choose the font, size, and other text attributes you need, including the font and font size. You might need a fairly large font size to ensure that the text is legible on the screen. You can choose any font that is available on your computer, but remember that if you move this project file to another computer that does not have this font, the text will use that computer's default font.

Paragraph styles Set margins, indicate whether you want the title to wrap, and set the width of the page if wrapping.

Fill Turn the fill on or off. If off, the text uses a default gray color. You can set the color of the selected text or set a multicolor gradient.

Letter Edge styles Set up to five independent edge styles for your text by using the five tabs. Click the check box to the left of each tab to turn a particular edge effect on or off.

Shadow styles Choose between drop, solid, and cast shadow styles to set up to five independent shadows by using the five shadow tabs. To turn a shadow on or off, use the check box next to that tab.

Type your title into the text area. You can copy and paste text from other sources and use tabs to position and align text as needed. Then, to format the text, make sure to have the text you want to change highlighted in the text area and set attributes in the individual tabs.

After you finish setting your text and styles, click the Apply button in the bottom-right corner, and the changes are applied to your title. You can now further refine your title in the Controls tab of the Viewer window.

Title 3D (Figure 9.31) has the controls listed in Table 9.1; the controls for Title Crawl (Figure 9.32) are presented in Table 9.2.

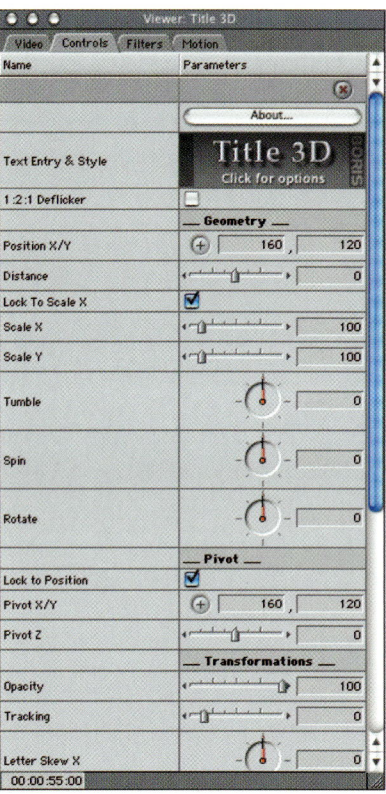

Figure 9.31
The Title 3D controls

▶ **Table 9.1** Controls for the Title 3D Effect

Control	Description
Title 3D options	Click the Text Entry & Style panel to reopen the text and style window.
Geometry controls	Change the size and orientation of the text block.
Pivot controls	Change the X, Y, or Z position of the text block on the screen.
Transformations controls	Set the text block opacity and tracking as well as the skew, scale, tumble, spin, and rotation of each letter.

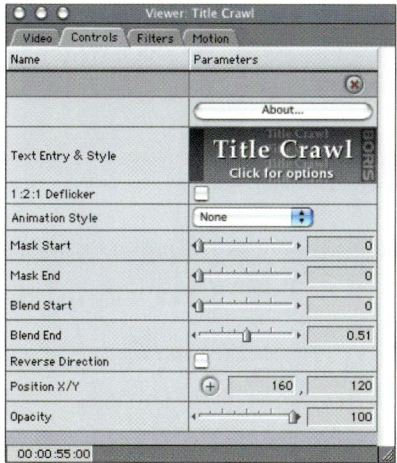

Figure 9.32 The Title Crawl controls

▶ **Table 9.2** Controls for the Title Crawl Effect

Control	Description
Title options	Click the Text Entry & Style panel to reopen the Title Options window.
Deflicker	Select this check box for output to video that will eliminate flicker.
Animation Style	Choose None, Crawl (horizontal), or Roll (vertical).
Mask Start/End	Clip the beginning or end of the title.
Blend Start/End	Fade the beginning and/or end of the title into the background.
Reverse Direction	Crawl moves left to right. Roll moves up to down.
Position X/Y	Set the X,Y coordinates for the center of the text block.
Opacity	Set the translucency of the text, enabling images from underneath to show through.

After you have the title the way you want it, open the Viewer's Video tab and then drag the title clip onto the Timeline, to the point where you want the title to appear (see Figure 9.33).

Figure 9.33 The new title being dragged into the Timeline

With the title in place, you can view the title in the Canvas. Title 3D is a real-time effect. However, Title Crawl is not a real-time effect, meaning that you have to render it to view it in the Canvas (👉 "Rendering Effects" in Chapter 6). You will have to render it before exporting your film.

If you want to edit your title, simply double-click it in the Timeline, and it will open in the Viewer.

Creating Final Cut Express Titles in Photoshop

If you need imagery for your title to be more complicated than what Final Cut Express can offer, you can use other software to create the imagery and then import and use that within your sequence. These will often come in the form of JPEGs, but Final Cut Express recognizes many picture formats, including Adobe Photoshop files (.psd).

If you are creating titles in a graphics program such as Photoshop, it's important to keep a few things in mind. Photoshop files are usually created to be viewed on a computer monitor, whereas Final Cut Express files are often meant to be seen on a TV monitor. To ensure that your title looks as good as possible in the movies, remember these points:

- Make sure you stay within the "title-safe" area. This will save you a lot of hassle later, when you would have imported that graphic and found that the words were too close to the edge of the screen.

- There is a difference between the pixel ratio of your computer and that of video shown on an NTSC monitor. If you import a 720 × 480 file into Final Cut Express and print it to video, the graphic will appear distorted. To avoid this problem, you will need to create your image files at a pixel ratio of 720 × 540. After your graphic is designed at this ratio, save it. Now, to make it work in Final Cut Express, resize it, squashing it a bit so that it will appear normal on a video screen. Choose Image > Image Size in Photoshop. Click the Constrain Proportions check box to deselect it and type in the new ratio of 720 × 480. Save this as your graphic (as a JPEG, Photoshop file, or other format), using a different name to create the final version of the file to be imported into Final Cut Express.

- Make sure the colors in the titles are "safe" for NTSC monitors. Use the NTSC colors filter (Filters > Video > NTSC Colors in Photoshop) to make sure the colors are consistent with the colors on an NTSC monitor.

- If you are using Alpha channels (transparencies) or want to use complex compositing effects, take special care when importing. The benefit is that these effects will give you more flexibility and options when layering your titles into the Final Cut Express sequence, and you can create more special effects than with a typical title clip.

- If you import a Photoshop file, it will be imported as a sequence rather than a clip, and its multiple layers will be found on the tracks inside this sequence. To import a Photoshop file as a clip, first flatten the image, eliminating multiple layers.

Setting Item Properties

You can set information about projects, sequences, and clips to help you keep them better organized. You can add comments or notes that will flag certain clips. If you are working with other editors, you can also add notes and other useful information so that it is clear how the clips are used.

Setting Project Properties and Item Comments

You can customize a project's properties by following these steps.

1. With the project you want to set properties for open in the Browser, choose Edit > Project Properties.
2. In the Project Properties dialog box (see Figure 9.34), set the following:
   - Choose how you want to display time for this project: either using timecode (standard) or number of frames. Typically you'll use standard timecode, but you may need to see exactly how many frames a sequence is running.
   - Enter column headings for up to four columns in the Browser. By default, these columns are labeled Comment 1–4 and are used to add notes to specific items (sequences, bins, or clips). However, you can customize these headings for your own needs. For example, you might want a column to list "to do" notes for the item and a column to specify the sequence in which a particular clip is being used. For this example, replace Comment 1 and Comment 2 with **To do** and **Sequence**, respectively.

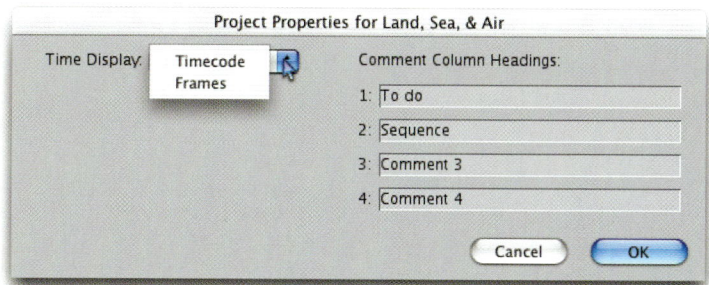

Figure 9.34
The Project Properties dialog box

3. After making changes, click OK.
4. With the Browser in list view, scroll across until you see the new To Do and Sequence column headings (see Figure 9.35).

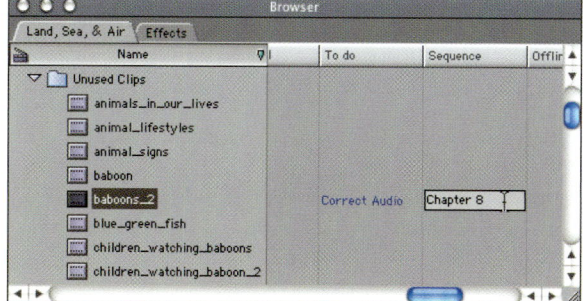

Figure 9.35
The new To Do and Sequence column headings

5. To add a comment, double-click in the column next to the item you want to add a note for, type your comments, and press Return to finish.

You can add notes for any item in the Browser, and this is a good way to keep track of clips in a large project.

If you want to move the comment column to the left to make it more visible while working, click and drag the column heading to the left and drop it in the desired position (see Figure 9.36).

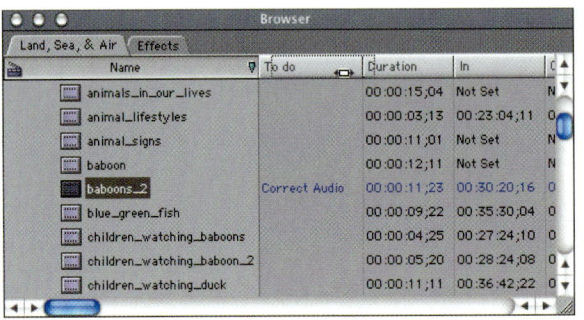

Figure 9.36 The column being dragged to a new position

Changing Sequence Settings

Sequence settings enable you to define how the sequence appears in the Timeline—including the relative size of audio and video tracks, the display of thumbnails, and whether clip overlay and audio waveforms should be shown.

1. To set sequence settings, click a sequence in the Browser to select it and then choose Sequence > Settings (⌘+0). You can also Control+click a sequence in the Timeline and select Sequence Settings. Either action opens the Sequence Settings dialog box (see Figure 9.37).

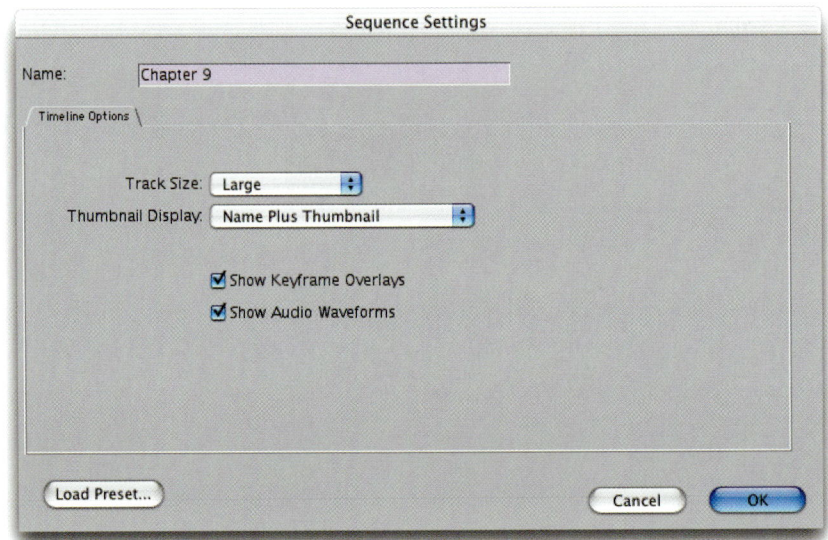

Figure 9.37 The Sequence Settings dialog box

2. In the Sequence Settings dialog box, set the following:
- Type a new name for the sequence.
- Choose the size that the tracks (video and audio) should appear in the Timeline (reduced, small, medium, or large). This will also affect the size that clips will appear in the Timeline independent of the actual magnification that has been set.
- Choose how thumbnail images should be displayed in clips. The Name option places a simple text label. Name Plus Thumbnail includes the name with the first frame in the sequence. Filmstrip displays frames across the width of the clip (see Figure 9.38).

Figure 9.38
The Timeline using Filmstrip mode for thumbnails

Note: When you are cutting a clip, Filmstrip mode is especially useful to help locate the right frame you are looking for.

- Check whether you want to see clip overlays as the default in the Timeline. This enables you to set opacity for video tracks and levels for audio tracks directly in the Timeline by clicking and dragging the overlay lines up or down.
- Check whether you want to see waveforms in the audio tracks of the Timeline (see Figure 9.39).

Figure 9.39
Clip overlays and waveforms visible in the Timeline with opacity being adjusted

- Click the Load Preset button and then choose one of the preset options in the Select Sequence Preset dialog box. Generally you will not want to change the preset from its default.

Click OK after you finish changing the settings. The new settings will have already taken effect while you were setting them, but you can still click Cancel and everything will return to the way it was.

Setting Item (Clip and Sequence) Properties

Every sequence and clip has certain properties that can be set to help you not only make changes to the In and Out points, but also edit and change information entered while capturing the clip.

1. To set sequence properties, click a sequence in the Browser to select it and then choose Edit > Item Properties (⌘+9). You can also Control+click a sequence in the Timeline and choose Item Properties. In the Item Properties dialog box (see Figure 9.40), you will be presented with three tabs.

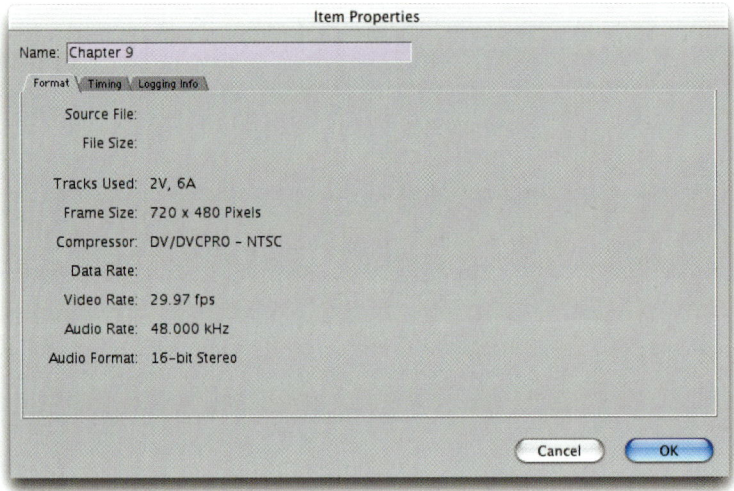

Figure 9.40 The Item Properties dialog box

2. Use the following tabs to view or change Item Properties:
   - The Format tab is the first tab you will see and contains information about the format of the sequence, none of which can be edited.
   - The Timing tab enables you to enter In or Out points for the sequence, or a total duration for the sequence, which will then be used to automatically set the Out point (see Figure 9.41).
   - The Logging Info tab enables you to change or reenter the information you could have entered while capturing your footage (☞ "Preparing to Capture" in Chapter 3, "Gathering Your Media").

3. Click the OK button after you finish changing the settings. The properties will be recorded with the sequence.

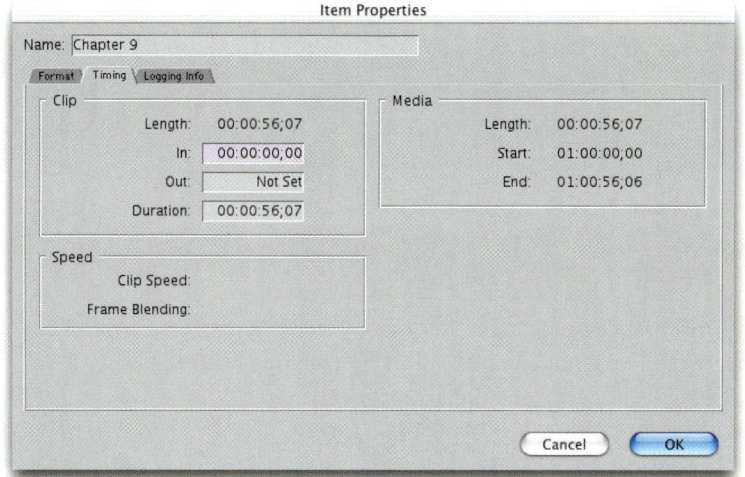

Figure 9.41 The Timing tab

Reconnecting Media

Sometimes a media file gets moved to a different folder, or for some reason Final Cut Express can't find the original media file to pull its media from. If this happens, the clip will appear offline (with a red slash through it) in the Browser. If the media file still exists on the hard drive, but Final Cut Express just can't find it, you can reconnect that media and help Final Cut find the media file so that it is reconnected to the clip.

> **Note:** When you first open a project, Final Cut Express will connect to the clips in that project. If they are not located in the same place as when the project was last closed, Final Cut Express will immediately ask whether you want to attempt to reconnect the clips. If this happens to you, go immediately to step 4.

To reconnect media, follow these steps:

1. Select one or more clips that you want to reconnect either in the Browser or in the Timeline.
2. Choose File > Reconnect Media. Alternatively, you can Control+click the clip(s) in the Browser and choose Reconnect Media from the contextual menu (see Figure 9.42).

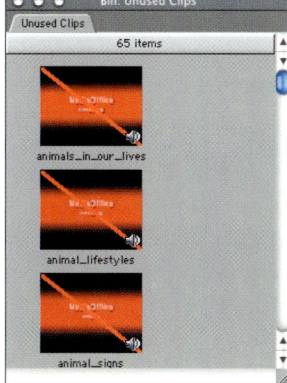

Figure 9.42
Offline clips selected to be reconnected

3. In the Reconnect Options dialog box, choose the kind of file that you want to reconnect (see Figure 9.43). Typically you'll want to select Offline because you will need to reconnect media that has become offline. Online is used if the clip is already connected and you want to change the connection, and Render enables you to connect to a rendered version of the clip.

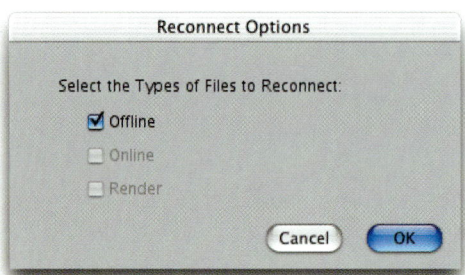

Figure 9.43
The Reconnect Options dialog box

4. In the Reconnect Options dialog, navigate to the folder and file with the original source media file (see Figure 9.44). When you have found it, click it and click the Choose button. To make life easier, you can also select the option to Reconnect All Files In Relative Path, which will automatically reconnect any other clips you had selected in that folder.

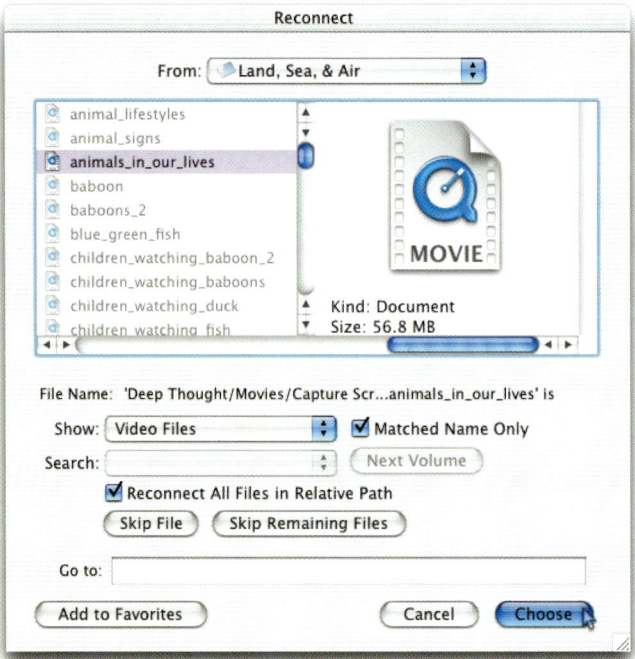

Figure 9.44
Browse for your media.

The file will now reconnect to the icon in the Browser, making it an online clip with media behind it. The thumbnails for the clips should no longer show the red stripe (see Figure 9.45).

Figure 9.45
The reconnected clips

Movie Night!

Vertigo, 1958

Director: Alfred Hitchcock

Vertigo is a great movie for many reasons, but its opening credits are one of the most famous title sequences in Hollywood history. Hitchcock often employed graphics, trick photography, and animation in his titles—*North by Northwest* and *Psycho* are two other famous examples—but *Vertigo* is perhaps the most complex and sinister. Using a spinning swirl as a motif to suggest hypnotism and psychological imbalance, the titles of the film play in front of a surrealist montage of falling bodies and blinking eyes.

Vertigo's story line focuses on a man (an especially creepy Jimmy Stewart) who becomes obsessed with a woman (Kim Novak). When it appears that she has died, he finds another woman who looks similar to her and he goes to painstaking effort to re-create the dead woman's style and dress on this new woman. The plot gets more complicated as it spirals into psychological necrophilia and a murder/detective story, but Hitchcock captures the unsettling and obsessive mood of the entire film in the opening minutes with his title sequence. For those first few moments, viewers are slowly taken out of their own lives and prepared for the world of Hitchcock's disturbing film.

Land, Sea,

10 Outputting Your Project

In order for the world to appreciate your work, you are going to have to distribute it. Video can now be delivered through many mediums—cinema, television broadcast, CD-ROM, DVD, the Web—and all of these require outputting your finished video. In this chapter, you will review the whole process of putting your video together and then learn how to output your video to tape, DVD, and the Web.

Chapter Contents
Putting it all together for output
Exporting a sequence
Outputting for video tape
Outputting for DVD
Outputting for the Web

Preparing Your Project for Output: Putting It All Together

Before you start burning DVDs and uploading files to the Web, you need to get your video ready. This section gives you an overview of the entire editing process—from laying down the clips to adding your final titles—and then shows you how to combine multiple sequences to create a single movie.

On the DVD: Chapter 10

Open the Final Cut Express project file labeled Land, Sea, & Air. Then double-click the Chapter 10 sequence in the Browser, and it will open in the Timeline.

In this chapter, you will be combining the skills you learned in the preceding six chapters to see how to put a finished work together and then output it for different media. We have set up a completed film using multiple video and audio tracks, transitions, filters, motion, keyframes, audio-fades, and everything else we have talked about. However, there is no "correct" final edited version. We encourage you to play around with this sequence. Try adding your own edits. Adjust clip lengths, change the in and out points, add music, add different filters and effects. The possibilities are endless even in this short film.

If you get to a point where you do not like what you have done, you can always close the project without saving and then reopen it to start over.

Every clip in the tutorial video for this chapter can be opened, changed, moved around, and edited. Because you have a saved version on the DVD, feel free to pick through the cut. This is a space for experimentation, so try out anything you can think of.

The previous six chapters have covered how to edit your video into a cohesive project, but before you get into outputting the video, let's quickly review the steps for putting your vision together, starting with some editing theory on how to think about putting clips together.

For this exercise, we decided to create a short video using clips of land, sea, and air animals with a complementing musical score.

The Juxtaposition of Shots

Viewers watch a movie and experience the total effect of the story: direction, acting, camera work, lighting, sound, and music. All of these parts come together to create a whole that tells a story, makes a point, conveys an idea, or creates a mood. Editing is the process that composes the total effect of the film, taking the many parts and turning them into a completed whole. The way in which shots are placed together creates meaning just as surely as the words spoken by actors, the music, and the cinematography. The juxtaposition of shots allows the editor control over the message, the sense of space and time, and the perspective the audience experiences.

Editing can be approached in many ways, but there are four primary methods for editing two shots together:

- Temporal relationships
- Match cuts
- Spatial relationships
- Rhythm

Editing Based on Temporal Relationships

When one shot cuts to another, the viewer instinctively looks to see what the new image tells them and how it relates to the previous image. By editing shots together to create a sense of time passing, you move the story or scene along. As an editor, when you receive the raw footage for a scene that you will cut together, you have a lot of control over how long that scene will last—both in actual screen time and in the time that appears to pass in the world of the film.

Imagine a scene in which a woman walks out of her house and down the street to a bus stop. This action in real life might take eight minutes, but most likely you don't want to spend eight minutes of screen time showing the whole thing (or maybe you do, but that's another story). To shorten the action so the viewers know without seeing the whole thing that she has performed these actions, you might choose a few short shots to cut together to suggest this action. The viewers might see her open the door, followed by a quick shot of her feet walking down the street, followed by her waiting at the bus stop. This sequence of three shots might take up only 15 seconds of screen time, but the viewer knows that these actions took longer than the time they were displayed. By cutting, an editor can create a sense of the progression of time, by presenting shots in a specific order.

Editing with Match Cuts

Another effective way to transition between shots or scenes is to use a visual link between the last frame of the outgoing shot and the first frame of the incoming shot. A prime example of this is in *2001: A Space Odyssey*, which uses the shot of a bone tossed in the air being transformed, through the power of editing, into a spaceship. This is a form of *match cut*, with the shape and orientation of the bone matching the shape and orientation of the spaceship.

Editing for Spatial Relationships

Einstein proved that time and space are not inseparable, and when editing, the way you treat space will also affect the portrayal of time. The most common cinematic shorthand for establishing space—"start wide, get closer"—can be seen in just about every television sitcom after a commercial break. The scene starts with an *establishing shot* of the exterior of a house or street. *The Cosby Show*, *Seinfeld*, *The Drew Carey Show*—they all start with this kind of shot, which not only tells the viewer which character's house they are entering, but often also reminds them which city they are in. Then the show cuts to a wide shot of the actual space where the scene takes place, such as the interior of an apartment. Here the viewer can see the entire room, all the characters and where they are standing, as well as the doors, couches, walls, and so forth. As the characters interact and move, the show cuts to closer and closer shots, often ending up with intercut shots of individual characters. Think of it as a spatial zoom in, with cuts.

Sometimes this same technique is used to create a sense of claustrophobia, as in Carl Dryer's *The Passion of Joan of Arc*. This film is told almost entirely in stark close-ups, so that while the viewer rarely gets a master shot of the whole scene, they feel a sense of closed and restricting space from the montage of tight shots.

Editing for Rhythm

Editing for rhythm, meaning the video is either cut to the beat of the soundtrack music or the editor creates their own visual beat through the pacing of the editing of shots, is an increasingly popular editing form, especially with the dawn of nonlinear editing, which allows for shorter shots, more rapid-fire editing, and quickly trimmed edits. Although this technique is not new—having been around since at least the 1920s—a new style of fast-paced cutting has emerged. In America, what used to be almost completely in the realm of commercials, trailers, and music videos has now become a dominant style in feature films. This is partly because the technology makes fast, beat-driven editing easier, but also because more and more Hollywood directors cut their teeth on editing by making commercials and music videos (such as *Adaptation*'s Spike Jonze and *Fight Club*'s David Fincher).

Many movies now have sequences that are edited by rhythm. Bob Fosse's film version of the musical *Cabaret* contains many sequences that are cut together to create a rhythmic pulse, imbuing a more visceral effect on the audience, in the same way that a live musical performance might.

Laying Down the Edits

Each film has unique characteristics and thus its own process for creation. Yet whether you are creating a commercial for a carpet company or a four-hour historical epic, you will always start (after the footage is captured, anyway) by sorting through the footage and laying down the clips in the Timeline.

1. Begin by sorting through your clips and setting the rough In and Out points for each by using the Viewer (see Figure 10.1; ↵ "Setting In and Out Points in the Viewer" in Chapter 4, "Editing Basics").

Figure 10.1
Set In and Out points for your clips.

2. Bring clips into the Timeline (↵ "Bringing Clips into the Timeline" in Chapter 4) and place them in a roughly sequential order based on the way that you want the final video to appear. Watch the clips closely and test different arrangements to find the order that tells the story you want.

   For this example, we wanted to create a simple montage of clips showing animals of the land, sea, and air, so we laid these clips down in that rough order, grouping them by category. To show where each group begins, we added markers defining the groups (see Figure 10.2).

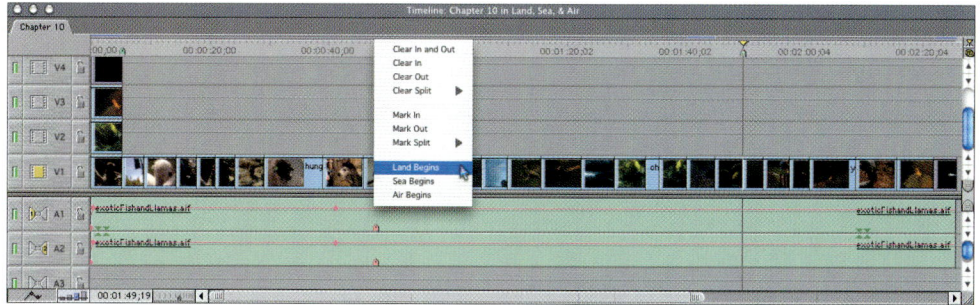

Figure 10.2 Clips and markers added to the Timeline

3. After you've established the basic clip order, it is time to refine their trim to create a more polished video (see Figure 10.3). The *trim* is their In and Out points and edit types. (For more details on refining a clip's trim, ↵ "Trimming Clips: Roll, Ripple, Slip, and Slide" in Chapter 5, "Cutting Your Video.")

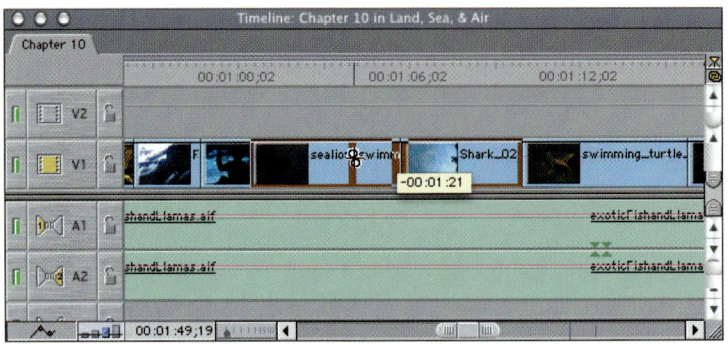

Figure 10.3
Trimming clips in the Timeline

After you have your basic edits in place, you can begin adding transitions to see how they will affect the flow of your video.

Adding Transitions

After a rough cut of the film is created, you are ready to add transitions between shots and audio if needed. For most edits you will probably want to use a straight cut, in which the clips simply move from one to the next without any fanfare. However, you might decide that a straight cut is too abrupt in some cases or that the imagery in the incoming and outgoing clips would be enhanced by a cross-dissolve or other transition between the two. This will be especially true at points where the scene is changing or you want to indicate the passage of time.

Follow these steps to add transitions between clips in a sequence:

1. In the Timeline, select the cut to which you want to add a transition (see Figure 10.4).

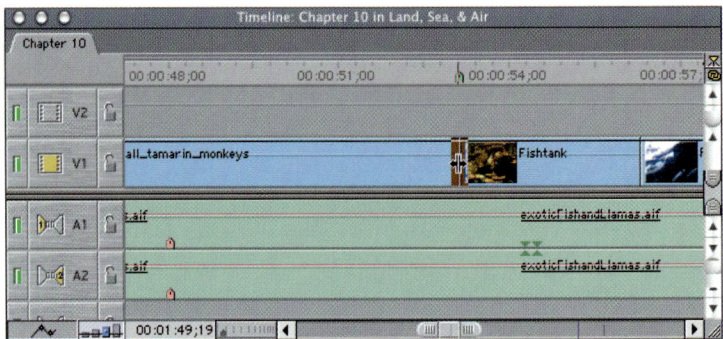

Figure 10.4
Edit selected in the Timeline

2. Add the transition you want by doing one of the following:
   - Choose the transition in the Browser's Effects tab and drag it to the edit point (see Figure 10.5).
   - Choose Effects > Video and choose one of the transitions from the submenus.
   - Control+click the edit itself in the Timeline to bring up a pop-up window that lets you add the default transition, which is generally Cross Dissolve.

For this exercise, we added a Ripple transition (Dissolve > Ripple Dissolve) between the last clip showing a land animal, and the first showing sea animals, and adjusted this to last 3 seconds.

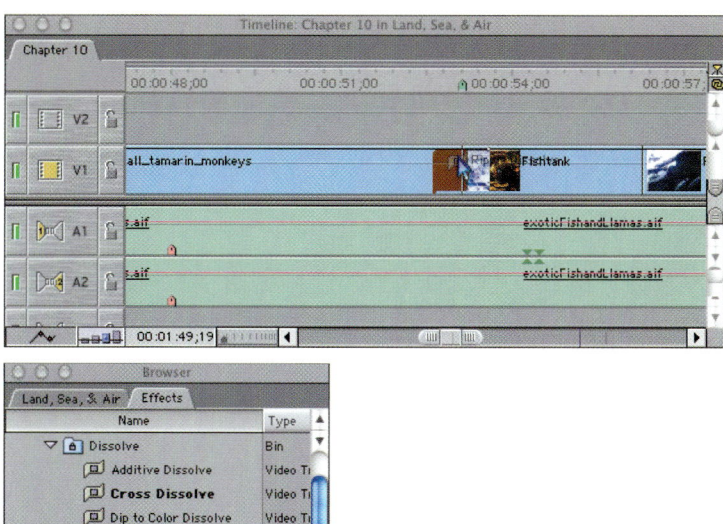

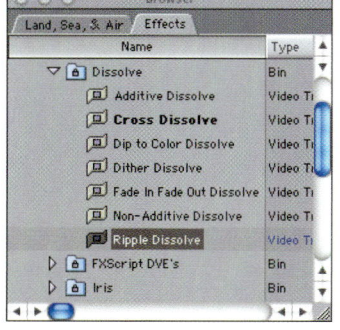

Figure 10.5
Transition being dragged from the Browser into the Timeline

3. If you want to make finer changes, double-click the transition to open it in the Transition Editor (see Figure 10.6). You can adjust the starting and stopping points for the transition as well as lengthen or shorten the transition by dragging the edges of the transition in the Timeline. (For more details on adding and refining transitions, ↝ Chapter 6, "Adding Transitions.")

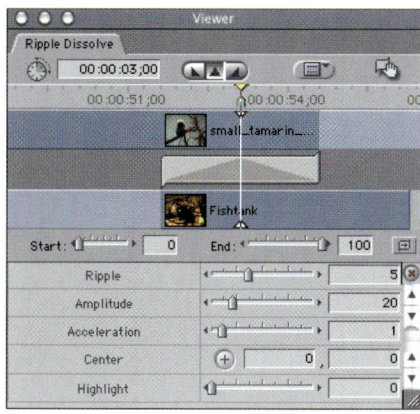

Figure 10.6
The Transition Editor

After the transition is added, you will need to render it to view it in the Canvas (see Figure 10.7) unless it is a real-time effect such as Cross Dissolve. (For more details on rendering, ↝ "Rendering Effects" in Chapter 6.)

Figure 10.7
The transition being viewed in the Canvas

Adding Filters and Other Effects

Adding effects is always one of the last tasks you should do. Because the effects require rendering, it's easiest to place all your cuts, fine-tune the trim, and have everything lined up the way you want it before you start monkeying with effects.

To add filters and other effects to your sequence, follow these steps:

1. In the Timeline, double-click the clip to which you want to add a filter; this opens it in the Viewer. For this example, we selected the clip showing the child petting rays in order to add a color correction filter to lighten the image.

2. To add a filter to the clip, do one of the following:

   - Drag the filter from the Effects tab in the Browser to the clip in the Viewer (see Figure 10.8).

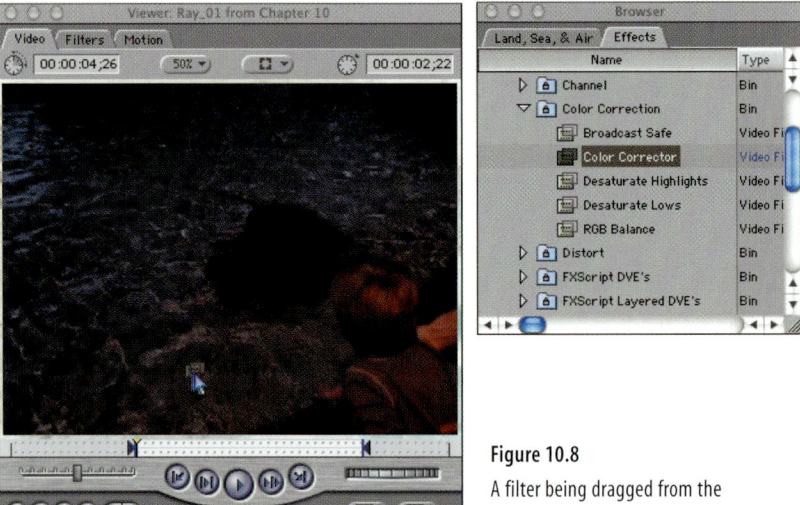

Figure 10.8
A filter being dragged from the Browser into the clip in Viewer

   - Choose Effects > Video Filters and then choose a filter from the submenus.

3. In the Viewer, choose the Filters tab and adjust the filter controls as desired (see Figure 10.9; ↪ "Adding Effects with Filters" in Chapter 7, "Adding Video Effects").

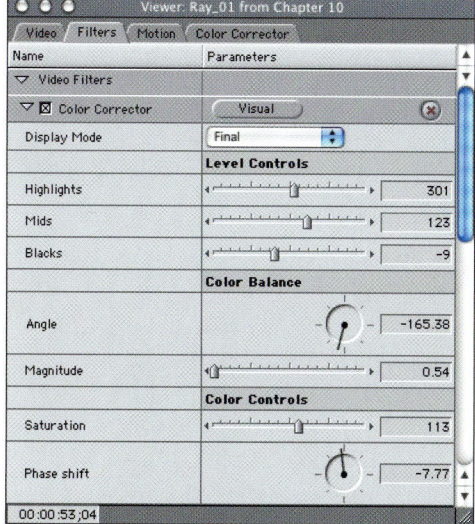

Figure 10.9
The Filters tab in the Viewer showing the color correction controls

After the filter is added, you will need to render it to view it in the Canvas (see Figure 10.10; ↪ "Rendering Effects" in Chapter 6).

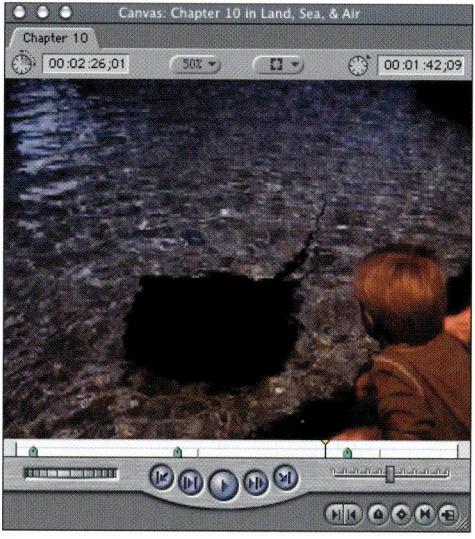

Figure 10.10
The clip with the filter applied in the Canvas

Adding Titles and the Soundtrack

After your video is cut, you can add titles to it. Most of the time you'll want a title card at the beginning and end, but you can certainly add titles between shots as well. When you make a title, think about the style and aesthetics of your movie. Is it a serious documentary or a flashy music video? How does this affect your titling?

Note: We recommend using the Boris 3-D Titling Generator instead of the built-in Final Cut Express title generator to create more elaborate titles. You can get more Boris titles, transitions, and filters from their website, www.borisFX.com.

To add titles and a soundtrack to your sequence, follow these steps:

1. In the Timeline, create a space where the title can be added. For this example, we cleared a few seconds at the beginning of the Timeline by moving all clips to the right, leaving a gap (see Figure 10.11).

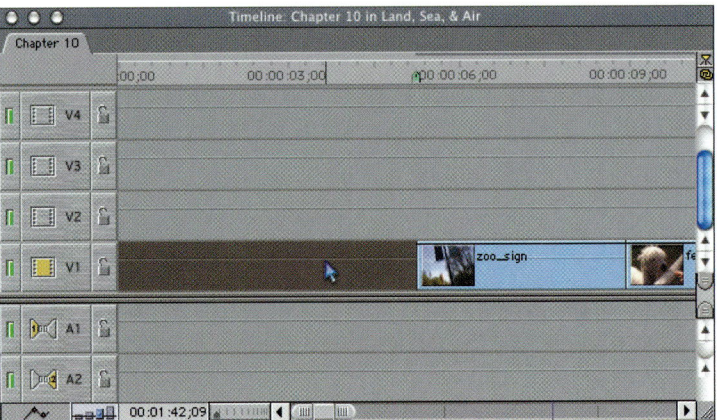

Figure 10.11
A gap added for the title

2. If you want background imagery, add the clips to the title area. We layered three clips—showing a land animal, a sea animal, and an animal of the air—and cropped them so that each occupies a third of the screen (see Figure 10.12). The three clips are placed on three separate video tracks so that they can play at the same time.

3. In the Browser, double-click the title generator of your choice and make changes in the Viewer to create your unique title. We used the Boris Title Crawl (Video Generators > Title Crawl).

4. Drag the title from the Viewer onto a video track in the Timeline so that it is on top of any other background imagery. We added the title to the fourth video track so that it will appear above all three of the clips from step 2. For the end of the movie, we added a fade to black and then a simple text title reading "The End."

5. Render your title so that you can view it in real time and make adjustments as necessary (see Figure 10.13).

6. To add the musical score, drag the sound file from the Browser into one of the audio tracks.

    For this example, we deleted all of the audio tracks for individual clips (so that they do not interfere with the music) and then added the file exoticFishandLlamas.aif (located in the Resources folder in the Browser) to the first audio track.

7. Adjust the soundtrack as needed so that it fits the video footage (see Figure 10.14).

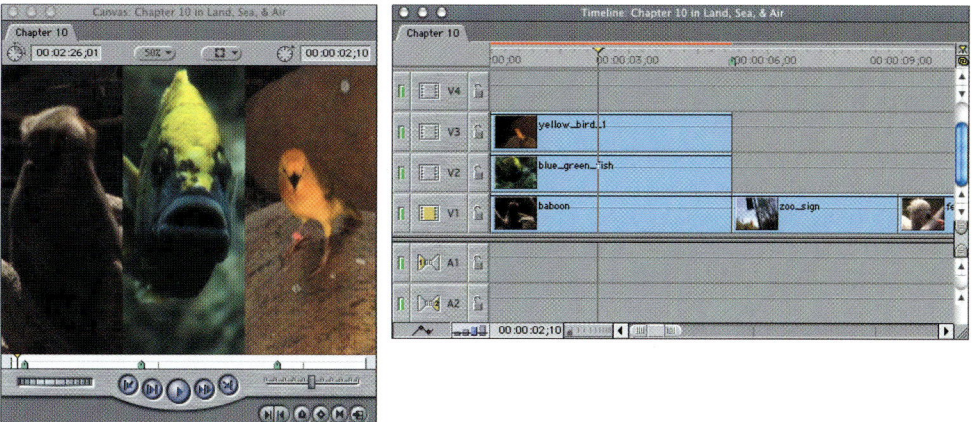

Figure 10.12 The clips in the Timeline have been cropped so that they appear side by side in the canvas.

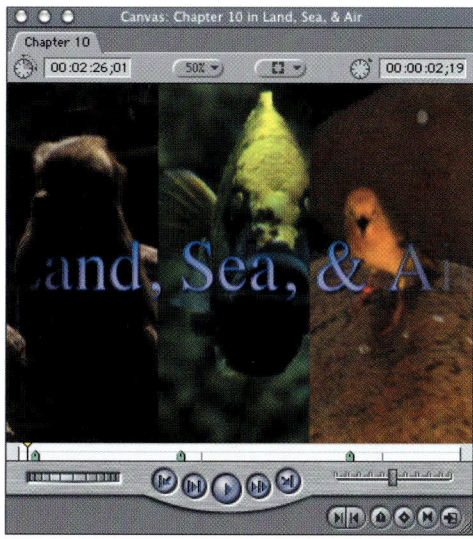

Figure 10.13
The final title in the Canvas

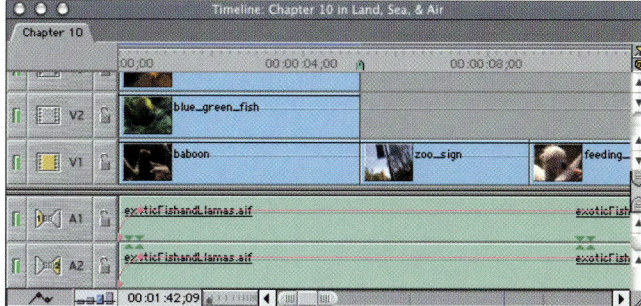

Figure 10.14 The soundtrack in the Timeline

Knowing When You Are Finished

Sometimes it is tempting to keep tinkering with a project until you get it "just right", but, as with any creative effort, you could keep tweaking your work for the rest of eternity and never be completely satisfied. If you have deadlines (or a life) it is important to know when to say when. First, make sure you've solved any technical problems, such as poorly exposed video, audio jumps between cuts, or awkward video edits. Make sure your audio levels are set correctly throughout the piece, and use keyframes to make any necessary adjustments. If you're not sure about the content, show the piece to friends or someone you trust to judge and comment on your work. Getting a second or third opinion, even from someone who is not an editor, can give you a fresh perspective.

Nesting Sequences

If you've been editing with more than one sequence in a project (for example, you are editing each scene of a short film in a separate sequence) you'll need to combine all the sequences after you've edited them all separately.

To nest one sequence within another sequence as a clip, follow these steps:

1. Create a new master sequence in your project (⌘+N) to lay all your other sequences into.

2. Name this sequence (see Figure 10.15); for this exercise, call it **Master Sequence**. Then open this master sequence in the Timeline by double-clicking it.

Figure 10.15 The new master sequence

3. From the Browser, drag the sequences you want to add (in sequential order) into the open master sequence, just like clips, laying them one after another in the order you want them to appear (see Figure 10.16).

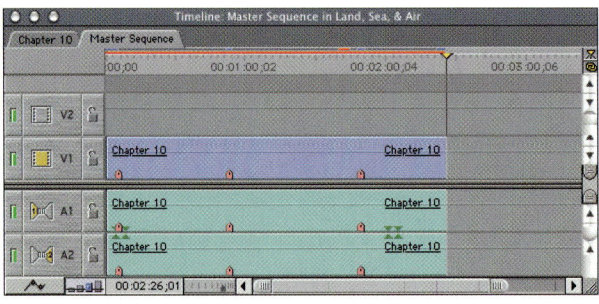

Figure 10.16
Sequence 10 added to the master sequence

> **Note:** All markers will be included with the nested sequence, but as clip markers, not Timeline markers.

The sequences you are adding are referred to as *nested* sequences, meaning they are sequences within another master sequence. Treat these nested sequences as you would any other clip added to a sequence. You can treat the edges of the nested sequences like any clip—so you can perform trim edits or transitions on them, and you can split the clip by using the Razor Blade tool. However, double-clicking the nested sequence will open the sequence in the Timeline (rather than the Viewer), and any changes made in the nested sequences' sequence tab will be reflected in the master sequence.

> **Note:** Rendering in the source sequence will also render in the nested sequence.

After you've laid out all your sequences into the master sequence, watch the entire movie.

Exporting a Sequence

After you have finished your film, you will want to export it as a Final Cut movie or a QuickTime file (both file formats can be read by QuickTime). Exporting creates a single media file that contains the entire sequence with all filters, keyframes, effects, and so forth in the finished sequence without the need for rendering.

Exporting a sequence as a movie can be very helpful because it creates a single media file that you can use as a clip in any Final Cut sequence whether you are using Final Cut Pro or Final Cut Express. You can also back up the file onto an external hard disk for archival purposes.

Exporting as a Final Cut Movie

The easiest and most versatile way to output your movie is as a Final Cut movie, which is based on the QuickTime format.

Follow these steps:

1. Open the sequence you want to export from the Browser. If you don't want to export the whole sequence, you can set In and Out points in the Timeline to define which part to include when exporting. For this exercise, practice exporting the sequence Chapter 10 (see Figure 10.17).

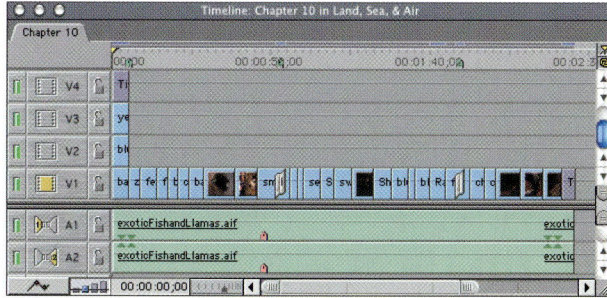

Figure 10.17
The sequence to be exported

2. Choose File > Export > Final Cut Movie.

3. In the Save dialog box (see Figure 10.18), type a name for the file (use a .mov suffix to keep file types clear) and designate where to save it on the hard disk. In addition, set the following options:

   Include Choose whether to include the audio, video, or both tracks in the exported movie.

   Markers Choose how markers should be treated when saving the movie. For example, you can set up markers to denote DVD chapter breaks if you are exporting to DVD Studio Pro, or you can have Final Cut Express include all the markers from the sequence into the final movie. This is very helpful if you'll need to refer to these markers later.

   Make Movie Self Contained Select this check box to have the exported movie contain all of the media required for playback. If this option is left unselected, the file will only point to the original media files on the hard disk, producing a significantly smaller file. Generally, if you are sending the file to another computer, you should select this option to ensure that the movie is not separated from the media used to create it.

After setting these options, click Save.

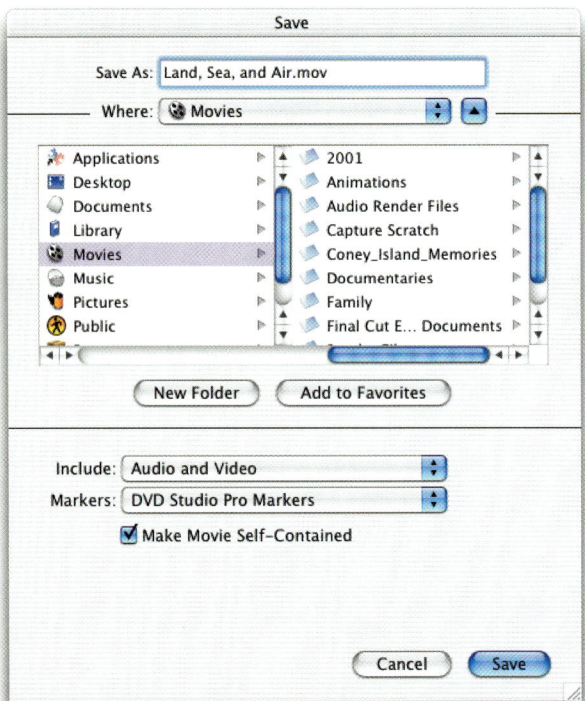

Figure 10.18
The Save dialog box

If effects had not been rendered, they will be rendered first. Then a progress bar appears (see Figure 10.19), letting you know how much longer it will take to save your movie. The Final Cut file is saved to your hard disk with an icon like the one shown in Figure 10.20 and is ready for you to play back. You can play this file directly in Final Cut Express, Final Cut Pro, or QuickTime.

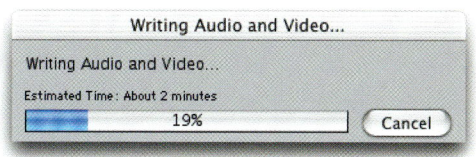

Figure 10.19
The Writing Audio And Video progress bar

Figure 10.20
A Final Cut file

Using an Exported Sequence in Final Cut Express (or Pro)

An exported movie is now a media file and can be imported back into Final Cut Express to create a clip. In fact, both Final Cut Express and Final Cut Pro can exchange files in this manner.

Exporting a sequence into a movie erases all cuts and individual clips, squashing everything into one big clip. Not only can you play an exported QuickTime file in Final Cut Express, you can also import it (⌘+I) back into any Final Cut product (Pro or Express) as a single clip and use that in other sequences. The advantage of this is that you won't need to render anything in the imported clip to see it play in real time, even when you use it in another sequence. Remember, though, that you also can't make any changes to the original cut after it has been made into a movie without changing the original project file and exporting it again.

Exporting as a QuickTime (or Other Format) Movie

In addition to exporting the movie in the Final Cut format, you can also export the movie in QuickTime and other video and audio formats. Generally, QuickTime is the most obvious format to export in, especially if you wish to use your files on the Web. However, you can also export in formats such as MPEG-4 for video or AIFF for CD audio to only export the audio tracks (no video).

To create a QuickTime version of your sequence, follow these steps:

1. In the Timeline, open the sequence you want to output.
2. Choose File > Export > QuickTime to open the Save dialog box.
3. In the Save dialog box, choose the general file Format you want to use. For this example, we used the QuickTime Movie format. Then, choose the general settings for the format from the Use drop-down list. These options will change depending on the format you are using; the QuickTime Movie settings are shown in Figure 10.21.

Note: ↪ "Exporting Still Images," next, for details on outputting still images by using the Export menu.

Figure 10.21

The Use drop-down list showing QuickTime Movie options

4. If you need to change the export options for the chosen format, click the Options button. The options vary from format to format, and how you set them depends on what you are going to be using the video for. For this exercise, keep the default settings. Later in the chapter we talk about how to set these options for output to Web and DVD

5. Type a name for the new file, locate where you want to save it on the hard disk, and click Save.

After a few seconds or minutes (depending on the size of your movie), the new file is saved to your hard disk and is ready for you to use. The icon used by the file will depend on the file format type you used when saving it (see Figure 10.22).

Figure 10.22

A QuickTime file

> ### Adding a Global Effect to the Finished Product
>
> If you decide to add an effect to the entire sequence (for example, if you want to make the entire video black-and-white), you should first export the sequence as a movie (or print it to video and recapture it as a single clip). You can then import the movie or clip into a new sequence and apply the across-the-board effect over this new single clip. This will save you a lot of rendering time in subsequent editing and also ensure that the effect is uniformly applied.

Exporting Still Images

Although, naturally, you are going to want to export your entire video as a "motion picture," at times you might want to export a single still image or sequence of images. For example, if you are making a poster for your movie, you will probably want to export still TIFF-formatted images. Or if you need still images on your website, you'll want to export images as JPEG-formatted files.

> **Note:** To export a frame, you do *not* need to create a freeze-frame clip as described in Chapter 9, "Adding Titles and Finishing Up."

To create a single still image or series of still images from your video, follow these steps:

1. In the Viewer, Timeline, or Canvas, place the playhead in the frame you want to export as a single image or simply within the clip to export the clip as a series of still images. For this exercise, move the playhead to the marker labeled Still Image in the Chapter 10 project (see Figure 10.23).

Figure 10.23
The frame selected for export

2. Choose File > Export > QuickTime.
3. In the Save dialog box (see Figure 10.24), choose one of the following for the general Format:
   - Still Image to export only the selected frame.
   - Image Sequence to export multiple still images from the selected clip. Final Cut Express will automatically create each file and number them.

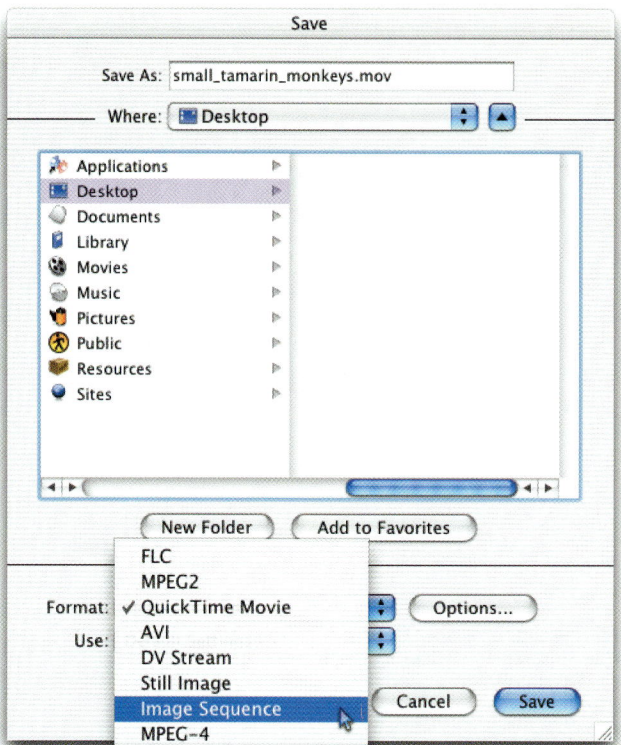

Figure 10.24
The Save dialog box

4. Choose one of the Use settings (generally leave this on Default Settings or Previous Settings) and then click the Options button if you need to change the export options—for example, if this is the first time you are exporting images.

5. In the Export Image Sequence Settings dialog box (see Figure 10.25), set the following options and then click OK:

   Format   Choose a file format for the still image(s). Generally, if the image is for print, use the TIFF format, but if the image is destined for the Web, use JPEG.

   Frames Per Second   If you are outputting a sequence, enter the number of still images to be created for each second of the clip between its In and Out points. The lower the number, the fewer still images will be produced. For example, if the clip lasts 2 seconds, and you set this value to 3, you will get 6 still images created from the sequence. If you are exporting only a single still image, leave this blank.

   Insert Space Before Number   Select this check box to use a space between the clip name and its number in the sequence. For example, if you name the clip Green Fish, the files will be numbered Green Fish 1, Green Fish 2, Green Fish 3, and so forth.

   Options   Click this button to set the compression settings for the file format type you selected. One common setting for all file formats is Depth. Generally, you will want to leave this on Best Depth to produce the highest-quality still images.

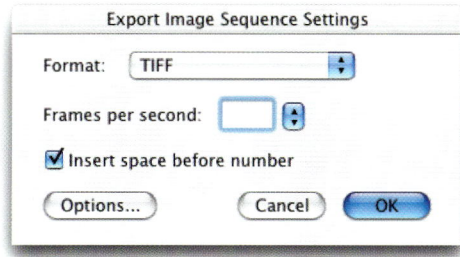

Figure 10.25
The Export Image Sequence Settings dialog

6. Back in the Save dialog, type a name for this still image or to be used as the base title for the series of images and choose where you want to save it.
7. Click the Save button, and your new file or files are created (see Figures 10.26 and 10.27).

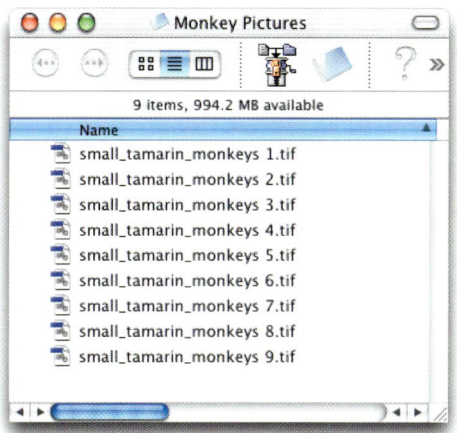

Figure 10.26
The series of images have been output.

Figure 10.27
The still image

These files can be opened in Photoshop, Illustrator, and most other graphic or photo programs, including Final Cut Express itself.

Note: Theoretically, you could use this method to create a freeze-frame for Final Cut Express, but a much easier technique is described in Chapter 9.

Using Photoshop to Fix Interlacing in Still Images

You might notice that some exported stills look as if every other line has shifted over. This is due to *interlacing* used with some video formats, but it can be quickly corrected in graphics programs such as Photoshop by using the De-Interlace filter. (Still images from Final Cut Express are all 72dpi, so you might also want to use Photoshop to change the resolution to 300dpi if your image is going to be printed.) To fix interlacing in a still video image, follow these steps:

1. Open the image to be fixed in an image-editing program that has the De-Interlace filter. For this example, we used the workhorse of digital editing software, Photoshop.

2. In Photoshop, access the De-Interlace filter (Filter > Video > De-Interlace).

3. In the De-Interlace dialog box, choose whether to eliminate Odd or Even fields and whether the new fields should be created by duplicating fields or through interpolation. Then click OK. The eliminate option will depend on the image, but generally Interpolation produces sharper results.

The image's quality should improve noticeably. If not, or if you want to try different options, choose Edit > Undo (⌘ +Z) to undo the filter and then start with step 2 again.

If you have a batch of images that you need to de-interlace, Photoshop enables you to create that action by using the Actions palette to quickly apply the filter. You can then use the Batch command (File > Automate > Batch) to create a droplet, enabling you to simply drop a folder of images onto an icon to have them all de-interlaced at once.

Printing to Video

Printing to video puts your edited project onto a fresh piece of DV tape stock. Whether you are creating a master tape for dubbing or a rough version to hand out and show around, you'll need a new DV tape to record your movie onto. Although Final Cut Express has a built-in command for printing to video, there is an alternate more direct method you can use by simply recording directly from Final Cut Express. Both methods will be covered here.

> **Note:** A *master tape* is a tape containing the final product of the video project. Typically, two master tapes are made: one that is never touched and is archived, and another from which all subsequent dubs are made.

Using the Print To Video Command

The more professional method to make your video is to use Final Cut Express's Print To Video process, which gives you more control over the parameters of printing. Although this method has been known to drop more frames than simply recording directly from Final Cut Express (see next section), but this is a rare occurrence as long as you have plenty of memory. Print To Video is better to use if you need to add elements such as color bars and tone, a slate with information, or black handles to the video sequence that will be printed; these will give your video a more professional appearance.

To output your video to tape using the Print to Video command, follow these steps:

1. In the Timeline, open the sequence you want to print. If you don't want to record the entire sequence, set In and Out points in the Timeline around the part you want to record.
2. Choose File > Print To Video (Control+M) to open the Print To Video window (Figure 10.28).

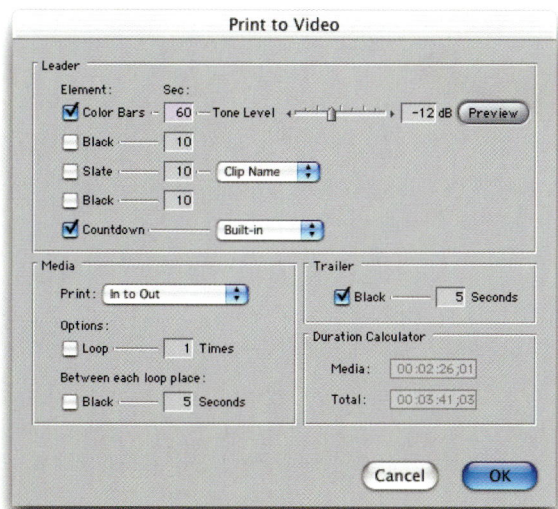

Figure 10.28
The Print To Video window

3. Customize the way your video will be recorded:

   Color Bars   Selecting this option is always a good idea for any video that's going to be given to someone else for use. This puts the standard color bars and tone at the beginning of the tape so that anyone else can calibrate their monitor and adjust their sound to match the recording levels on the video tape. It's usually a good idea to put at least 10 seconds, and 60 seconds is the broadcast standard. Generally, you will want to include color bars only for your master copy or if you are outputting for broadcast.

   Tone Level   Use this setting to control the level of the tone that plays under the color bars. Keep this setting at a standard –12dB unless the person or company you are delivering the tape to tells you differently. As with the color bars, you will want to include tone level only for your master copy or if you are outputting for broadcast.

   Black   Select this check box to put a slug of black at the beginning, before a slate. It's a good idea to include at least 10 seconds of black here.

   Slate   Use this option to put a text slug of information before the video. Either choose to display text that you type yourself in the box provided in this window, or have Final Cut Express use the clip names, sequence name, a picture file such as a professionally designed slate, or other title. If you're typing in your own slate, it's always a good idea to include the name of the project, the running time of the piece (use the abbreviation *TRT* for *total running time*) and the date of that version of the edit. Make sure you choose a time that allows everything in the slate to be read.

   Black   Select this second Black check box to add another slug of black after the slate. This is obviously necessary only if you are using a slate.

   Countdown   Use this option to add a countdown before the video. This is used for tapes intended for on-air broadcast. If you're not sure you need one, contact the person you are delivering your tape to. Most broadcasters have branded countdowns, which can be inserted into Final Cut Express. To choose a countdown film file, choose File from the Countdown drop-down list, click the folder icon, and then open the file you want to use.

   Print   Choose to print an entire sequence or just the part of the sequence between the In and Out points in the Timeline.

   Loop   Select this option to play the sequence in a loop. It will play the sequence as many times as you specify or until the tape runs out.

   Black   Select this option under the Media section to place a designated number of seconds of black between loops.

   Trailer   Selecting the Black check box puts a designated number of seconds of black at the end of the sequence. This is highly recommended, and you should always include at least 10 seconds of black at the end.

   Duration Calculator   This shows you the duration of the sequence (Media), as well as the duration of the sequence plus all the other elements such as color bars, countdown, and so forth (Total).

4. After you've set your parameters, click OK. Anything that hasn't been rendered in the sequence will now be rendered, and the sequence will also be prepared to print to video. Then the media is prepared (this is actually a rendering process and might take a few minutes), and a progress bar shows you the relative amount of time remaining.

5. After the media is prepared, you are prompted to start your deck recording and then click OK. This starts printing your sequence to video.

When the printing is done, stop the tape and rewind it to make sure everything recorded properly. Double-check the audio to make sure the levels are acceptable, and not too quiet or too loud. You can never be too careful.

Recording Directly from the Timeline

Recording directly from the Timeline is the easiest and fastest method for laying down your project to videotape. Some editors prefer this method, because it has been known to reduce the possibility of dropped frames. It requires simply playing the sequence in the Timeline just as if you were watching it while editing, but with the video deck recording the sequence onto tape. This might not be as elegant as Print To Video, but it works.

To output your video directly to tape, follow these steps:

1. Place the playhead in the Timeline at the beginning of your sequence or wherever you want the video to begin recording (see Figure 10.29).

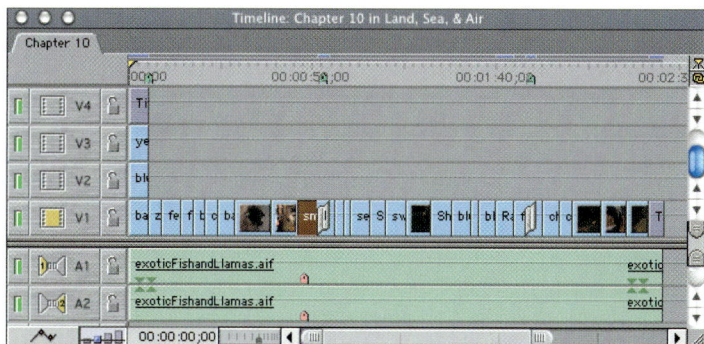

Figure 10.29
The playhead at the beginning of the sequence and ready to record

2. If you want a few seconds of black at the beginning, add a black slug (from the Video Generators bin in the Browser's Filters tab or from the Viewer's Video Generator pull-down window) at the beginning. You can use an Insert edit to do this (see Chapter 4, "The Seven Editing Methods"). Adding this leader is a good idea because you'll get a freeze-frame at the beginning of your tape if you start recording with your playhead on an image.

3. Press the Record button on your video deck. Wait a moment until it engages the tape and begins recording. Most decks will show the timecode on their front display panel, so wait until you see the timecode rolling.

4. Press the spacebar to begin playing the sequence. If you want to record a specific part of the sequence, set In and Out points in the Timeline to delineate this

footage and, instead of pressing the spacebar, choose Mark > Play > In To Out (or press Shift+\). This starts the playhead at the In point and stops it at the Out point. Make sure you've turned off looping by choosing View > Loop Playback if you don't want the footage to repeat.

5. Put a black slug at the end of your sequence so the video ends on a black screen. Otherwise, the last image in your sequence (or the frame at the set Out point) will end as a freeze-frame.

6. After the edit has run its course and your sequence has played, let the tape record a little longer and then press Stop.

After recording, rewind the tape and play through your newly recorded video to make sure it recorded properly. It's important to check the audio and make sure the levels are clear and are not too soft or too loud, causing the audio to peak and distort. You now have a videotape of your project.

> **Watch Out for Dropped Frames**
>
> Whenever you are creating a finished video, you should always have the Report Dropped Frames check box selected in the Preferences window (choose Edit > Preferences or Option+Q). This will alert you when a frame is dropped while printing, so you can stop the process and start over. Otherwise, if frames are dropped, the quality of your print suffers. It's a good idea to increase your RAM, and even restart the computer, before using Print To Video.

Burning to DVD

Unlike recording to video, Final Cut Express cannot output ("burn") directly to DVDs. Instead, you have to output your sequence or sequences as DV files and then use a separate authoring program (such as iDVD or DVD Studio Pro, both from Apple) to create a DVD that can play on standard DVD players.

In this section, you will learn how to prepare your project to be used by DVD authoring software. You will also look at how to burn computer files directly to a DVD as a data disc (rather than a stand-alone DVD that can be used in a standard DVD player), which is one of the best ways of transferring large video files from one computer to another.

Saving Your Project for DVD

Although you must rely on other software to create a stand-alone DVD, you still need to output your files by using Final Cut Express. This process follows the same pattern described earlier in this chapter for exporting a movie as a QuickTime file, but you have two options as to the format you use to output:

QuickTime   Although not a native format for DVD, Apple's iDVD software can take a file output in broadcast-quality QuickTime and compress it for use on DVD.

MPEG-2   All DVDs use MPEG-2 as their compression standard. If you have DVD Studio Pro installed on the same computer that you are using Final Cut Express on, then MPEG-2 will show as one of the output options during export. MPEG-2 is a *codec* used for creating small but high-quality digital video.

The process for saving a file for QuickTime is described previously in this chapter (↩ "Exporting as a QuickTime [or Other Format] Movie"). To save a file in the MPEG-2 format, follow these steps:

1. In the Timeline, open the sequence you want to output and choose File > Export > QuickTime to open the Save dialog box.

2. In the Save dialog box, choose the MPEG2 format (there are no general settings in the Use options).

> **Note:** It is important to note that these options will appear only if you have DVD Studio Pro or another MPEG-2 codec loaded on your system.

3. Click the Options button to open the QuickTime MPEG Encoder dialog box. Set the options and click OK (see Figure 10.30). The QuickTime MPEG options are as follows:

    Video format   Choose between NTSC and PAL video formats. To avoid distortion, choose the format in which you edited your video; this should already be preselected.

    Aspect ratio   Choose an aspect ratio: either 4:3 (television) or 16:9 (cinema). To avoid distortion, choose the ratio that you have used in editing; this should already be preselected.

    Save Audio   Select this check box to include the audio as part of the MPEG-2 file. This will increase the file size.

    Field Dominance   Choose Automatic (recommended), Upper, or Lower. This needs to be set based on the field dominance used when the video was captured and the equipment being used. Generally, the Automatic option is your safest bet.

    Bitrate   Use this slider to set the image quality as a factor of the number of bits used to record each second of video. The higher the value, the better the image quality, but the larger the file size.

    Info   This section displays information about the file that will be created based on the settings, including a thumbnail of the currently selected frame and an estimated file size.

    Write Protocol File   Select this check box to create a text file with the information about how the file was created. This can be handy if you are not mastering the DVD yourself and need to provide the person who will do so with details they need to get the best results.

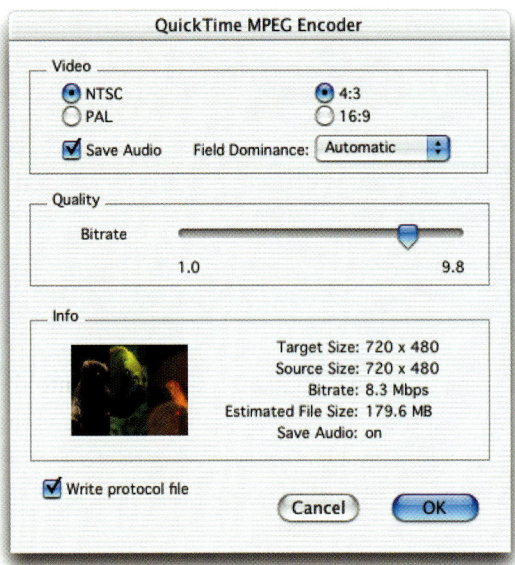

Figure 10.30
The QuickTime MPEG Encoder

4. After setting the options and entering a filename (making sure to keep the .m2v extension), click Save. Your computer will churn away, compressing the video and showing a progress bar.

After the file has been created, you are ready to use it with your DVD authoring software to master your DVD.

Should I Use iDVD or DVD Studio Pro?

There are many DVD authoring programs on the market, but the two primarily used on the Mac both come from Apple; which you choose will depend on the kind of projects you are working on and the amount of money you want to spend.

The case for iDVD For production of home or semiprofessional DVDs (such as weddings, corporate videos, and school plays), when all that is required are simple menus used to view video, iDVD will probably fit the bill. Not only is it extremely cheap (free with a Mac equipped with the DVD-burning SuperDrive) it is an easy-to-use program that does not require a huge learning curve to master. But its simplicity does not mean that you will have to skimp on creativity. iDVD provides built-in templates to speed production but does not limit your ability to create your own backdrops or buttons, and, for power users, can even use AppleScripts to better integrate with your workflow.

The case for DVD Studio Pro For production of professional DVDs (such as broadcast, film, and product training), when high-quality output is expected, you will need to invest in DVD Studio Pro. In many ways, DVD Studio Pro is an extension of the Final Cut products (Pro and Express) and uses many similar interface elements. After you have mastered Final Cut Express, moving to DVD Studio Pro should not prove a daunting challenge. DVD Studio Pro also provides a bevy of professional templates, but also enables you to create nonlinear interactive DVDs by using a Timeline similar to Final Cut Express.

Creating a DVD Data Disc

If you are attempting to transfer large files, such as video files, one of the best ways is to simply burn them to a DVD, using the DVD as a data disc. When most people hear the term *DVD*, they immediately think of media for viewing movies. However, DVDs can hold up to 4.3GB of information, making them the best way to transfer raw video files short of carting around an external hard disk.

To burn files to a DVD, follow these steps:

1. Insert the DVD-R disc into your drive. After a few seconds, you will see the DVD icon on your desktop.
2. Drag the file or files you want to add to the DVD from the Finder onto the disk icon. A progress dialog appears, letting you know how long it will take to prepare the files. This might take several minutes depending on the size of the files being transferred, but this will not actually place the data on the disk yet. You can continue to drag files to the disk until you eject it.
3. Eject the DVD to burn the collected data. You will be asked whether you want to burn the data or not.
4. Choose Burn. The computer will then begin placing the data on the disk, displaying a progress bar and estimated time remaining. This will take at least as long as it did to prepare the data in step 2. After burning, you will again have to wait as the data that was burned is verified which can also take a lot of time. You can click Cancel during this phase if you do not want to wait. This will not affect the disk itself and you cannot make changes if the data is corrupted, but you run the risk of unknowingly having a corrupted disk..

After the DVD is burned, you can take it to any other computer with a DVD drive (even if the drive cannot itself burn DVDs) and use the files. Of course, Final Cut Express files will work only on Macs with Final Cut Express installed, and video files will play only on PCs with QuickTime installed. If you are transferring Final Cut Express project files and captured video clips, you might need to reconnect the files after they are loaded into Final Cut Express (&~ "Reconnecting Media" in Chapter 9).

> **Which Format Should I Use: DVD-R or DVD+R?**
>
> There are several DVD formats, but you will want to stick with DVD-R (that's DVD *dash* R) and *avoid* the DVD+R (DVD *plus* R) formatted discs. Both DVD-R and DVD+R are used to record data once and then they can be used only for playback. However, the Apple SuperDrive and other Apple-compatible DVD burners can use only DVD-R 4.7GB General Use media. These discs are playable in most standard DVD players and computer DVD-ROM drives. For more details, see the DVD FAQ: www.dvddemystified.com/dvdfaq.html.

Exporting to the Web (or Other Multimedia)

Increasingly, the Web is becoming a popular medium for video. Although it still has its drawbacks, the Web is the best way to get your work out to the widest audience. Whether you are creating a preview for a larger video, a portfolio of your video work, or an entire movie for viewing online, adding a properly exported QuickTime movie to your web page requires adding only a few simple lines of code and using a few simple tools:

HTML editor   You will need some way to generate the Hypertext Markup Language (HTML) code used to create your web page. If you are doing a lot of video work with the Web, then it will be worth your while to invest in a program such as Macromedia Dreamweaver or Adobe GoLive. These programs provide easy-to-use tools not only for creating web pages without needing to know any code, but for easily embedding Quick-Time movies into the pages. However, if you are on a more modest budget, all you need to create the web page is a simple text-editing application—such as TextEdit, which comes standard with every Mac—and the upcoming code provided in Listing 10.1.

Web server   You will need a web address and hard disk space on a computer that can serve up web pages and that is called, aptly, a *server*. Generally, the server is a computer that you are renting space on through a *hosting service*. If you have, for example, a Mindspring or .Mac account, then you already have some server space. However, even small QuickTime movies can eat a lot of space, and most hosting services place bandwidth restrictions on the amount of data that can be transferred from your web space for a given month. For most websites, bandwidth is rarely an issue. However, after you start delivering large video files from your site, you might find that you quickly hit your limit. Before you place your movies online, check with your hosting service to see the exact amount of storage space you have and your available bandwidth, and whether you need to increase your bandwidth to accommodate your videos.

Note: If you are looking for a Mac-friendly web hosting service, we recommend MacServe.net (www.macserve.net).

FTP software   You will need a File Transfer Protocol (FTP) program (sometimes called a client) to transfer the web page and video files from your computer to the server. Although Mac OS X has come a long way in its capability to network directly with other computers over the Internet, you will probably still need an FTP program to upload your files for live viewing on the Web. Such a program enables you to hook directly into the server and place files in it that can then be accessed by a web browser. You will, however, need to get the exact settings indicating how to do this from your hosting company.

Note: If you need an FTP client, we recommend Transmit from Panic (www.panic.com/transmit/) or CaptainFTP (captainftp.xdsnet.de).

Saving Your Project for the Web

To create a QuickTime version of your sequence for display on the Web, follow these steps:

1. In the Timeline, open the sequence you want to output.
2. Choose File > Export > QuickTime to open the Save dialog box.

Note: Although this section covers the Web, these instructions could be used to create QuickTime files for use on other computer-based media such as CD-ROMs. Your settings will be slightly different, though, depending on where the file will end up.

3. In the Save dialog box, choose QuickTime from the Format drop-down list and then one of the preset options from the Use drop-down list (see Figure 10.31). Which option you choose depends on the Internet speed you expect your audience will be using to view your video and the desired quality of the images you want to deliver:

   - Choose LAN if the viewer is on an extremely fast connection such as an Ethernet connection or a T1 or T3 line. This will produce the largest images with the best quality.
   - Choose one of the DSL/Cable settings if the viewer has a fast Internet connection. The lower the level you choose, the more compressed your video will be (and thus the lower quality) in order to cut down on file size.
   - Choose Modem for the lowest quality but smallest file sizes. You can also choose Modem – Audio only if you do not want to send any video at all, which will substantially reduce the file size.

For this exercise, name the file **LandSeaAir.mov** in a folder called **media** with the DSL/Cable-Medium setting.

Note: If these options do not appear, make sure that you have QuickTime Pro installed on the computer you are using. This should have come free with your Final Cut Express installation disk.

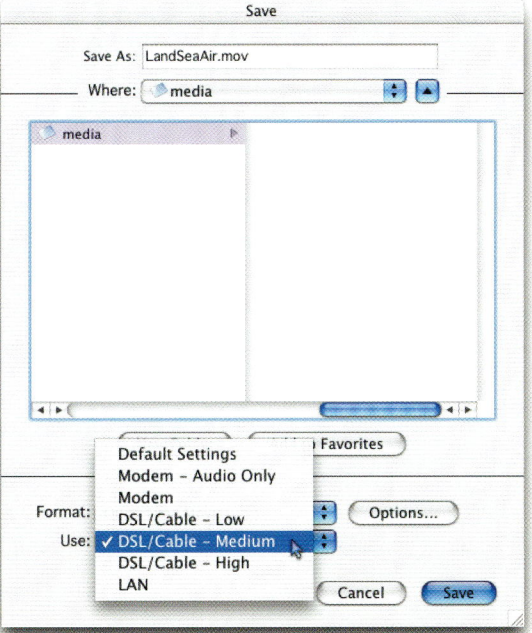

Figure 10.31
The Save dialog with the QuickTime Use options showing

4. At this point, you can click OK to begin saving your video or you can click Options to fine-tune your optimization settings in the Movie Settings dialog box (see Figure 10.32). The default settings for QuickTime work well for most uses, but you might want to tweak these for your specific needs:

   Video Settings   Click this button to access options that set the compression method for the video portion of your work. The default MPEG-4 is best for most uses.

   Video Filter   Apply a video filter to the entire sequence while exporting. This is especially helpful if you are compressing the video and want to add a slight blur to offset the artifacts created by compression.

   Video Size   Set the pixel dimensions of the final video output. Generally, if you set this manually, you will want to make sure to keep the dimensions in proportion. Of course, the larger the physical dimensions, the larger your file size will be. Reducing the video size is often a good way to improve the image quality.

   Sound Settings   Click this button to access options that set the compression method for the audio portion of your work. Generally, MPEG-4 for audio will be your best bet.

   Prepare For Internet Streaming   Choose from three settings indicating how the video should be treated when played over the Internet. The Fast Start setting enables you to have the video start playing before the entire file is downloaded. The Compressed Header option works faster but requires your audience to be using the newer versions of QuickTime. Hinted Streaming is used if you will be streaming the video; this requires special server software to work.

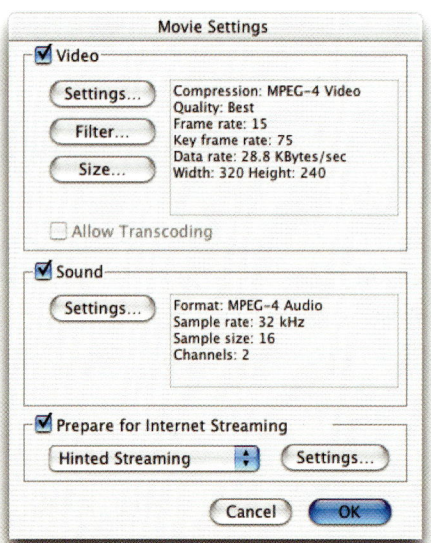

Figure 10.32
The Movie Settings dialog box

Now that your file has been saved in the media folder, you will need to add it to a web page.

Placing Your Video in a Web Page

After the QuickTime file has been created, your next step is to create a web page to display the movie and then upload all of these files to a web server, where they can then be viewed.

To create a web page for your video, open a text editing program or a specialized web page editing program, create a new file, and add the code shown in Listing 10.1.

▶ **Listing 10.1** Inserting Video into an HTML Page

```html
<html>
<head>
    <meta http-equiv="content-type"
        content="text/html;charset=iso-8859-1">
    <title>Land, Sea, and Air</title>
</head>
<body>
    <object>
        <param name="loop" value="true">
        <param name="playeveryframe" value="true">
        <param name="cache" value="true">
        <param name="controller" value="false">
        <param name="autoplay" value="true">
        <param name="src" value="media/LandSeaAir.mov">
        <embed style="float: left" src="media/LandSeaAir.mov"
            width="320" height="240" autoplay="true" controller="false"
            cache="true" type="video/quicktime" playeveryframe="true"
            loop="true">
    </object>
</body>
</html>
```

In this example, we will be showing the movie called LandSeaAir.mov, which is located in the folder called media. This code looks as though it "embeds" the video file into the web page twice, first using the <embed> tag and then again using the older <object> tag. However, the video will appear only once on the page. The web browser will use whichever of the tags it recognizes first, ignoring the other one. Using redundant tags, though, ensures that any web browser can view your video regardless of which tag it recognizes.

To tailor this code to your needs, you will need to change the source (src) for both tags (media/LandSeaAir.mov) to the folder and file you are using. In addition, you will need to set the width and height values in each tag to be the width and height for your movie. You can also set other attributes:

loop can be set to true or false depending on whether you want the movie to repeat after it finishes playing.

cache can be set to true or false if you want to have the movie stored by the browser's cache when for faster replay. True is generally recommended for faster replay.

autoplay can be set to true to have the movie start playing immediately after loading, or to false to wait for the viewer to click the Play button.

playeveryframe can be set to true to force the browser to play every frame of the movie without skipping, even if this means slowing down because of a slow computer. Setting this option to false will cause the video to skip frames if they do not arrive in time to be played.

volume can be set from 0 to 100 for the volume the movie plays at. This can be adjusted by the viewer if the controls are present.

controller can be set to true to allow show player controls: volume, play/pause, progress bar. A false value will keep the controller from showing which prevents the viewer from changing the volume, pausing the video, or jumping around in the video.

 Note: You can also add any other standard HTML content you want to this page, including background graphics and text, but we have kept the page simple here.

Next, save your new HTML file in the same folder as the media folder created in the previous exercise (see Figure 10.33). You can name this file anything you want (we called ours index), but do not use any spaces and end the filename with the extension .html.

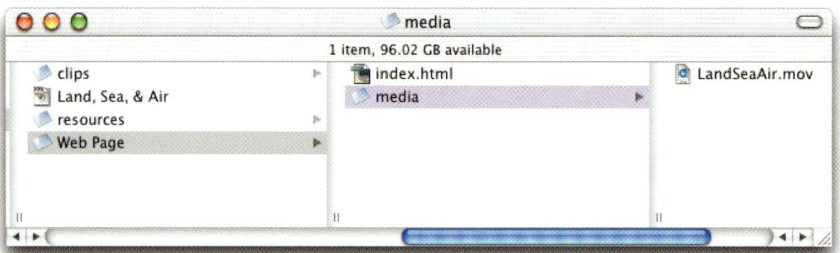

Figure 10.33 The HTML file is saved in the same folder as the media folder containing the movie.

Use your FTP software to upload the HTML file and video file to your web server. Exactly how you do this will depend on the FTP software you are using. With Transmit, you would log onto your web server (by using its FTP address as opposed to its actual web address), navigate to the folder you want to add the files to, and then simply drag the folder containing your web page and video file to the target folder (see Figure 10.34).

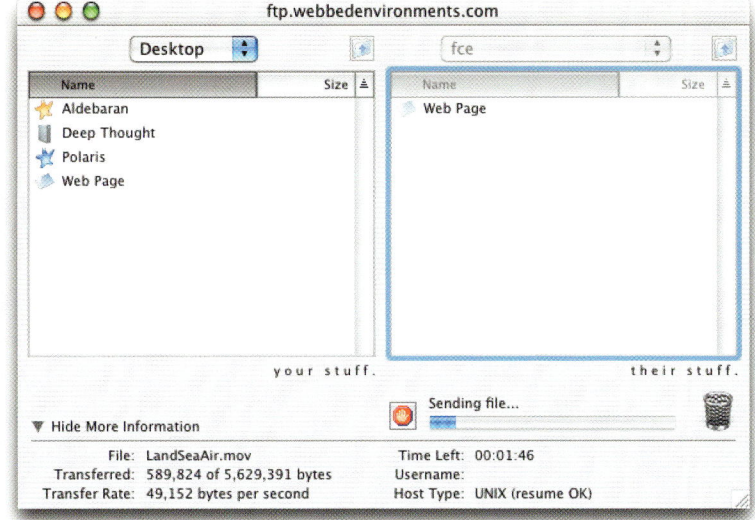

Figure 10.34 The folder with the web page being uploaded

You will then need to wait while the files are uploaded. This could take some time, depending on the size of the video file and the speed of your Internet connection.

You can now visit this web page by using a browser to display the movie (see Figure 10.35). You can see this video playing on our website at

    http://www.webbedenvironments.com/fce/WebPage/index.html

Figure 10.35
The video playing in a web browser

Glossary of Terms

A-roll The primary *footage* in a sequence. Usually contains running narration or dialog and shows the main action. See also *B-roll* (see Chapter 5).

Alpha channel A layer of data in a *clip* that stores the *opacity* information for a *frame*. Alpha channels are used in many forms of digital imaging and exist in many of the files that you can *import* into Final Cut Express. In DV editing, they are primarily used when *compositing* multiple clips or adding titles (see Chapter 7).

anamorphic An image's *aspect ratio* that has the horizontal proportions of 16:9. Anamorphic images are shot with a special lens that squashes the image. Final Cut Express has a feature that "unsquashes" the image to its undistorted horizontal size (see Chapter 3).

aspect ratio The dimension of the *frame* in which the image is presented. The standard for television is roughly a 4:3 aspect ratio. The *anamorphic* (also known as widescreen) ratio is 16:9 (see Chapter 3).

Audio Meter A Final Cut Express tool that displays the *decibel* level of both audio channels while a *clip* or a *sequence* is being played. This enables you to make sure the audio is not being distorted during playback (see Chapter 8).

B-roll Secondary *footage* used in a *sequence* to cut away from the main footage (the *A-roll*). It typically shows details related to the primary action in a separate image, such as pigeons scattering in the air as two characters walk down a city street (see Chapter 5).

Bezier handles Controls used to add curves in a *keyframe* path. These controls stick out as "handle bars" perpendicular to the path and can be rotated to change the curve (see Chapter 9).

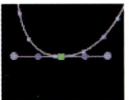

bin A folder in the *Browser* that enables you to organize your *clips*, *sequences*, and other *media* (see Chapter 3).

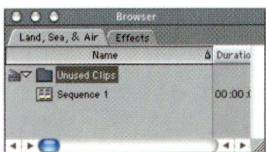

Browser The window where the *project files*, *bins*, and all your *clips* are stored and organized. The Browser also contains the Effects tab, which contains *filters* and *generators* (see Chapter 2).

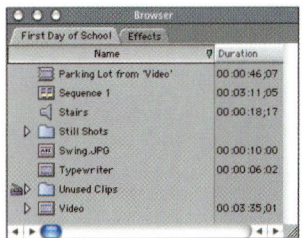

Canvas The window that shows the *footage* contained in the *Timeline*. The Canvas will show whatever *frame* is under the Timeline's *playhead*. The Canvas only plays the Timeline's *clips*—unlike the *Viewer*, it is not an area for adjusting clips. An external monitor will play whatever plays in the Canvas window (see Chapter 2).

capture To bring *footage* from a source tape into the computer's hard disk as a *media file* for use in Final Cut Express (see Chapter 3).

capture bin The designated *bin* where *clips* will be housed when you capture them (see Chapter 3).

clip The representation of a *media file*, containing video, audio, and/or graphics. Clips are housed in the *Browser* and are the individual pieces of *media* that you edit together in the *Timeline*. Clips can be manipulated, distorted, and trimmed without affecting the original media file they represent. Clips are used as the building blocks for any video sequence (see Chapter 3).

color bars A standard graphic of different-colored bars used to calibrate monitors correctly. The color bars can be added quickly to a *project* by using the drop-down menu in the bottom-right corner of the *Viewer*. This way, others viewing or broadcasting your project can make sure they've calibrated their equipment correctly (see Chapter 2).

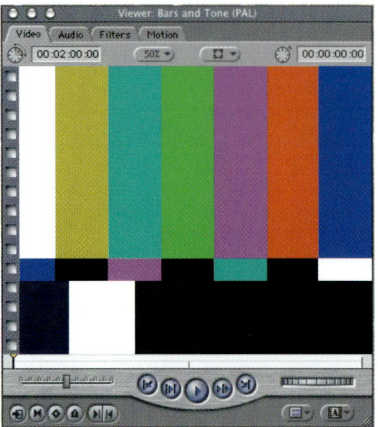

cut The edit point between two *clips* in the Timeline (see Chapter 4). Cuts can either be straight cuts, with one clip going directly to the next, or *transitions*, in which *effects* such as cross-dissolves are used between the two clips (see Chapter 6).

decibel (dB) A logarithmic measure of sound intensity (level) in the audio of a *clip*. In Final Cut Express, the audio level can be viewed by using the *Audio Meter* and adjusted by changing the level in the *Viewer's* Audio tab. Generally the audio level for a clip should fall somewhere between –12dB and –3dB (see Chapter 8).

deck The common name for any piece of equipment that plays and/or records video and audio tape. A deck is used to play back your source tape *footage* when *capturing*, as well as to record a Final Cut Express *sequence* back to tape when printing to video (see Chapter 1).

digital video (DV) A video format that stores information in the computer's language of 1s and 0s, enabling the video to be edited nondestructively in computer memory and preventing loss of quality from transfer to transfer.

dissolve A common type of *transition*, the dissolve changes a straight cut into a fade out of one clip as the incoming clip fades up (see Chapter 6).

drop frame timecode A type of *timecode* that adjusts itself for *NTSC's* 29.97 frame rate by dropping a *frame* from its count at regular intervals (see Chapter 3).

edit point See *cut*.

effect The umbrella term for *filters*, *motion*, *transitions*, *generators*, and anything that manipulates a clip beyond basic trimming (see Chapters 6 and 7). In Final Cut Express, all effects are located in the *Browser's* Effects tab.

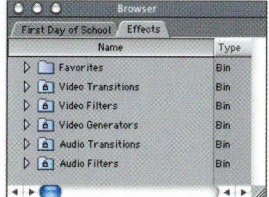

fine cut   A version of your edit that is near the final version, with exact edits, mixed sound, and so forth.

FireWire   A type of cable connection between computers and DV *decks* or cameras (and even external hard disks) that allows for extremely rapid transfer of digital information. Developed by Apple Computer as their implementation of the *IEEE 1394* standard. The equivalent Sony implementation is known as *i.LINK* (see Chapter 1).

footage   See *media*.

frame   One still image that, played within a series of other frames, creates the illusion of movement in video.

frames per second (fps)   The number of *frames* shown in a second of *footage*. The more frames shown per second, the more seamless the illusion of continuous motion. The *NTSC* (North American) standard runs at 29.97fps, whereas *PAL* (used in Europe and elsewhere) uses 25fps.

gain   In audio, the degree to which a signal is amplified, controlling the loudness of the sound (see Chapter 8). In video, the level of the whites.

gamma correction   In Final Cut Express, an *effect* that alters the midtones of an image, leaving the deep blacks and bright whites alone. Technically, the term refers to adjustments to a video signal to compensate for properties of a cathode ray tube. The Final Cut Express effect controls the way this adjustment is applied to a *clip*.

generator   An *effect* that creates a new *clip* inside Final Cut Express that has not been *captured* from a video or audio source. These kinds of clips include *slugs* and titles (see Chapter 9).

IEEE 1394   A standard defining a type of connection between computers and DV *decks* or cameras (and even external hard disks) that allows for very rapid transfer of digital information. Apple Computer's implementation is known as *FireWire* and is compatible with most peripherals. Sony's version, known as *i.LINK*, comes on all Sony DV cameras (see Chapter 1).

import   To bring a file into Final Cut Express, for example, a media *clip*, a Photoshop file, a JPEG image, a TIFF image, or a track from a CD (see Chapter 3).

In point   An edit that *trims* a *media file* so that it begins at that designated *frame*. The 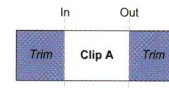 *Timeline* will not show *footage* before the In point during playback, but the *media* is still there on the hard disk and the In point can be changed at any time during the editing process to reveal more or less of the media (see Chapter 4). See also *Out point*.

insert edit   A type of edit that pushes all *clips* after it forward to accommodate the incoming clip (see Chapter 4). See also *overwrite edit*, *Ripple edit, Roll edit, Slide edit, Slip edit*.

i.LINK   Sony's implementation of the *IEEE 1394* standard, which is implemented by Apple Computer as *FireWire* (see Chapter 1).

jump cut   A *cut* that pieces together two *clips* of the same scene shot from a similar angle, typically less than 30 degrees' difference (see Chapter 5).

keyframe   A marker that enables audio levels or motion attributes to be changed over time in a *clip* (see Chapters 7 and 9).

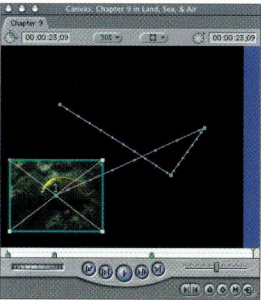

log and capture The two-stage process by which you create source *footage* ready for Final Cut Express to work with. Logging provides the essential information that the program will need about the *clip* so it can take the clip from a source tape. Capturing brings the media files from the source into the computer's hard disk and associates each file with its log information (see Chapter 3).

Logging bin The designated *bin* where offline logged *clips* will be created and *captured* (see Chapter 3).

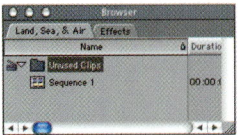

markers A way of designating and labeling certain *frames* in a *clip* or the *Timeline* (see Chapter 4). To navigate markers in the Timeline, Control+click in the ruler and choose from the list of markers at the bottom of the contextual menu.

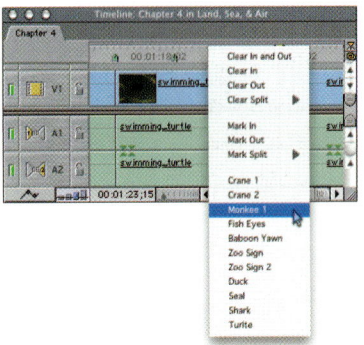

match cut A *cut* whose incoming and outgoing *clips* share a similar composition, graphic element, or movement (see Chapter 10).

media 1. The audio and video content of a *clip*. Used interchangeably with *footage* (see Chapter 3).

2. A physical storage device used to record data, such as CD, DVD, hard disk, film, or video (see Chapter 1).

3. General term for information delivery methods.

media file The actual file on your hard disk of the captured *footage* whose representation in the form of *clips* is being edited in Final Cut Express. The media file is unaffected by changes made to the clips (see Chapter 3).

Mini-DV tape A tape used for recording audio and video information with a *digital video* camera. Mini-DV tapes record this information digitally and can transfer this information directly into a hard disk through *FireWire* (see Chapter 1).

motion path A line or group of interconnected lines that show the path of a moving element in the *Canvas*. Motion paths are created by using *keyframes* to mark the movements (see Chapter 9).

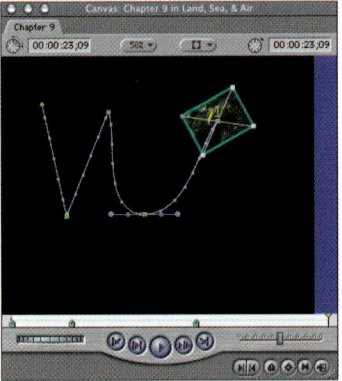

nested sequence A *sequence* that has been placed inside another sequence (see Chapter 10).

non-drop frame timecode A type of *timecode* that never drops a *frame* because it runs on a frame rate that uses whole numbers, such as the *PAL* system's rate of 25 frames per second (see Chapter 3). See also *drop frame timecode*.

NTSC National Television Standards Committee—the North American standard for video resolution and sample rate. It runs at 29.97 frames per second and with DV has a resolution of 720 × 480 pixels. See also *PAL*. (see Chapter 1)

opacity The transparency of a *clip* as defined by the properties of its *Alpha channel* (see Chapter 7).

Out point An edit that trims a *clip* so that it ends at that designated *frame*. All media after the Out point in a clip is ignored during playback, but the Out point can be changed during the editing process to reveal more or less of the media (see Chapter 4). See also *In point*.

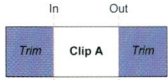

overwrite edit A type of edit that places the incoming *clip* over any *footage* in its way on the target track in the *Timeline* (see Chapter 4). See also *insert edit, Ripple edit, Roll edit, Slide edit, Slip edit*.

PAL Phase Alternating Line—the video standard used in much of Europe and most of the rest of the world. It runs at 25 frames per second and for DV has a 720 × 540 pixel ratio. See also *NTSC*. (see Chapter 1)

playhead In either the *Timeline, Canvas,* or *Viewer,* a vertical bar that designates which *frame* you are watching in a *clip*. You can drag the playhead to *scrub* quickly through a clip. (see Chapter 2)

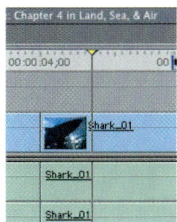

Print To Video The process of recording a sequence from Final Cut Express to a digital videotape, such as a *Mini-DV tape*, or to an analog *deck* (see Chapter 10).

project file The file on your hard disk that stores information about how your *clips* and *sequences* are organized in the *Browser* and how they are edited in the *Timeline*. It also contains information on *effects* and *rendering*. No media is actually contained in this file (see Chapter 3).

render To prepare an affected clip (that is, a clip that has an *effect* applied to it) for real-time viewing. Performed internally by Final Cut Express, rendering consists of actually calculating the effect and applying it frame-by-frame to the image. This creates a special render file in which the information describing the image has been modified. Editing the clip after the effect has been rendered will probably require that the effect be re-rendered (see Chapter 6).

Ripple edit A type of edit that trims or extends the duration of one *clip*, and moves the surrounding clips to accommodate the new time (see Chapter 5). See also *insert edit, overwrite edit, Roll edit, Slide edit, Slip edit*.

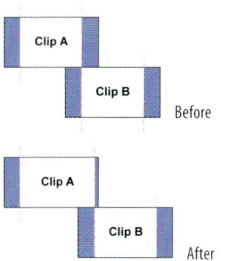

Roll edit A type of edit that changes the edit point between two *clips* without affecting their placement in the *Timeline*, thus keeping their combined length the same (see Chapter 5). See also *insert edit, overwrite edit, Ripple edit, Slide edit, Slip edit*.

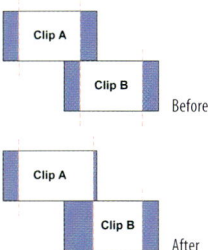

scratch disk The hard disk or disk partition where audio, video, and render files will be stored during editing. This can be your startup disk or any other hard disk mounted to your machine (see Chapter 2).

scrub   To move back and forth through a *clip* or a sequence by dragging the mouse back and forth over a scrub bar. (see Chapter 2)

sequence   A string of *clips* (containing audio, video, and graphic clips) that have been edited together. A sequence appears as an item in the *Browser,* and as tabs in the *Timeline* and *Canvas.* Only one sequence tab can be viewed at a time in the Timeline or Canvas; however, you can have *nested sequences* (see Chapter 10).

Slide edit   A type of edit that changes the placement of a *clip* in the *Timeline* but does not affect the duration or *In* and *Out points* (see Chapter 5). See also *insert edit, overwrite edit, Ripple edit, Roll edit, Slip edit.*

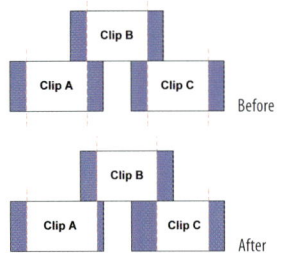

Slip edit   A type of edit that changes the In and Out points of a *clip* without changing duration or placement (see Chapter 5). See also *insert edit, overwrite edit, Ripple edit, Roll edit, Slip edit.*

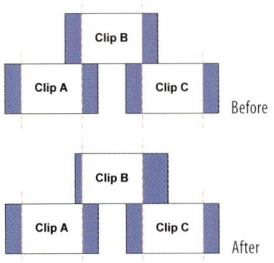

slug   A video *clip* that has no properties of its own until *effects* or filters are added to it. The default slug is black. See also *generator.* (See Chapter 9)

split edit   An edit in which a *clip's* audio and video do not start or end at the same time (see Chapter 8).

stereo pair   Two audio *clips* that are linked so that one plays from the left speaker and the other from the right speaker (see Chapter 8).

timecode   A coding system that designates each *frame* of video or audio with a number that incrementally increases with each frame. The format is 00:00:00:00, where the last two zeros represent frames, the previous two zeros represent seconds, the previous two zeros represent minutes, and the first two zeros represent hours (see Chapter 2).

Timeline   The Final Cut Express window where you view and make edits to a *sequence* of *clips* represented graphically, their length corresponding to the duration of the clip (see Chapter 2).

title-safe area   The area of the video *frame* that will be visible on any TV monitor; titles placed within this area will not be cut off. Final Cut Express provides a Title Safe guide that you can bring up in the *Viewer* or the *Canvas* window (see Chapter 9).

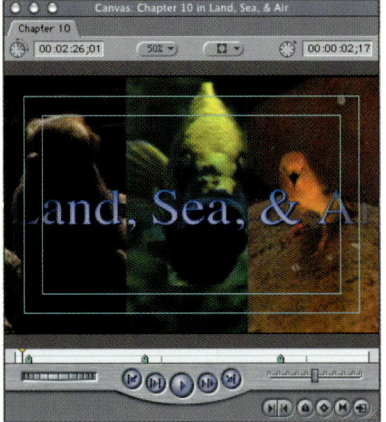

transition Any type of change between two *clips* that incorporates both images during the transition rather than being a *straight cut* in which one clip abruptly ends and the next begins. The most common transition is the cross-dissolve, in which the two clips seamlessly blend over the whole screen until the new clip replaces the old (see Chapter 6).

trim To add or subtract *frames* from a *clip's* edit (see Chapter 5).

Viewer The Final Cut Express window that you use to work with an individual *clip*—to view the clip, insert *In* and *Out points*, add filters or other *effects*, adjust the audio, or change the clip's motion (see Chapter 2).

Index

Note to the Reader: Page numbers in **bold** indicate the principle discussion of a topic or the definition of a term. Page numbers in *italic* indicate illustrations.

Numbers

3 Band Equalizer filter, **191–193**, *192*
3-D Simulation: Cube Spin transitions, **127**

A

A-roll footage, **100**, **265**
Abort Capture options, *36*, **36**
Adaptation, 234
Add composite mode, **168**
Adobe After Effects, **31**
Adobe GoLive, 258
Adobe Illustrator, **31**
Adobe Photoshop
    creating titles in, 222
    de-interlacing images, 250
alignment, transitions, *121*, **121–122**, 124
All Tracks Forward tool, 212
Alpha channels, 141, 222, **265**
anamorphic, **265**
anchor points, *157*, 159
animated titles, 211–213, *211–213*
animating clips using keyframes, *See also* video effects
    combining effects, 208
    creating motion paths, 204–207, *204–207*
    editing motion paths, 207–208, *208*
    overview of, 203–204
Apple DVD Studio Pro, 30, 254, 255, **256**
Apple iDVD, 30, 254, **256**
Apple iPhoto, 30, 53–54, *53*
Apple iPod MP3 players, 6
Apple QuickTime. *See* QuickTime
aspect ratios
    changing, 161, 162–163, *162–163*
    defined, **265**
    for widescreen films, 172
audio, **175–195**
    adding
        pauses, 189
        soundtracks, 240, *241*
        transitions, 187–188, *188–189*
        voice-overs, 201–203, *201–203*
    adding filters
        3 Band Equalizer, 191–193, *192*
        Echo, 193
        Hum Remover, 193
        overview of, 191
        Reverberation, 193–195, *194*
        Vocal DeEsser, 193
        Vocal DePopper, 193
    adjusting levels
        with Audio Meter, 179–180, *180*
        entire clips at once, 178–181, *178*, *180–181*
        instant volume changes, 182
        using keyframes, 181–184, *182–184*
    adjusting tracks separately, 177, 180, *181*
    Audio Meter, *18*, **19**, *28*, **28**, **265**
    Audio tab in Viewer, 176, 178–179, *178*, 180
    Ch 1/Ch 2 tabs in Viewer, 176, 180, *181*
    decibels, 177, **266**
    exporting, 245
    gain, 177, **267**
    importing, 189–191, *190–191*
    overview of, 175
    sound tone (of "silence"), 189
    split edits of video and
        defined, **185**, **270**
        editing in Viewer, 186–187, *186–187*
        overview of, 184–185
        using Ripple edit, 185–186
        using Roll edit, 185, *185–186*
    spread, 177, *178*, 179
    stereo pairs
        combining/splitting, 177
        defined, *176*, **176**, **270**
        versus linked clips, 176
    terminology, 177
    video tracks and
        linked together, 184–185
        linked/unlinked, moving, 78
        linking, 91, 93–94, *93*
        unlinking, 91–93, *92–93*
    waveform, 177, *178*, *178*, 179

B

B-roll footage, **54**, **100**, **265**
batching images, 250
Belmondo, Jean-Paul, 13
Bevel Border filter, **147–148**, *148*
Bezier handles, 208, **265**
bins, *See also* media
    capture bins, 40, 42, **266**
    creating, 54
    defined, **42**, **265**
    deleting, 54
    logging bins, 268

organizing media into, 54–55, *55*
　　　properties of items in, 56, *56*
blend modes. *See* composite modes
blocking unwanted images, 172
blue rendered effects, 123
Blue Velvet, 195
Blur filter, Gaussian, **144–145**, *145–146*
Bonnie and Clyde, 13
Border filters, Bevel, **147–148**, *148*
Boris FX titles. *See* titles, advanced
Boris software, 31
Breathless, **13**
Browser window, *See also* interface
　　　defined, *18*, **19**, **20**, **265**
　　　editing clips in, 74
　　　Effects tab, 22–23, *22*
　　　list view, 55
　　　opening, 20
　　　project tabs, 20–22, *21–22*
　　　selecting clips in, 113
burning to DVDs, *See also* outputting
　　　using authoring programs, 254, 255, 256
　　　choosing DVD formats, 257
　　　creating DVD data discs, 257
　　　overview of, 254
　　　saving in MPEG2 format before, 255–256, *256*
　　　saving in QuickTime format before, 254, 255
Burns, Ken, 31

C

Cabaret, 234
Cabinet of Dr. Caligari, The, 131
Canvas window, *See also* interface
　　　changing timecode views, 40
　　　defined, *18*, **19**, **27**, *27*, **265**
　　　Edit Overlay window, 74–75, *74–75*, 86
　　　Slide edits in, 111–112, *112*
　　　Slip edits in, 110, *111*
CaptainFTP software, 258
Capture window
　　　defined, *38*, **38–39**
　　　Logging tab, *38*, 39, 41, *41*
　　　setting markers, 43–44, *43*
　　　troubleshooting, 42
capturing video, *See also* media gathering
　　　using Capture Clip, *38*, 46–48, *46–48*
　　　using Capture Now, *38*, 45–46, *45*, 48
　　　using Capture Project, *38*, 49–51, *49–50*
　　　defined, **35**, **266**
　　　dropped frames and, 37
　　　FAQs on, 42
　　　long clips, 48
　　　preparing for
　　　　　in Capture window, 38–42, *38–39*, *41*
　　　　　changing timecode views, 40
　　　　　creating capture bins, 40, 42
　　　　　in Logging tab, 41–42, *41*
　　　　　naming clips, 41–42
　　　　　reviewing source tapes, 25, 39–40, 46

　　　　　setting markers, 43–44, *43*
　　　　　setting preferences, 35–37, *36–37*
　　　　　setting Reel names, 41, *41*, 42
　　　short clips, 48
　　　stopping, *45*, 46
　　　and storing, 44, *44*
CD formats, 7
CD Track Names feature, Get, 51
centering images, **156–157**, *157*, **158–159**
channels
　　　Alpha channels, 141, 222, 265
　　　RGB color, inverting, 141–142, *142*
　　　UV, inverting, 142, *143*
Cheadle, Don, 57
Civil War, The, 31
Clip controls in Viewer, *23*, **24**
clipboard, **78–79**, *78–79*
clips, **35**, **266**, *See also* audio; media; sequences; video clips
color bars, **266**
color channels, inverting, **141–142**, *142*
color composites. *See* composite modes
color correction, **150**
Color Corrector filter, *See also* video effects
　　　advanced controls, 152
　　　brightening/darkening images, 150–153, *151–152*
　　　changing contrast, 152, 153
　　　daylight vs. tungsten and, 153–154
　　　defined, **151**, *239*
　　　fixing white balance, 153–155, *154–155*
　　　resetting defaults, 155
color saturation, changing, **134–138**, *135–138*
coloring drop shadows, 166, *166*
composite modes, *See also* video effects
　　　Add, 168
　　　changing, 167, *168*
　　　Darken, 171
　　　defined, **167**
　　　Difference, 169
　　　Hard Light, 170
　　　Lighten, 171
　　　Multiply, 169
　　　Normal, 167, 168
　　　Overlay, 170
　　　overlaying, 172
　　　Screen, 170
　　　Soft Light, 171
　　　Subtract, 169
　　　Travel Matte (Alpha, Luma), 172
contextual menus, *19–20*, **19–20**
contrast, changing, 152, 153
Controls tab in Viewer, *See also* Motion tab; Viewer
　　　defined, *209*, **209**
　　　Title 3D controls, 220, *220*
　　　Title Crawl controls, 221, *221*
copying
　　　clips to hard disks, 51
　　　filter effects, 139, *139*, 140
　　　and pasting with clipboard, 78–79, *78–79*
　　　and pasting, shortcuts for, 139
Cosby Show, 234
Crawl, Title (Boris), *218*, **218**, *221*, **221**, 222, 240, *241*

Crawl titles (Final Cut), 212, *212*
cropping images, *160–161*, **160–161**, *See also* cuts; editing; trimming
Cross Fade audio transitions, **187–188**, *188–189*
cross-dissolves, *See also* transitions
    adding, 117–118, *117–119*
    changing alignment, 121, *121*
    defined, **115–116**, *116*
    editing duration, 119–120, *120*
    fade to black using, 126, *126*
    overview of, 127
Cube Spin transitions, **127**
cuts, *See also* editing; trimming
    defined, **266**
    fine cuts, 267
    jump cuts, 267
    match cuts, 233–234
    straight cuts, 115, 236

D

Darken composite mode, **171**
daylight vs. tungsten light, **153–154**
De-Interlace filter, **250**
decibels (dB), **177**, **266**
decks, *12*, **12**, **266**
deleting
    bins, 54
    clips
        gap deletes, 95–96, *95–96*
        lift deletes, 95, *95*
        overview of, 94, *94*
        ripple deletes, 95, *95*
    filters, 138
    keyframes, 184
    markers, 65
    tracks, 86–87, *86*
    transitions, 118
Desaturate filter, *See also* video effects
    adding, 136–137, *136–137*
    defined, **134–135**, *135*
    multiple filters and, 138, *138*
Difference composite mode, **169**
Digital 8 format, **11**
digital video. *See* DV
Display control panel, 8, *9*
displays. *See* monitors
dissolves, *See also* transitions
    defined, **266**
    Fade In Fade Out, 126, 127
    Ripple, 128
distorting images, *See also* video effects
    with Fisheye filter, 143–144, *143–144*
    using Motion controls, 161–163, *162–163*
    reasons for, 163
distributing. *See* outputting
Douglas, Michael, 57
dragging and dropping
    clips into Timeline, 72–74, *72–73*
    media files into projects, 53–54, *53*
    media files into/out of bins, 55

Dreamweaver program, 258
Drew Carey Show, The 234
drop frame timecodes, **266**
drop frame timecodes, non-, **268**
drop shadows, *165–167*, **165–167**
dropped frames, **37**, **254**
Dryer, Carl, 234
Duration window, 120, *120*
DV cameras, **11**
DV decks, *12*, **12**, **266**
DV (digital video), **266**
DV-NTSC setup option, **17**, *17*
DVCAM format, **11**
DVD burners, **6–7**, *See also* burning
DVD Studio Pro software, 30, 254, **255**, **256**

E

Easy Setup command, 16–17, *17*
Echo filter, **193**
Edge wipe transitions, **130**
Edit Marker dialog box, 63, *64*
editing, **59–87**, *See also* cuts; outputting; trimming
    in Browser window, 74
    clips into Timeline
        by dragging, 72–74, *72–73*
        using Edit Overlay window, 74–75, *74–75*, 86
        using function keys, 76–77
        overview of, 71–72
        sub-clips, 81, *81*
        tracks, 83–85, *83–85*
    cropping images, 160–161, *160–161*
    using Fit To Fill, 76
    using Insert Edit, 73, *73*, 76, 267
    with multiple tracks
        adding tracks, 83–85, *83–85*
        deleting tracks, 86–87, *86*
        overview of, 82–83
        setting target tracks, 85–86, *85*
    nonlinear editing, 82
    overview of, 59
    using Overwrite Edit, 73, *73*, 76, 269
    previewing titles while, 217
    redoing edits, 83
    using Replace Edit, 76
    sequences
        creating, 66–67, *67*
        defined, **66**, **270**
        inserting clips into, 74–75, *74–75*
        item properties, 56, *56*, 226, *226–227*
        naming, 67, *67*
        opening, 67, *67*
    split edits of audio/video
        defined, **185**, **270**
        editing in Viewer, 186–187, *186–187*
        overview of, 184–185
        using Ripple edit, 185–186
        using Roll edit, 185, *185–186*
    using Superimpose, 76–77
    in Timeline window
        adding markers, 63–64, *63–64*

adding tracks, 83–85, *83–85*
versus Browser window, 74
changing views, 60–61, *60–61*
with clipboard, 78–79, *78–79*
clips into, 71–77, *72–75*
editing markers, 65
insert edits, 73, *73*
marker options, 62
moving clips, 77–78, *77*
moving markers, 65
navigating markers, 65–66, *66*
overview of, 60
overwrite edits, 73, *73*
sequences, 66–67, *67*
setting In/Out points, 61–62, *62*
titles, 217, 222
transitions
alignment, 121–122, *121*, 124
duration, 119–120, *120*, 124
opacity, 124
Ripple edits, 125, *125*
Roll edits, 125, *125*
in Transitions Editor, 124–125, *124–125*, 237, *237*
trimming clips into sub-clips before
using In/Out points, 68–71, *68–71*, 79–80, *80*
using markers, 80–81, *81*
overview of, 68
undoing edits, 83
in Viewer, 74
effects, **266–267**, *See also* audio; titles; transitions; video effects
Effects tab, *22*, **22–23**
The Elephant Man, 195
eMac computers, *3*, **3**
Eraserhead, 195
Explode transitions, **128**
exporting. *See* outputting
Extend Edit command, *100*, **100**
external DVD disks, 7
external hard disks, 5–6
external microphones, 13
external video devices, 17, *18*
External Video For Playback option, **17**
Eyedropper tool, fixing white balance, 154–155, *154–155*

F

Fade In Fade Out dissolves, *126*, **127**
Fade to Black transitions, *126*, **126**
Fallen Angels, 173
FAQs on capturing video, 42
feathering edges, 161, *161*
Fight Club, 234
files. *See* media
Film Gimp software, **31**
films. *See* movies
filters, audio, *See also* audio
3 Band Equalizer, 191–193, *192*
Echo, 193
Hum Remover, 193
overview of, 191

Reverberation, 193–195, *194*
Vocal DeEsser, 193
Vocal DePopper, 193
filters, video, *See also* video effects
Bevel Border, 147–148, *148*
Color Corrector, 150–155, *151–152*, *154–155*, 239
De-Interlace, 250
Desaturate, 134–138, *135–138*
Fisheye, 143–144, *143–144*
Gaussian Blur, 144–145, *145–146*
Image Mask, 172
Invert, 141–142, *142–143*
Mirror, 146, *147*
Solarize, 149–150, *149–150*
Widescreen, 172
Final Cut Express, *See also* interface
deleting preferences files, 16
Easy Setup command, 16–17, *17*
navigation shortcuts, 25, 39–40, 46
starting, 16–18, *17–18*
supportive software, 30–31
Final Cut movies, exporting sequences as, *243–245*, **243–245**
Fincher, David, 234
finishing videos. *See* outputting
FireWire cable, *See also* IEEE
defined, **7–8**, 267
DV decks and, *12*, *12*
external hard disks and, 5–6
Fisheye filter, *143–144*, **143–144**
Fit To Fill edit method, **76**
footage. *See* video footage
Fosse, Bob, 234
frames, *See also* keyframes
de-interlacing, 250
defined, **267**
dropped frames, 37, 254
exporting as still images, 247–250, *247–249*
freeze-frames, 199–200, *200–201*
unrendered, viewing, 122
FTP (File Transfer Protocol), 258, 262
function keys. *See* shortcut keys

G

gap deletes, *95–96*, **95–96**
Gauss, Carl Friedrich, 144
Gaussian Blur filter, **144–145**, *145–146*
generated clips, **214**, **267**
Godard, Jean-Luc, 13
GoLive program, Adobe, 258
green dot on motion paths, 206, *206*
green highlight bars, 103
green markers, 64, *64*
green render lines, 122
green triangles (stereo pairs), 176, *176*

H

Hard Light composite mode, **170**
hardware setup, **1–13**
DV cameras/formats, 11

DV decks, 12, *12*
DVD burners, 6–7
FireWire and, 7–8
hard disks
    external FireWire disks, 5–6
    internal disks, 5
    iPods as, 6
    overview of, 5
    recommended features, 6
    SCSI disks, 6
lights, 13
Macintosh computers
    eMacs, 3, *3*
    iBooks, 3, *4*
    iMacs, 2, *3*
    Power Macs, 4, *5*
    PowerBooks, 4, *4*
    requirements, 2
microphones, 13
monitors
    adding speakers, 10
    mirror displays and, 8
    overview of, 8
    reference monitors, 9–10
    second monitors, 8, *9*
    video standards, 10
overview of, 1
scratch disks
    defined, **16**, **269**
    preferences, 37, *37*
    setting up, 16–17, *17*
help. *See* troubleshooting
Hill, Benny, 198
Hitchcock, Alfred, 229
hosting services, **258**
hot keys. *See* shortcut keys
HTML, creating web pages in, **261–262**, *262*
HTML editors, **258**
Hum Remover filter, **193**

I

iBook computers, **3**, *4*
iDVD software, 30, 254, **256**
IEEE 1394, **267**, *See also* FireWire
i.LINK, **267**, *See also* IEEE
Illustrator, Adobe, 31
iMac computers, **2**, *3*
Image Control filters, Desaturate, **134–138**, *135–138*
Image Mask filter, 172
images. *See* video
importing, *See also* media gathering
    audio clips, 189–191, *190–191*
    defined, **267**
    video clips, 51–52, *52*
In/Out points
    creating sub-clips from, 68–71, *68–71*, 79–80, *80*
    In points, defined, **267**
    Out points, defined, **269**
    setting in Timeline, 61–62, *62*
Insert Edit method, 73, *73*, **76**, **267**

Insert Reel dialog box, 50, *50*
Insert Tracks dialog box, 84, *84*
interface, **15–31**, *See also* Final Cut; Timeline; Viewer
    arranging windows, 18, *18*, 30
    Audio Meter, *18*, **19**, 28, *28*, 265
    Browser window
        defined, *18*, **19**, **20**, **265**
        editing clips in, 74
        Effects tab, 22–23, *22*
        list view, 55
        opening, 20
        project tabs, 20–22, *21–22*
        selecting clips in, 113
    Canvas window
        changing timecode views, 40
        defined, *18*, **19**, **27**, *27*
        Edit Overlay window, 74–75, *74–75*, 86
        Slide edits in, 111–112, *112*
        Slip edits in, 110, *111*
    clip progress through, 27
    contextual menus, 19–20, *19–20*
    defined, *18*, **19**
    navigation shortcuts, 25, 39–40, 46
    overview of, 15
    Tool palette, *18*, 28–30, *28*
interlacing, fixing, **250**
internal DVD disks, 7
Invert filter, **141–142**, *142* 143
inverting colors, **141–142**, *142–143*
inverting images, **149**, *150*
iPhoto software, **30**, 53–54, *53*
iPod MP3 players, 6
iris transitions, **129**, **131**
Item Properties dialog box, *See also* media; sequences; video clips
    Format tab, 56, *56*, 226, *226*
    Logging Info tab, 56, 226
    Timing tab, 56, 226, *227*
iTunes, Get CD Track Names feature, 51

J

Jarmusch, Jim, 113
Jaws wipe transitions, **130**
Jazz, 31
Jonze, Spike, 234
justification, **215**

K

keyframes, *See also* frames
    adjusting audio using, 181–184, *182–184*
    animating clips using
        combining effects, 208
        creating motion paths, 204–207, *204–207*
        editing motion paths, 207–208, *208*
        overview of, 203–204
    defined, **182**, **267**
    deleting, 184
Kurosawa, Akira, 87

L

laying edits out in Timeline, **234–236**, *235*
lift deletes, *95*, **95**
Lighten composite mode, **171**
lights, choosing, 13
Link tool, *See also* trimming clips
    defined, **90**, *90*
    linking A/V tracks, 91, 93–94, *93*
    moving linked/unlinked clips, 78
    toggling on/off, 92, *92*
    unlinking A/V tracks, 91–93, *92–93*
linked A/V tracks, 184–185
linked clips vs. stereo pairs, 176
locking tracks, 105
Log Clip dialog box, 47, *47*
logging bins, **268**
Logging tab, *41*, **41–42**
Lower Third titles, *210*, **210**
Lucas, George, 87
Luhrmann, Baz, 82
Lynch, David, 195

M

Macintosh computers, *See also* hardware
    eMacs, 3, *3*
    iBooks, 3, *4*
    iMacs, 2, *3*
    Power Macs, 4, *5*
    PowerBooks, 4, *4*
    requirements, 2
Macromedia Dreamweaver program, 258
Man Ray, 149
markers, *See also* editing
    adding to Timeline, 63–64, *63–64*
    contextual menus, 66, *66*
    creating sub-clips using, 80–81, *81*
    defined, **63**, **268**
    deleting, 65
    editing, 65
    extending, 65
    moving, 65
    navigating, 65–66, *66*
    options, 62
    setting for captures, 43–44, *43*
    shortcut keys for, 62
    snapping to, 64, 77
masking unwanted images, 172
match cuts, 233–234
Matrox rendering device, **123**
mattes, **172**
Matrix, The 140
media gathering, **33–57**
    capturing video
        using Capture Clip, *38*, 46–48, *46–48*
        using Capture Now, *38*, 45–46, *45*, 48
        using Capture Project, *38*, 49–51, *49–50*
        defined, **35**, **266**
        dropped frames problem, 37
        FAQs on, 42
        long clips, 48
        short clips, 48
        stopping, *45*, *46*
        and storing, 44, *44*
    dragging/dropping files, 53–54, *53*
    importing audio clips, 189–191, *190–191*
    importing video clips, 51–52, *52*
    media/media files, defined, **268**
    and organizing in bins
        creating new bins, 54
        deleting bins, 54
        dragging files in/out of, 55
        overview of, 54
        setting item properties, 56, *56*
        tips for, 55
    overview of, 33
    preparing for video capture
        in Capture window, 38–42, *38–39*, *41*
        changing timecode views, 40
        creating capture bins, 40, 42
        in Logging tab, 41–42, *41*
        naming clips, 41–42
        reviewing source tapes, 25, 39–40, 46
        setting markers, 43–44, *43*
        setting preferences, 35–37, *36–37*
        setting Reel names, 41, *41*, 42
        reconnecting to source media, 49–51, *49–50*, 227–228, *227–229*
        starting new projects before, 34–35, *34–35*
Menu bar window, *18*, **19**
menus, contextual, *19–20*, **19–20**
microphones, adding, 13
Mini-DV format, **11**, **268**
Mirrione, Stephen, 57
mirroring images, **146**, *147*
monitors, *See also* hardware setup
    adding speakers, 10
    mirroring displays and, 8
    overview of, 8
    reference monitors, 9–10
    second monitors, 8, 9
    video standards, 10
Morris, Errol, 31
motion paths, **268**, *See also* animating
Motion tab controls, *See also* Controls; video effects; Viewer
    Basic Motion controls
        Anchor Point, *157*, 159
        Center, 156–157, *157*, *158–159*
        defined, **156**, *157*
        Rotation, 156–157, *157*, *158*
        Scale, 156–158, *157*
    Crop controls, 160–161, *160–161*
    defined, *156*, **156**
    Distort controls, 161–163, *162–163*
    Drop Shadow controls, 165–167, *165–167*
    Opacity controls, 163–165, *164–165*
Moulin Rouge, 82
mouse, quick trims with, **98–99**, *99*
Movie Settings dialog box, *260*, **260**
movies
    Adaptation (Jonze), 234
    Blue Velvet (Lynch), 195

Bonnie and Clyde (Penn), 13
Breathless (Godard), 13
Cabaret (Fosse), 234
The Cabinet of Dr. Caligari (Wiene), 131
The Civil War (Burns), 31
The Elephant Man (Lynch), 195
Eraserhead (Lynch), 195
Fallen Angels (Wong), 173
Fight Club (Fincher), 234
Jazz (Burns), 31
Moulin Rouge (Luhrmann), 82
North by Northwest (Hitchcock), 229
The Passion of Joan of Arc (Dryer), 234
Psycho (Hitchcock), 229
Rashomon (Kurosawa), 87
Star Wars (Lucas), 87
Stranger Than Paradise (Jarmusch), 113
The Thin Blue Line (Morris), 31
Traffic (Soderberg), 57
Vertigo (Hitchcock), 229
moving clips, 77, **77–78**
moving markers, 65
MPEG-4 compression format, 260, *260*
MPEG2 compression format, **255–256**, *256*
Multiply composite mode, **169**

N

naming clips, 41–42
naming sequences, 67, *67*
navigating markers, 65–66, *66*
navigation clips, 25, 39–40, 46
nested sequences, *242*, **242–243**, **268**
non-drop frame timecodes, **268**
Normal composite mode, 167, *168*
North by Northwest, 229
Novak, Kim, 229
NTSC (National Television Standards Committee), **10**, **268**

O

offline source media, reconnecting to, *49–50*, **49–51**, *227–229*
opacity, *See also* composite modes
 changing, 163–165, *164–165*
 defined, **163**, **268**
 of drop shadows, 166, *166*
 Normal mode, 167, *168*
 of transitions, 124
Out points. *See* In/Out points
Outline Text titles, *210*, **210**
outputting, finishing and, 197
outputting videos, **231–263**
 burning to DVDs
  using authoring programs, 254, 255, 256
  choosing DVD formats, 257
  creating DVD data discs, 257
  overview of, 254
  saving in MPEG2 format before, 255–256, *256*
  saving in QuickTime format before, 254, 255

editing clips together before
 adding filters, 238–239, *238–239*
 adding soundtracks, 240, *241*
 adding titles, 239–240, *240–241*
 adding transitions, 236–237, *236–238*
 knowing when to finish, 242
 laying edits out in Timeline, 234–236, *235*
 with match cuts, 233–234
 nesting sequences, 242–243, *242*
 overview of, 232–233
 for rhythm, 234
 for spatial relationships, 234
 for temporal relationships, 233
exporting sequences
 adding global effects, 246
 as Final Cut movies, 243–245, *243–245*
 and importing back into Final Cut, 245, 246
 in MPEG2 format, 255–256, *256*
 overview of, 243
 as QuickTime movies, 245–246, *246*, 254
 of still images, 247–250, *247–249*
exporting to Web
 creating web pages, 261–262, *262*
 FTP software in, 258, 262
 HTML editors in, 258
 overview of, 257–258
 placing movies in web pages, 262–263, *263*
 saving as QuickTime movies before, 258–260, *259–260*
 Web servers in, 258
overview of, 231
printing to videotape
 directly from Timeline, 253–254, *253*
 dropped frames and, 254
 master tapes, 251
 overview of, 251
 using Print To Video, 251–253, *251*, **269**
Overlay composite mode, **170**
Overlay window, Edit, 74–75, *74–75*, 86
overlaying composite modes, 172
Overwrite Edit method, 73, *73*, 76, **269**

P

Page Peel transitions, **128**
PAL (Phase Alternating Line) standard, **10**, **269**
The Passion of Joan of Arc, 234
pasting. *See* copying
pauses, adding to audio, 189
Pen tool, audio keyframing with, *182–184*, **182–184**
Penn, Arthur, 13
Perspective filters, Mirror, **146**, *147*
Photoshop
 creating titles in, 222
 de-interlacing images, 250
pink line through audio tracks, 184, *184*
Play controls in Viewer, 23, *24*
playheads, 69, *69*, **269**
post-roll footage, **46**
Power Mac computers, 4, *5*
PowerBook computers, *4*, **4**

pre-roll footage, **45**
preferences files, deleting, 16
Preferences window
    General tab, 36, *36*
    opening, 254
    Report Dropped Frames option, 254
    Scratch Disk tab, 37, *37*
printing to videotape, *See also* outputting
    directly from Timeline, 253–254, *253*
    dropped frames and, 254
    master tapes, 251
    overview of, 251
    using Print To Video, 251–253, *251*, 269
problems. *See* troubleshooting
project files, **269**
project tabs in Browser, **20–22**, *21–22*
projects, *See also* audio; media; video
    organizing in bins, 54–56, *56*
    reverting to previous, 98
    saving, 34–35, *35*
    setting properties, 223–224, *223–224*
    starting, 34–35, *34–35*
proxy effects, 122, 123
Psycho, 229

Q

QuickTime Explode transitions, **128**
QuickTime Movies
    saving files as
        for DVD output, 254
        overview of, 245–246, *246*
        for Web export, 258–260, *259–260*
QuickTime MPEG Encoder dialog box, 255–256, *256*
QuickTime software, 30
QuickTime Zoom transitions, **129**

R

Rashomon, 87
Razor Blade tool, *96–97*, **96–97**
RBG (Red/Blue/Green) channels, inverting, **141–142**, *142–143*
reconnecting to source media, *49–50*, **49–51**, **227–229**, *227–228*
red render lines, 122, *122*
red slash over clips, 49, *49*, 227
Redo command, 83
Reel names, setting, 41, *41*, 42
reference monitors, **9–10**
rendering, *See also* transitions
    defined, *122*, **122**, **269**
    Matrox cards and, 123
    proxy effects, 122, 123
    real-time effects, 122, 123
    selections, 123
    viewing after, 123, *123*, *237*, *238*
    viewing effects without, 123
    viewing unrendered frames, 122
Replace Edit method, **76**

Report Dropped Frames option, **254**
Reverberation filter, **193–195**, *194*
reversing transitions, 124
reversing video playback, *198–199*, **198–199**
reverting to previous edits, 98
rhythm, editing for, **234**
ripple deletes, *95*, **95**
Ripple dissolves, **128**
Ripple edits, *See also* editing; trimming
    defined, **102**, **108**, **269**
    in split edits of A/V, 185–186
    in Timeline, 109–110, *109–110*
    of transitions, 125, *125*
    in Trim Edit window, 108–109, *108–109*
Roll edits, *See also* editing; trimming
    defined, **101**, **106**, **269**
    in split edits of A/V, 185, *185–186*
    in Timeline, 107, *107*
    of transitions, 125, *125*
    in Trim Edit window, 106–107, *106*
room tone, **189**
rotating images, **156–157**, *157*, 158
RT (real-time) effects, rendering, 122, 123

S

saving finished videos, *See also* outputting
    as Final Cut movies, 244, *244*
    in MPEG2 format, 255–256, *256*
    as QuickTime Movies
        for DVD output, 254
        overview of, 245–246, *246*
        for Web export, 258–260, *259–260*
    as stills/image sequences, 247–249, *248–249*
saving new projects, 34–35, *35*, *See also* storing
scaling images, **156–158**, *157*
scratch disks, *See also* hardware
    defined, **16**, **269**
    preferences, 37, *37*
    setting up, 16–17, *17*
Screen composite mode, **170**
Scrolling Text titles, **211**, *211*
scrub, *69*, **69**, **270**
SCSI hard disks, 6
Seberg, Jean, 13
Seinfeld, 234
selecting clips, 94, 103, *104*, 113
sequences, *See also* editing; outputting; video clips
    changing settings, 224–226, *224–225*
    creating, 66–67, *67*
    default tracks in, 82
    defined, **66**, **270**
    inserting clips into, 74–75, *74–75*
    item properties, 56, *56*, 226, *226–227*
    naming, 67, *67*
    nesting, 242–243, *242*
    opening, 67, *67*
    organizing in bins, 55, *55*
servers, **258**
Setup For options, **16–17**, *17*
shadows, drop, *165–167*, **165–167**

shortcut keys
    Clip controls, *23*, 24
    copying/pasting, 139
    deleting clips and gaps, 95, *95*
    edit methods, 76–77
    locking tracks, 105
    Mark commands, 62
    navigating clips, 25, 39–40, 46
    navigating markers, 66
    opening Preferences window, 254
    Play controls, *23*, 24
    Redo command, 83
    reviewing footage, 25, 40, 46
    selecting/deselecting clips, 94
    transition alignment, 121, *121*
    Undo command, 83
    zoom tools, 97–98
Show Displays in Menu Bar option, 8, *9*
sizing images, 156–158, *157*
Slide edits, *103*, 111–113, *112*, **270**
Slip edits, *102*, 110, *111*, **270**
slow motion, *198–199*, **198–199**
Snap tool, *See also* trimming
    defined, *90*, **90**
    snapping to markers, 64, 77
    snapping tracks into position, 90–91, *91*
    toggling on/off, 91, *91*
Soderberg, Steven, 57
Soft Light composite mode, **171**
Solarize filter, *149–150*, **149–150**
sound tone, **189**, *See also* audio
soundtracks, adding, **240**, *241*
spatial relationships, editing for, **234**
speakers, adding, 10
speed, playback, changing, *198–199*, **198–199**
Spielberg, Steven, 130
split edits of audio/video, *See also* audio; editing; video
    defined, **185**
    editing in Viewer, 186–187, *186–187*
    overview of, 184–185
    using Ripple edit, 185–186
    using Roll edit, 185, *185–186*
spread (audio), **177**, *178*, *179*
Star iris transitions, **129**
Star Trek, 149
Star Wars, 87
starting Final Cut Express, **16–18**, *17–18*
stereo pairs, *176*, **176–177**, **270**, *See also* audio
Stewart, Jimmy, 229
still images. *See* frames
storing, *See also* saving
    captured media, 44, *44*
    favorite filters, 140, *140*
straight cuts, **115**, **236**
Stranger Than Paradise, 113
Stretch: Squeeze transitions, **129**
Stylize filters, Solarize, *149–150*, **149–150**
sub-clips. *See* trimming clips
Subtract composite mode, **169**
Superimpose edit method, **76–77**
Sync Adjust Movies Over *x* minutes, *36*, **36**

T

temporal relationships, editing for, **233**
Text bin in Effects tab, 210, **213–214**, *214*, *See also* titles
The Thin Blue Line, **31**
3 Band Equalizer filter, **191–193**, *192*
3-D Simulation: Cube Spin transitions, **127**
timecodes
    changing views, 40
    defined, **270**
    drop frame timecodes, 266
    non-drop frame timecodes, 268
    option, 36, *36*
Timeline window, *See also* editing; interface
    defined, *18*, **19**, *25*, **25–26**, **270**
    laying edits out in, 234–236, *235*
    printing to videotape from, 253–254, *253*
    trimming clips in
        using Ripple edits, 109–110, *109–110*
        using Roll edits, 107, *107*
        selecting clips, 103, *104*, 113
        using Slide edits, 111–113, *112*
        using Slip edits, 110, *111*
titles, **209–222**
    advanced titles
        adding, 221–222, *221*
        editing, 222
        overview of, 217, 218–219, 240
        setting parameters, 219–221, *219–221*
        Title 3D, 217–219, *218*, 220, *220*, 222
        Title Crawl, 218, *218*, 221, *221*, 222, 240, *241*
    basic titles
        adding, 209, *209*, 213–216, *214–216*
        animated titles, 211–213, *211–213*
        Crawl, 212, *212*
        Lower Third, 210, *210*
        Outline Text, 210, *210*
        overview of, 210
        previewing while editing, 217
        Scrolling Text, 211, *211*
        setting parameters, 215–216, *215*
        Text (simple), 211, *211*, 213–216, *214–216*
        Typewriter, 213, *213*
    clearing space for, 212, 240, *240*
    creating in Photoshop, 222
    customizing title clips, 217
    overview of, 239–240
    previewing while editing, 217
    Title Safe guide, 209, 222, **270**
Tool Bench window, Voice Over tab, *200–203*, **200–203**
Tool palette, *18*, *28*, **28–30**
tracks, *See also* audio; editing; video
    adding to Timeline, 83–85, *83–85*
    defaults, in sequences, 82
    deleting, 86–87, *86*
    insert edits of, 73, *73*
    locking, 105
    overview of, 82–83
    setting target tracks, 85–86, *85*
    snapping into position, 90–91, *91*
Traffic, 57

transitions, **115–131**, *See also* video effects
   3-D Simulation: Cube Spin, 127
   audio transitions, 187–188, *188–189*
   cross-dissolves
      adding, 117–118, *117–119*
      changing alignment, 121, *121*
      defined, **115–116**, *116*
      editing duration, 119–120, *120*
      fade to black using, 126, *126*
      overview of, 127
   defined, **115**, **271**
   deleting, 118
   dissolves
      defined, **266**
      Fade In Fade Out, 126, *127*
      Ripple, 128, 236
   editing
      alignment, 121–122, *121*, 124
      duration, 119–120, *120*, 124
      opacity, 124
      Ripple edits, 125, *125*
      Roll edits, 125, *125*
      in Transitions Editor, 124–125, *124–125*, 237, *237*
   irises, 129, 131
   overview of, 236–237, *236–238*
   Page Peel, 128
   QuickTime: Explode, 128
   QuickTime: Zoom, 129
   rendering
      defined, *122*, **122**, **269**
      Matrox cards and, 123
      proxy effects, 122, 123
      real-time effects, 122, 123
      selections, 123
      viewing after, 123, *123*, 237, *238*
      viewing effects without, 123
      viewing unrendered frames, 122
   reversing, 124
   Stretch: Squeeze, 129
   when to use, 126
   wipes
      defined, **115**
      Edge, 130
      Jaws, 130
Transmit (FTP client), 258
transparency. *See* composite modes
Travel Matte (Alpha, Luma) composite mode, **172**
trimming clips, *See also* editing
   cutting in two, 96–97, *96–97*
   defined, *68*, **68**, **89**, **235**, **271**
   deleting clips
      gap deletes, 95–96, *95–96*
      lift deletes, 95, *95*
      overview of, 94, *94*
      ripple deletes, 95, *95*
   into sub-clips
      defined, *68*, **68**, **79**
      using In/Out points, 68–71, *68–71*, 79–80, *80*
      using markers, 80–81, *81*
   locking tracks, 105
   quick trims
      edit points and, 98–100, *99–100*

      using Extend Edit, 100, *100*
      with mouse, 98–99, *99*
      overview of, 98
      using Razor Blade, 96–97, *96–97*
   reverting to previous edits, 98
   Ripple edits
      defined, **102**, **108**, **269**
      in Timeline, 109–110, *109–110*
      in Trim Edit window, 108–109, *108–109*
   Roll edits
      defined, **101**, **106**, **269**
      in Timeline, 107, *107*
      in Trim Edit window, 106–107, *106*
   Slide edits, **103**, 111–113, *112*, **270**
   Slip edits, **102**, 110, *111*, **270**
   Snap and Link tools in
      defined, *90*, **90**
      linking A/V tracks, 91, 93–94, *93*
      snapping tracks into position, 90–91, *91*
      toggling Link on/off, 92, *92*
      toggling Snap on/off, 91, *91*
      unlinking A/V tracks, 91–93, *92–93*
   in Timeline
      Ripple edits, 109–110, *109–110*
      Roll edits, 107, *107*
      selecting clips, 103, *104*, 113
      Slide edits, 111–113, *112*
      Slip edits, 110, *111*
   in Trim Edit window
      accessing, 103
      defined, **103–105**, *104*
      Ripple edits, 108–109, *108–109*
      Roll edits, 106–107, *106*
   Zoom In/Out tools in, 97–98, *97*
troubleshooting
   dropped frames, 37, 254
   not finding source media, 49–51, *49–50*, 227–228, *227–229*
   not seeing video controls, 42
Truffaut, Francois, 13
tungsten light vs. daylight, **153–154**
2001: A Space Odyssey, 233
Typewriter titles, *213*, **213**

U

Undo command, 83
UV (ultra violet) channels, 141, 142, *143*

V

Varda, Agnes, 13
Vertigo, 229
video clips, *See also* audio; media; sequences; tracks
   animating using keyframes
      combining effects, 208
      creating motion paths, 204–207, *204–207*
      editing motion paths, 207–208, *208*
      overview of, 203–204
   changing speed, 198–200, *198–199*
   clips, defined, **35**, **266**

freezing frames, 199–200, *200–201*
generated clips, 214, 267
naming, 41–42
navigation shortcuts, 25, 39–40, 46
organizing in bins, 55, *55*
progress of through interface, 27
reconnecting to source media, 49–51, *49–50*, 227–228, *227–229*
reversing, 198–199, *198–199*
setting item properties, 56, *56*, 226, *226–227*
video devices, external, 17, *18*
video distribution. *See* outputting
video editing. *See* cuts; editing; trimming
video effects, **133–173**, *See also* transitions
 adding globally, 246
 animating clips using keyframes
  combining effects, 208
  creating motion paths, 204–207, *204–207*
  editing motion paths, 207–208, *208*
  overview of, 203–204
 color correction
  advanced controls, 152
  brightening/darkening, 150–153, *151–152*
  changing contrast, 152, 153
  daylight vs. tungsten and, 153–154
  defined, **150**, *239*
  fixing white balance, 153–155, *154–155*
  resetting defaults, 155
 using composite modes
  Add, 168
  changing modes, 167, *168*
  Darken, 171
  defined, **167**
  Difference, 169
  Hard Light, 170
  Lighten, 171
  Multiply, 169
  Normal, 167, 168
  Overlay, 170
  overlaying, 172
  Screen, 170
  Soft Light, 171
  Subtract, 169
  Travel Matte (Alpha, Luma), 172
 using filters, *See also* filters
  adding beveled borders, 147–148, *148*
  blurring images, 144–145, *145–146*
  changing color saturation, 134–138, *135–138*
  copying filters, 139, *139*, 140
  defined, **134**
  deleting filters, 138
  distorting images, 143–144, *143–144*
  inverting colors, 141–142, *142–143*
  inverting images, 149, *150*
  masking unwanted images, 172
  mirroring images, 146, *147*
  multiple filters, 138, 145, 146
  overview of, 238–239, *238–239*
  reordering list of, 138, *138*
  solarizing images, 149–150, *149–150*
  steps in applying, 134–137, *135–137*

storing favorites, 140, *140*
turning on/off, 138
widescreen effect, 172
using Motion tab controls
 adding drop shadows, 165–167, *165–167*
 centering images, 156–157, *157*, 158–159
 changing aspect ratios, 161, 162–163, *162–163*
 changing opacity, 163–165, *164–165*
 cropping images, 160–161, *160–161*
 defined, *156*, **156**
 distorting images, 161–163, *162–163*
 feathering edges, 161, *161*
 rotating images, 156–157, *157*, 158
 scaling images, 156–158, *157*
 setting anchor points, *157*, 159
 multiple effects, 145
 overview of, 133, 140, *141*
video filters. *See* filters; video effects
video footage
 A-roll footage, 100, 265
 B-roll footage, 54, 100, 265
 post-roll footage, 46
 pre-roll footage, 45
 reviewing, 25, 40, 46
Video Generators bin, 22, *22*
Video Generators/Text bin, 210, **213–214**, *214*, *See also* titles
video standards, **10**
Viewer window, *See also* interface; Motion tab
 Audio tab, 176, 178–179, *178*, 180
 Ch 1/Ch 2 tabs, 176, 180, *181*
 changing timecode views, 40
 Clip controls in, *23*, 24
 Controls tab
  defined, *209*, **209**
  Title 3D controls, 220, *220*
  Title Crawl controls, 221, *221*
 creating sub-clips using In/Out points, 68–71, *68–71*, 79–80, *80*
 creating sub-clips using markers, 80–81, *81*
 defined, *18*, **19**, *23*, **23–25**, **271**
 editing clips in, 74
 editing split edits in, 186–187, *186–187*
 Mark options, 62
 Play controls in, *23*, 24
 Video Generators/Text submenu, 214, *214*
views in Timeline, changing, *60–61*, **60–61**
Vocal DeEsser filter, **193**
Vocal DePopper filter, **193**

W

waveform (audio), **177**
Web, exporting videos to, *See also* outputting
 creating web pages, 261–262, *262*
 FTP software in, 258, 262
 HTML editors in, 258
 overview of, 257–258
 placing movies in web pages, 262–263, *263*
 saving as QuickTime movies before, 258–260, *259–260*
 Web servers in, 258

websites
    Boris FX, 240
    DVD FAQs, 257
    FTP clients, 258
    Mac-friendly web hosting, 258
    Monsoon speakers, 10
    viewing book's video, 263
Widescreen filter, 172
Wiene, Robert, 131
windows. *See* interface
wipe transitions, *See also* transitions
    defined, **115**
    Edge, 130
    Jaws, 130
Wong Kar-Wai, 173
world tone, **189**

X

The X-Files, 213

Y

yellow filmstrip icons, 85, *85*

Z

Zoom transitions, **129**
zooming in/out
    of edits, 97–98, *97*
    of Timeline, 60–61, *60–61*
    of waveform displays, *178*, 179

Take Your Digital Images to the Next Level...

With *Photoshop Elements 2 Solutions*, noted photographer and author Mikkel Aaland has thoroughly updated his best-seller to include all the smart new features in the latest version of the program. This book is an invaluable guide for turning your ordinary images into extraordinary images. Coverage includes:

- **Getting Photoshop Elements up and running**
- **Sharpening out-of-focus pictures**
- **Touching up faces and fixing red-eye**
- **Making standout product shots**
- **Enhancing outdoor and real-estate shots**
- **Fusing photos into amazing panoramics**
- **Combining images into realistic-looking composites**
- **Optimizing photos for the web and e-mail transmission**
- **Creating PDF slide shows and professional-looking picture packages. And more...**

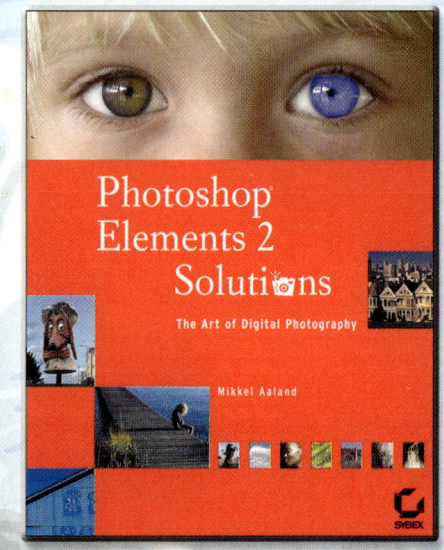

Photoshop® Elements 2 Solutions: The Art of Digital Photography
By Mikkel Aaland
ISBN: 0-7821-4140-4 • US $40
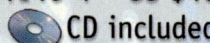 CD included

"*There are several books that have been published recently about Photoshop Elements 2 and this is one of the best I have read. If you are serious about learning Adobe's Photoshop Elements 2, I would suggest you buy this superb book.*" —Ann Roberts, Photoshop Etc.com

CD Description

The enclosed CD comes with more than 100 practice images from the book, plus utilities to make your work easier, tryout versions of fun and useful plug-ins, and a demo of Sybex's Photoshop 6 Learning Studio software.

www.sybex.com

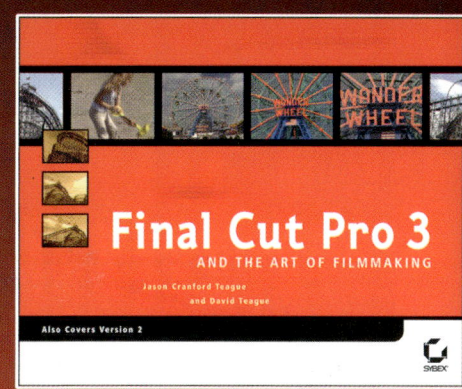

Final Cut® Express Solutions
by Jason Cranford Teague and David Teague
ISBN: 0-7821-4248-6 • US $39.99
DVD included

Final Cut Pro 3 and the Art of Filmmaking
by Jason Cranford Teague and David Teague
ISBN: 0-7821-4027-0 • US $60.00
DVD included

Discover Digital Video

iMovie™ 3 Solutions: Tips, Tricks, and Special Effects
by Erica Sadun
ISBN: 0-7821-4247-8 • US $39.99
CD included

Digital Video Essentials: Shoot, Transfer, Edit, Share
by Erica Sadun
ISBN: 0-7821-4198-6 • US $29.99
CD included

SYBEX®
www.sybex.com

Using the Companion DVD

The *Final Cut Express Solutions* DVD provides all the tools you need to work through the projects in this book, including project videos, source images, and audio files. You can access videos and source files from the DVD interface by clicking Movie Files or Chapter Files.

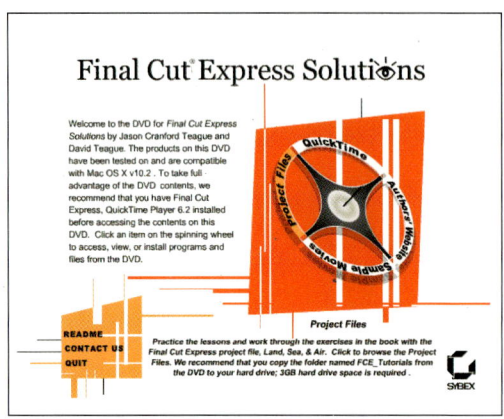

Using the Project File with the Exercises

The best way to develop skills is to practice them. And practice is also essential for developing judgment about which techniques and effects are best suited to particular situations. Beginning in Chapter 4, "Editing Basics," you can use the Final Cut Express project file Land, Sea, & Air, which contains several dozen clips and sequences. Each sequence includes clips for the exercises in the chapter, and there are markers in the Timeline to help your find your place. Generally, the first clips after the marker will be unaltered and are for you to practice on. The last clip of the sequence (separated by a few seconds of blank space) shows how the clip should appear after the exercise.

To use the exercises with the DVD, you first need to copy the folder FCE_Tutorials from the DVD onto your hard disk. You will need at least 3GB of free hard disk space. This folder contains the Land, Sea, & Air project file, a folder of video clips, and a folder of sound file resources. Follow these instructions to install the files:

1. Insert the DVD in your drive and wait for the icon to appear on your desktop.
2. Open the DVD by double-clicking the icon. Drag the folder FCE_Tutorials to your computer's hard disk. It might take several minutes for all of the files to transfer.
3. You can then move this folder anywhere you want on your hard disk. However, we refer to the file in our instructions as if it is in the top directory of your hard disk, so you will need to keep in mind where you placed it and adjust accordingly.